The Nature of Research

Inquiry in academic contexts

Angela Brew

London and New York

First published 2001
by RoutledgeFalmer
11 New Fetter Lane, London EC4P 4EE

Simultaneously published in the USA and Canada
by Routledge
29 West 35th Street, New York, NY 10001

RoutledgeFalmer is an imprint of the Taylor & Francis Group

© 2001 Angela Brew

Typeset in Baskerville by
Keystroke, Jacaranda Lodge, Wolverhampton
Printed and bound in Great Britain by
MPG Books Ltd, Bodmin

British Library Cataloguing in Publication Data
A catalogue record for this book is available from the British Library

Library of Congress Cataloging-in-Publication Data
Brew, Angela, 1943–
    The nature of research: inquiry in academic contexts / Angela Brew.
    p. cm.
    1. Research. 2. Universities and colleges—Research. I. Title.
    Q180.A1 B68 2001
    001.4—dc21   00–045947

ISBN 0–415–21406–8 (hbk.)
ISBN 0–415–21407–6 (pbk.)

Contents

Acknowledgements

To all the academics who have shared their ideas with me and especially all the new researchers who have participated in workshops to develop their research – I have learned much and am grateful. Special thanks go to all of the experienced researchers who participated in the study, Conceptions of Research in Three Academic Domains, and to the University of Sydney for providing funding to support it.

Chapter 1

Introduction

What you participate in, that you become.

(Henryk Skolimowski)

This was no ordinary city. It had become a place of pilgrimage for those who were looking for what was of value in their lives. While all of the buildings had an air of tranquillity about them, there was one which was particularly striking. Dominating the side of the hill on which it was situated, here was a palace of no mean proportions. Designed to reflect the heights of human endeavours and to personify all that was beautiful, the architect had become renowned for the process of inquiry which had characterized its design and building. So as she entered, her spirit was lifted and she experienced a sense of joy that infused the light, airy walls and galleries. Standing in the central hall, she had a sense of her own special place in the universe.

There were a few people milling about, quietly taking in the lofty space. Others sat in silence on low benches or cross-legged on the white marble floor deep in contemplation and meditation. Her urge was to continue, yet it was apparent that for some, this entrance space was enough. At the far end, a wide staircase, its red carpet contrasting with all the white and glass of the walls, floors and ceilings, seemed to draw her in. And so she advanced, going slowly up, then wandering here and there, wherever it seemed she had to go. This was her quest, her journey. She passed through halls and galleries. Some were like the art galleries of the past with pictures on the walls and sound and light installations. Some halls had exhibits in cases. She had heard tell of places called museums. She thought they might have been like that. At times there were collections of objects in cases together with a series of questions: what might these objects mean, how does she make sense of them? She wandered into a dark space where there were holographic people from the past asking questions about aspects of their lives as they saw them. And then into a space that looked like a quaint old shopping mall. Yet here, there was no inducement to buy anything. That era was over. Here there were opportunities for self-fulfilment, great teachers to talk to and ideas for consideration.

At length, she entered a long wide corridor resplendent with ancient gilded wall-paintings and tapestries and adorned with a ceiling of lofty frescoes reaching to an imaginary sky. She lingered, marvelling at the wonder of the paintings. At the end of this splendid place was a large window. It looked out towards the city with its backcloth of mountains. She sat on a low bench and contemplated its beauty.

So deeply was she immersed in the tranquillity of the view and her own thoughts that she did not see the young man approach and stand in front of her. She looked up. The man said: 'We are waiting for you, if you would like to come with me.' Still in her state of reverie, she rose and followed him. They seemed to be going from one building to the next, through corridors, across courtyards, down grassy slopes, through archways and round corners. She had no idea who the young man was nor where he was taking her. No matter. There was something she had to learn and the only way to learn it was to walk into the unknown.

At last, the young man stopped in front of a large, studded wooden door. He knocked. A small door within the great one opened and they stepped inside. 'Here you are,' he said. A dog bounded up to her and she backed away. 'Don't be afraid. Come,' her companion said, 'I will take you to see the Professor.' More walking through more corridors, yet in comparison these were narrow and claustrophobic. There were glass cases here and there with exhibits that terrified the once tranquil visitor: a case with spiders, another with ancient weapons. Never mind the Professor; she wanted to escape. The places they passed didn't give her any more comfort either: the Haunted House Room, the Nightmare Room, the Dangerous Microbes Centre, the Experiential Space and Aeronautics building, the Family and Children Centre and an arrow to the Tower of Terror. She was glad when her guide stopped. 'Here we are,' he said, opening a door. They entered a bright, spacious room where the Professor was waiting. 'Welcome,' she said.

'Thank you, but could you please explain to me where this is?'

'Yes,' the Professor kindly replied. 'This is the Department of Fear. You are here to help us with our inquiries, I understand, because you have things you wish to learn and we are working on the same issues.'

It wasn't until the Professor had spoken that she realized that freedom from fear was precisely what she desperately sought. She said:

'So does that mean you study the causes of fear and seek to eliminate them?'

'Not necessarily,' replied her host. 'We study many things. Fear can have beneficial as well as harmful effects. The important thing is to understand the world so that we can find the right balance. Since that balance is different for different individuals we are particularly interested in exploring with them what is right for them in different circumstances. I would like to invite you to meet our team of researchers and hopefully you will join them.'

'I am happy to meet with them and find out what they are working on, but I do not know anything about the subject you are studying so I would not be a very good team member.'

'But you are an expert. It is a subject you have had a great deal of experience in. Here in the Department we study all kinds of experiences so that the quality of life can be improved. Shall we go and meet the others?'

As he stands on the banks of the river seeing his own reflection in the water, Hermann Hesse's character Siddhartha is reminded of something he had forgotten; the person he once was. He has been searching for truth from great teachers, from worldly pleasures and riches, from family relationships and from an old ferryman. The river flows and laughs at him as he sees within it that answers do not lie in any of the places he has searched and that wisdom grows only by coming face to face with oneself (Hesse 1973). This is a powerful metaphor for academic research today. For while academic research is a systematic process for understanding aspects of our experience, we too have found that truth is problematic. We too have found we have to look elsewhere to develop wisdom, including within ourselves.

Anyone coming into the research arena or wanting to understand more about the nature of research faces a number of puzzles. There is a crisis in the academy causing universities to critically question their role, status and function in society. There is growing interference from outside the academy in the setting of research agendas. An educated public is increasingly interested in research findings. Huge changes in higher education are affecting the amount of time available for research. Increased speed and global access to information makes heavy demands of academics who are trying to keep pace and is changing the character of research. At the same time there are intellectual crises which have thrown ideas about knowledge and methods of investigation right into the melting pot. Academic research occupies contested space. Some of the contests are such that their outcome may prove a matter of life or death for the world as a whole and all its species, including our own.

Suggesting that the world the modern university has to face is a world which is 'not just unknowable; it is radically unknowable', Barnett (1997b: 4) argues that a university is 'a site of organized inquiry for generating and managing uncertainty' (Barnett 1997b: 18). In this context, he suggests, the pursuit of traditional disciplinary research has to give way to new forms of inquiry, requiring self-knowledge on the part of the researchers and the ability to engage with policy-makers and bureaucrats as well as to communicate with the world outside the academy. We have to learn how to live in what Barnett calls a super-complex world where there are no certainties and, he argues, academic research has to teach us how to do it. This may mean looking differently at aspects of the world and at our experiences of it, in ways we have not yet seriously engaged with.

My concern in this book is to illuminate more fully some of the taken-for-granted aspects of the nature of research, those which tend often not even to be talked about. I am concerned to break down some of the mystique surrounding research, to question its taboos and to lay bare some of its secrets. Throughout the book these are graphically illustrated using analogies with different kinds of pictures. At times, research is viewed as if it were a rich, complex and colourful painting. Sometimes we will look closely and examine its texture – the brush strokes, how it feels. At other times we look from a number of different angles and notice the way the painting changes as we perceive perhaps unusual aspects. At times I look as if from the other side of the room or I look at the room in which the research picture is placed and notice how it is arranged. A picture appears different when it is viewed from close up from when it is viewed from afar. Sometimes we are so close to the research agenda it is difficult to see how its picture could be different. So at times I look at research as if from very far away indeed. But the picture changes too. Sometimes what we see is more like a tapestry and I examine the warp and the weft. At other times the research picture resembles one of those computer-generated pictures which look at first sight like a pattern. A crowd stands round and one person says: 'Dinosaurs? Don't be daft!' and another says: 'Oh yes, yes, I can see them now!' I look through the picture to see the hidden one which initially was not immediately visible. Sometimes the picture is like a giant television screen made up of a matrix of separate screens, each of which contributes part of the picture; I contrast looking at one screen with views of research seen by looking at the whole.

As we explore that rich tapestry which is academics' attempts to come to know the world, so we have to ask ourselves whether the ways research is doing this and the areas research is investigating are the right ones, or whether, like Siddhartha, researches are looking in the wrong way and in the wrong places. This book specifically addresses those who are new to the world of academic research: new academics, postgraduate research students and research assistants who have their research careers before them. It challenges them not only to understand the nature of inquiry in academic contexts as it currently is, but also to take up the important task of changing it.

CONTESTED SPACE

Every research act takes place within a social and intellectual context. So to understand the nature of academic research we have to see it in relation to its various contexts. On one level this is the department, the research team, the laboratory or the library in which researchers work. On another level the research context is the intellectual tradition which defines not only the methods used and the kinds of questions considered appropriate but also the ways in which ideas, universities, research teams, communities and libraries are organized. On another level again, the context is the subject discipline, department or institution to which researchers are attached, and on yet another, it is the social and political context of country and world. But the contexts and the activities of research intermingle. There are no clear-cut boundaries between them and they often compete or pull in different directions. Different contexts make competing demands.

Academic research is increasingly being judged on the basis of whether or not it is funded; money from one source even being seen as more valuable than money from other sources. Yet sources of funding are becoming difficult to find, particularly for the inexperienced researcher. Governments are now driving the research agenda. Their funding formulas have implications for the ways in which research is pursued. Collegial collaboration is inevitably compromised by increased competition for research funds. Freedom of choice of the individual academic to pursue or not to pursue research and choice of subjects and issues to research are increasingly being curtailed. Curiosity-driven, passionate commitment to scholarship which is not bounded by project objectives and deadlines appears to be becoming a thing of the past. So what are the longer-term consequences of these trends? In the contested space which research now must occupy, there are winners and losers. Yet who the winners and losers are depends on the perspective of the viewer, and whether we are taking a shorter- or a longer-term perspective.

Not all research carried out in universities requires huge amounts of funding. The larger share of research activity takes place not in the academy but in industry; research in universities is the pauper in comparison with industrial research. Nevertheless, research, particularly scientific and medical research, does require relatively large expenditure from the public purse, and there is concern in society about getting value for money and whether current funding priorities are appropriate. Indeed, if we look at the social context in which universities and academic research are located, we see that research is frequently viewed with suspicion. Some even question why people in universities should conduct research at all. After all, it is only in the relatively recent history of universities that research has been undertaken. Academic research is tied to national strategy and planning and research has a relationship with how the country is viewed vis-à-vis other countries. So research is important. Yet society is still imbued with outdated and erroneous images of academics who spend all day reading, taking tea, drinking sherry and going on long vacations. Although this is now changing, the term *academic* is still used derogatively, as if it had nothing to do with the so-called real world.

Research funding committees have set up punitive regimes requiring researchers to demonstrate sustained performance. But what is the effect of pressure to publish brought about by the measurement of research output? Is this also stifling open exploratory inquiry and placing impossible demands on academic life? Meanwhile for the public at large, research is increasingly treated as a curiosity and used as entertainment. In other words, both for society and for the governmental funding agencies, it has become focused on public performance of different kinds. In a consumer-oriented society, time and opportunity for reading and reflection are considered mere luxuries. Products become more important than processes. Economic benefit becomes a major, if not the major, criterion for judging whether an activity should be engaged in at all, particularly if it is, as research is, one which requires public funding. All of these factors influence the research agenda. Academics no longer control it. The research domain has become contested space within the wider public arena.

Added to this have been the huge changes in universities in recent years. These include the move towards a mass higher education system, with increased numbers of students; changes in university funding regimes involving devolution of budgetary responsibility; external quality assessment regimes; changes in the academic year including moving to semesterized course structures; amalgamations of institutions bringing into universities a number of professional areas formerly outside the academy; and changes in the status of non-university tertiary institutions (e.g. polytechnics). In addition, higher education has become global. This includes increased international competition, with students migrating across the globe as well as the challenges of designing curricula that are inclusive and take account of diversity. All of these changes have an effect on attitudes towards research and on the research being carried out. Academics in some institutions are questioning whether research can be sustained. Is research in conflict with other activities, such as teaching for example? In some countries, whole institutions are just starting to develop a research culture and are questioning what in practice that should mean. Should institutional managers encourage academics to put research at the top of their priorities? How are tensions between teaching and research to be resolved? Should some people do research and others concentrate on teaching? Again research occupies contested space.

Global access to information via the Internet presents a further range of challenges. This too is having both positive and negative effects on research. On the one hand, access to information from a wide range of sources, communication with colleagues across the globe through email and the speed of document and data transfer from one site to another, all contribute to the new world in which research operates. On the other hand, the amount of information which is readily available places heavy demands on academics. Add to this increased publication as a consequence of the funding regimes mentioned above, and the question that needs to be asked is: what are the longer-term effects of the use of information technologies for the research of the future? There is simply too much information in any given area for researchers to access. So what are the consequences of information overload? Moreover, since global networks make research findings available to a wider audience, what are the effects of the work of researchers being open to anyone, whether in academia or not, who is able to access it?

But that is not all. Academic research is carried out according to conventions which define what counts as knowledge, what counts as an appropriate method for looking and what counts as evidence. So every research act is located in a tradition of coming to know. This is not a static process. During the course of the twentieth century, ideas about knowledge radically shifted. For example, the philosophy of science together with developments in science throughout the century challenged traditional assumptions about the nature of knowledge and the nature of reality, and the relationship between knowledge and reality. From another direction came critiques from, for example, feminism, poststructuralism, postmodernism and postcolonialism which also drew attention to the social context in which traditional assumptions about knowledge are situated. None of these trends is self-contained or clearly bounded. However, what this critical questioning adds up to is a fundamental challenge to many basic beliefs about research. For example, the idea of research as increasing our knowledge was questioned. This has implications for any ideas about progress we might have had. The idea that there are no grand theories which explain everything is having a serious impact in many academic areas. Postmodernism and post-positivism, for example, caused researchers to rethink the status of theories as truths about the universe. Feminist, gay and postcolonial research established the gendered nature of much academic research and highlighted the implications of its locatedness in the dominant, Western, heterosexual culture. Whether or not they agree with such ideas, academics have to take account of the debates which are causing many to question what they are doing as research. After all, if research is conventionally conceived as the pursuit of knowledge and is based on the idea that it increases our knowledge, when that idea is challenged we are in deep trouble.

University research has traditionally defined for society what knowledge is while of course also being a major contributor to it. But, knowledge is now produced as much outside universities as within them (Gibbons *et al.* 1994). In an information-hungry society, there is pressure on universities to create more and more of it. Yet at the same time, philosophically, academics have, so to speak, pulled the rug from under their own feet. There is a quite widely held view that knowledge is in crisis (see for example, Barnett and Griffin 1997). What this all adds up to is that the ownership and creation of knowledge have clearly become contested space. In undertaking research in any academic context nowadays we have to negotiate our way through this mine field.

On the basis of all of the tensions which research is currently facing we have to conclude that academic research is in trouble. It has moved into the public sphere at the very time when its bases, financial and epistemological, have been undermined. This critical questioning about the nature of knowledge, the emergence of postmodernity, the use of postpositivist methodologies, together with the breaking down of boundaries between disciplines, sit alongside the objectivist, outcomes-oriented approaches of government policies and funding formulas. To say, in this context, that research occupies contested space is perhaps an understatement. It is a polite way of describing irreconcilable differences in which academic research, while maintaining a stiff upper lip, currently flounders.

In view of all of this turmoil and the pressures on research coming, as they do, from outside as well as from within the academy, it is timely to look at research and the ways in which it is changing. I shall argue in this book that it is within this very quagmire that the strengths of research and its future directions can be discerned. Exploring the different contested dimensions will enable us to give substance to aspects of research waiting in the wings: ideas, methods and techniques waiting to fly; ideas which, more often than not, have their wings clipped to protect or promote the interests of the powerful. In these new ideas and methods lie the germs of the transformation needed for the enormous tasks of dealing with the various crises facing the world.

If the world's problems are to be solved there is a big job to be done. The process of research must move us beyond the despair of postmodernism and the drudgery of commodified knowledge. There are choices to be made and if we make the wrong choices or preclude some of the more creative approaches then we are in deep trouble. We must discover anew how to inquire in ways which not only take our understanding of the world forward but also provide exemplars which model how we and others might live.

Research can only do this by acknowledging its disasters as well as its achievements; its rigidities as well as its creativity; its power and its powerlessness; its openness and its dogmatic closed-mindedness. A shift of focus is needed if research is to be of value in the new century. This shift of focus will come about in recognizing that research has been extremely successful in exploring, in limited ways, a limited range of phenomena. We must now be open to new problems and new questions, and to finding new ways of searching for new solutions. This means recognizing that answers to the world's problems will be found in unexpected places. They will be unexpected answers.

The shift of focus will come about by a changed emphasis on the value of the processes of research, a critical questioning at every stage of the relationship of the research to society. Rules for research must be defined within each research project, ethical behaviour and the nature of knowledge must become part of research discourse within each local context. The process, i.e. how we research, is important. There is no golden city at the end of the journey. The competing tensions between these different agendas have to be resolved on every level, with every research project, in every research context, by every individual researcher and research team. This means that, in the activities carried out as research, in the ways research is communicated and in the consciousness of the researcher, inquiry has to become reflexive. For the shift of focus will also come about by recognizing that we have to put ourselves back into the picture. We need to understand the social and the psychological forces which direct our actions and to recognize that we cannot do this in research while we continue to cut ourselves off from it.

THE AUTHOR AND THE BOOK

For me, research is not just an activity I engage in; it is a subject which fascinates me and about which I have researched a great deal. I cannot remember a time when I was not interested in that rich tapestry of questions about how we come to know and in what that knowing consists. I have spent my career helping university students to learn academic content better than they do, helping academics teach it better than they do and in questioning the basic assumptions about what it is we are all doing. On my journey, I have taught or studied many subjects and examined how people learn them. In my work as an academic developer I meet and talk daily with academics across the disciplines and provide guidance to many on teaching, learning and research issues. I am always interested to talk to academics about their subject, how they research it and how they teach it. I am fascinated by how students come to understand academic ideas. How *do* we come to know? Research is a crucial activity in this process.

So that the nature of this book should be clear, it is important also to tell you what I am not. First of all, I am not male. I am not a university manager. I am not a politician. I am not a member of a research funding body and I am not a scientist. All or any of these people would perhaps be more obvious authors of a book on research. That, in itself, tells us something about the nature of research. It is frequently discussed and written about by the establishment. However, the book that each would write would not be this one. Research is a big topic. This book focuses principally on the experience of research in academic contexts as I see it. I am aware that a significant proportion of academics are entering higher education, often from the professions, without traditional research training, so I consider what research is like for those who carry it out; what the issues are with which they are currently confronted; what the dilemmas and concerns are and where this all might be heading. I examine higher education research from the perspective of those who practise it and from the perspective of its relationship to the wider society. The aim is to explore what makes academic research what it is today, to look at some of the decisions facing the academy and indicate some directions for it to follow in the future.

I draw from different areas of scholarly literature, from my own experiences of research, from the research I have carried out concerning the ways research is experienced in higher education, and from the many discussions about research which I have had with academics in many disciplines in a range of countries, to provide a point where ideas about research as it is experienced can meet. I am interested in what research means to people in an academic context so I link theories about research ideas and methods to empirical evidence about practice, bringing together ideas from a number of different traditions of literature to inform the discussion. I am concerned about the decisions that may face the researcher of the future, so as well as exploring present dilemmas, I try to anticipate those which may lurk just over the horizon.

A number of research projects I have pursued over a period of about twenty years are used to inform and illustrate the book. These have included my doctoral thesis work, which set out to develop an entirely new research methodology appropriate to the then emerging post-positivist research tradition. More recently I have been exploring ways the relationships between teaching, research and learning might better be understood. I have also empirically investigated ways research is changing. This has included looking at supervisory practices which either inhibit or encourage non-traditional doctoral research theses (ones which do something excitingly different!) and it has also included developing criteria for the evaluation of research that breaks its traditional rules.

My recent empirical work has investigated the ways senior academic researchers conceptualize their research. In it I have also looked at how researchers view the relationship between research and scholarship, how they see their research contributing to their personal learning, as well as at their perceptions of the ways research is changing. As the book proceeds, I want to draw on this study to illustrate the different ways practising researchers think about their research.

One of the problems we have is that of always looking at research from our own vantage point. Depending on how we personally think of research we will see different aspects. In this book I shall endeavour, as it were, to walk round the issues or to step back and imagine seeing them as if from a distance. Hopefully, working in an academic department which is outside a faculty structure puts me in a position to see issues a little differently, as when we step away from a painting and see it from the other side of the room. The nearer we are to events, Max Plank (1981; first published 1933) suggested, the more difficult it is to see their causal structure. Laplace, Plank said, had the idea of a super-intelligence which can stand outside of the facts occurring in the universe. A super-intelligence would be able to see causal relations in all the happenings of the world. This is reminiscent of those computer-generated fractal pictures. When the pictures are being created all that we see is a random, chaotic pattern. But as the pattern becomes established we can see that there is order in it.

The practice of research

To understand the nature of research we need first to look at its intellectual context. That is the focus of Part I. We examine research as it is practised, how it relates to scholarship, what the rules for doing it are, the kind of knowledge which results, and the problems and questions which are deemed important to pursue. The social context is the specific focus of Part II. However, this is not a dichotomy. Rather, while Part I takes as its point of departure the inner context of research in terms of the intellectual tradition in which it is situated, Part II looks from the perspective of the outer context of the university and society. For it is not possible to explore the academic climate within which research is situated without also looking at some of the tensions between intellectual and political agendas and the ways in which research takes on the socio-cultural mores of Western society. Nor is it possible to explore the social and political context without taking account of the intellectual context.

So in Part I, by exploring what it is conventionally said we are trying to do when we do research and critically questioning what is considered to be acceptable practice, the constraints of the past are compared to the opening up of new ways to tackle the problems facing us. The scene is set in Chapter Two, 'What is research?', by examining what we understand research to be. We take an imaginary walk round a bookshop to see where ideas about research are typically located. This is a book about research in general, yet research is most often discussed in a disciplinary context, so after looking at what is happening to disciplines I then draw on my investigation of how experienced researchers think about research and how it is changing to establish a framework for looking at variations in ideas about research in later chapters. We then turn in Chapter Three, 'Research and scholarship', to the nature of scholarship. I explore the tension between definitions of research and scholarship employed by government bodies and by academics, and examine how research has arisen historically. We see that there is contested territory between quantitative views of scholarship promulgated in, for example, government policy and the views of academics who ground their ideas of scholarship in qualitative notions of depth of preparation for research, expertise in specialist skills and knowledge, and/or the practice of professionalism. These qualitative ideas are significant in the context of finding new directions for research.

Another important tension is that between the need for creativity in research on the one hand and the desire for order through rule-based procedures on the other. Chapter Four, 'Following rules', examines how traditional rules about how to conduct and evaluate research are changing. Opening up how we research is having a subtle yet serious effect on the decisions facing all academic researchers. However, it is in the relaxation of traditional rules, moves in research from the use of rules which are externally imposed to ones which are internally developed and integral to the research process, and the tension between them, that we see the germ of transformation. The changes have only just begun to take place in the margins. Nevertheless within them we can glimpse ways in which research may be able to move beyond the rigidities of the present and lead the new thinking which is needed.

Ideas about knowledge determine the topics we choose to explore, the methods used to do the explorations as well as what we discover. But ideas about knowledge also go further because they determine how universities are organized and the relationship of research to action in the world, as well as the methods we use to evaluate research projects, research publications and even academic careers. A discussion of what we mean by knowledge, then, is important to our understanding of the nature of academic research. Chapters Five to Seven are concerned with how research is to find a new role for itself at a time when its philosophical and empirical bases are in disarray and when it has lost its authority to define for society what knowledge is and how to get it.

Since it used to be thought that research proceeded in a wholly rational manner, Chapter Five, 'Knowledge', explores rational explanations influencing what issues are researched. While these explanations have been critically questioned, we see that the research culture is still imbued with such notions and enshrines them in practice. Although rational explanations about the nature of knowledge underpin the issues that are researched, they do not determine them. So Chapter Six, 'Problems and questions', turns to look at a range of historical, social and cultural factors which also contribute to determining what knowledge is pursued and why. Noting that research serves a range of human interests we ask whose interests it serves in particular; whose priorities are addressed, and whose questions/problems are considered worthy of addressing. We see that caught up in any attempt to explain why research focuses on particular issues are questions of social justice. I argue that changing whose values and concerns are addressed is important in reordering research priorities. So in the final section of the chapter I give some examples of the kinds of issues left out and ask why. In defining for society new understandings about the nature of research, the reasons for excluding particular issues from consideration when they contribute to the public good or would solve a problem in society are important for they show how research might change and what prevents it doing so.

But there is another set of factors which powerfully influences the kinds of issues and questions being pursued. Failure to take account of psychological factors underpinning our ideas about what knowledge is, and how we come to know it, blocks moving forward to new definitions of research and new knowledge. Chapter Seven, 'New knowing', explores what some of the psychological blocks are and then looks at how the tensions between, for example, freedom and constraint, creativity and dogmatism, can be resolved and what needs to happen if new knowledge is to grow. This is vitally important if future academic research is to help people to thrive within a context of uncertainty, complexity and plurality.

Research in context

However, academic research never takes place in isolation. Huge challenges for the academy are posed by, for example, the integration of the academy and society, by political, social and cultural agendas, by new patterns of communication (information technology assisting researchers to pursue new areas while also providing new challenges), as well as through competing tensions within higher education, for example, between teaching and research. Influences and pressures from the context of academic research make the discussion of new rules and new issues to be researched in Part I appear hopelessly idealistic. Researchers, research teams and universities more generally cannot ignore them. So Part II looks at research in context, again highlighting the choices facing the academy. For while research occupies a problematic, contested social space, I argue that it nonetheless contains the means of transformation.

The most powerful and pernicious influences on academic research currently in focus are output views of research with their emphasis on performativity, enshrined most particularly in government policies and funding formulas. The products of research are viewed as commodities within such an economic model. Chapter

Eight, 'Research as a commodity', explores the dimensions and implications of focusing attention on performance and outcomes of research from individual projects on the one hand, to countries on the other. When research is considered as a commodity to invest in, the thoughts, minds and lives of those who do it are largely invisible. The chapter addresses the question of how and why the academy has apparently been so compliant with the economic model. At the end of the chapter, I allude to the tension between the potential of research to transform the lives of its practitioners through their engaging with ideas over a long period of time and the pressure to bring work to a speedy conclusion and publish it.

Research changes the way our society perceives the world around it. The view of research as a process of personal and social learning is left out of the economic model. So in Chapter Nine, 'Research and learning', I turn attention to the perspective of the relationship of research to learning on personal and collective social levels. The aim is to highlight some of the tensions which are foregrounded when we talk of research as a process of learning. The extent to which researchers see their learning connected to their research, as part and parcel of it, depends on their views of the nature of research, so the chapter looks at researchers' different views about what they learn while doing research. Ideas about collective, social learning are tied up with the idea of progress. So the chapter examines how research can find a new definition for itself and what needs to happen in the context of critical questioning of this idea.

If academic research is to teach society how to live it must become more like learning. Individual learning and social learning come together through teaching. In the broadest sense the aim of research is to teach. It teaches society how to see the world, but I argue it now has to move to teaching it how to live joyfully within it. Understanding the relationship between research and teaching, therefore, is vitally important but it means we have to conceptualize research as teaching. In Chapter Ten, 'Research and teaching', therefore, we pursue our understanding of the nature of research by looking at the relationship between teaching and research. Researchers have different conceptions of this and these are explored. Because of the intimate relationship between teaching and research in higher education, and the ways in which they similarly respond to what is essentially the same intellectual climate, trends in teaching and learning throw further light on the tensions and dilemmas highlighted in other chapters, and tell us about directions which are important for the future. Indeed, looking at directions in teaching and learning throws into stark relief some of the dilemmas which are more muted when we look at academic research alone.

Finally, the nature of the language used to talk about research supports the interests of those who have power in defining research agendas. So Chapter Eleven, 'Research as discourse', highlights narratives which underpin research, discussing the language, including the types of imagery and metaphor used. In this chapter we see the way in which different discourses or narratives share, and give expression to, the contested space which is research. We see there that there is nothing polite about it. The language of war indicates that behind the polite academic veneer, life is tough. I argue that we need to change the language if we are to change research practice.

Research has not yet reached crisis point, but a crisis is waiting in the wings. Since research is so central to university life, looking at research will tell us much about what the university of the future might be like. Academics cannot take research for granted. So the concluding reflections of Chapter Twelve, 'Research and the future', summarize how the academy can reclaim the research agenda by developing new forms of research which provide a new justification for its existence. Since research is such a key part of how a society sees itself, in resolving dilemmas within the academy, research must and, I argue, can in the future, be in a position to teach society how to live in a context characterized by uncertainty and complexity.

Part I

The practice of research

Chapter 2

What is research?

[N]owhere is so pleasant, as to while away a few idle weeks at one or other of the Universities.

(Charles Lamb)

Voicing the question they had all been wondering, Janine asked: 'Yes, but what is research?'

'Aren't we supposed to know?' Sean said, and everyone laughed.

Amir tried an answer: 'It's a systematic process of inquiry.'

'Everyone knows what research is,' retorted James, then added: 'don't they?'

'But when I go and buy a car I engage in a systematic process of inquiry. That doesn't tell you very much.'

'Anyway it's a non-question.'

'Yes but we're being asked to do it. You can't just say it doesn't exist. What is it that these academics do when they disappear to do some research?'

'Anyway . . . er . . . I don't think you can talk about research in general,' Anne said tentatively. 'You have to see it in relation to a particular subject, don't you? I mean . . . er, if you're doing research in a . . . well a science laboratory, that's different from doing research, say, where you're using, you know . . . a . . . manuscripts in a library.'

'That's right, so there's no one thing that research is. You can't reduce it to some essential quality.'

'But we're supposed to be doing it, so we have to know what it is we are supposed to be doing.' Janine was getting rather irritated.

'Did you know that the person at a supermarket checkout lifts the weight of a jumbo jet every day?' Everyone laughed and James continued: 'It's true, researchers have discovered it!'

'I heard a different one,' Sean said. 'Actually I read it in the paper. It said that if you want to get fit you shouldn't walk your dog because you don't get enough exercise. Apparently they compared dog owners with others over the same distance. . . .' He continued to outline the research findings. Everyone was smiling.

'Crazy!' James said, shaking his head. 'Researchers do some crazy things.'

'Anyway, I agree with Anne,' Amir said, returning to seriousness. 'You have to think about the particular questions and have a hypothesis. I don't think there is any essential thing which corresponds to research. It means different things in different contexts.'

'That's just too deep and meaningful for me,' said Janine. 'I just want to know what I've got to do. Then I can get on and do it.'

'I was in industry before,' said James, 'and the company I worked for, . . . they did research. Actually they did lots of it; not just market research but basic research into new products and things. I suppose that's the kind of thing academics are doing but with less money.'

'We're supposed to get a research grant . . .' Anne said wistfully.

'Surely you'll have to make your researchers a bit more knowledgeable than that. I mean, you've set up a conversation. I don't think academics would ask such basic questions.'

'No. No, I thought about that,' I replied, '. . . but perhaps they would wonder about them even if they didn't actually say them in a conversation.'

'So what's the point of it?' Graham was mystified.

'Well isn't research something you're supposed to know about?'

'Well, yes, I suppose so.'

'And isn't every bit of research located in a piece of fiction?'

'Mmm, I'm not so sure about that. . . .' Graham looked worried.

I said: 'Well, that's the reason. I, er, I suppose I want to explore where the boundaries are.'

'Well all right then,' he said grudgingly, 'but it's very risky.'

This book is about research as a phenomenon in higher education. It is a huge topic. Academic research is a key element of higher education. Research is central to university life and to the lives of thousands of people employed in institutions of higher learning. Indeed some would say that it defines higher education. But it is also hugely influential in society. It is intimately tied up with a country's prestige, its wealth, its history and its destiny. It is important in the everyday lives of millions who are affected by its achievements. It crosses national and international boundaries. Research can be highly controversial, intensely fascinating, inordinately frustrating and sternly demanding. It can stretch even the most intellectually able and can make or break careers or lives. The results of research can move mountains or can lie hidden in dust-ridden obscurity.

Curiously though, when I tell academics I am writing about research, they often question why on earth I should be doing that. I was explaining to a friend recently how my explanations were often met by a blank look of incredulity. 'Yes, because it's *there*, isn't it?' she replied, putting the palm of her hand right at the end of her nose. Research is an activity which is so close it is often not seen. Since so much of it is just taken for granted in a university, to the outsider or the new academic there is an air of mystery surrounding much research activity. Even walking through a university campus will not tell us a great deal about what researchers are doing. Apart from the obvious signs of experimental science and engineering being carried out (the laboratories full of equipment, people in white coats amid hydrogen and helium bottles), and apart from the hushed floors of libraries, most research is almost invisible. Yet when we look beyond the surface we can find people working on all manner of intensely interesting topics. Indeed, when you say the word 'research' to people in higher education, they all have views about what they and others are or are not doing; what they and others should and should not be doing. Many of these ideas are about research in a specific discipline or subject area. Many are to do with government policy on research or the priorities of funding bodies. Other ideas are concerned with personal competence, with career, or with intellectual trends which dictate the kinds of research considered acceptable. But what is going on behind common assumptions? What are the forces directing people's actions? And what are the tensions influencing research decisions?

FINDING OUT ABOUT RESEARCH

If you are new to university life or to being a postgraduate student you will have noticed that research is something highly valued in your institution. You may also have picked up that you are supposed to get research grants and to publish. On the other hand you probably have some ideas about the kinds of things you would like to research. So how do you find out more? In the workshops I have run for new researchers, I have found that many think that the questions about research they want answered are so basic they do not like to ask them of their more experienced colleagues. So how do you find out about research?

Supposing you are in a bookshop and want to find a book which will tell you all about research and answer your questions, where do you look? The most obvious place perhaps would be to look at books on research methods. There are a few useful general ones to be found in the section devoted to student study guides, but much more common are those which are specific to different disciplines or different methodologies. This tells us something about research: it is rarely discussed outside of the disciplinary or theoretical context. If you then open one of the books on research methods, with few exceptions, what you will not find is a discussion of what research is! You probably will not even find a discussion of the purpose of research. This tells us something else about research. It is a given. Much is written about it in specific terms, for example, laboratory research, qualitative research, statistical methods in research, action research, etc. Much is talked about it. Many people spend their lives doing it and huge sums of money are spent on it. The assumption is, everyone in universities knows what research is.

Continuing our search for ideas about research in general, we will find inspirational historical studies providing accounts of how famous researchers carried out their research and how famous research institutions became established. Indeed there has been a growth in such work in recent years. In addition, there is the sociology of science literature which provides graphic accounts of what scientists do in laboratories. We may find our bookshop has a sizeable section labelled 'science'. Much of this is written with a general readership in mind so it popularizes science, turning research into entertainment. Here we will find out about some extraordinary research findings and work we never imagined was being done. There is also work in this section which exposes the social nature of research. Notice too that among books on science are some serious studies of the nature and scope of research. We will return to the implications of framing research as science in Chapter Eleven.

We will have to search in the scholarly literature on higher education to encounter discussions of the relationship between research and teaching, and on the relationship between scholarship and research. This provides perplexing evidence of the existence or non-existence of links between these facets of academic life. There, too, we will also discover documents written about research policy issues. Most recently many of these have been written, not by academics within universities, but by government agencies. Indeed, research policies are often made with only passing reference to the academic literature. Research output (e.g. citations, numbers and nature of publications, etc.) and the nature of the academic profession are other areas which we will find commented upon in scholarly journals. In the many writings on the nature of scholarship, we will find research discussed, for, as we shall see in the next chapter, attempts to define the scope of academic work, including research have, particularly in the United States, centred on redefinitions of the concept of scholarship.

Much of what is known or surmised about the process of research, however, is to be found not in empirical studies – of which, if science studies and the sociology of science are left out of the picture, there are very few – but in the theoretical literature related to research methodology. In the philosophy of science section of our bookshop we will see many topics which are of relevance to our quest to understand the nature of research. From that literature we see that the tradition of inquiry which characterized conventional academic research has been seriously challenged. We see academic research in a state of disarray. A relatively stable view of its methodology and purpose has given way to uncertainty and a diffuse pattern of studies. Even if they do not read this work, academic researchers are having to come to terms with its effects.

From all of these sources, the new researcher meets a confusing array of ideas. There will probably now be more questions to be resolved than at the beginning. The diffuse nature of writings about research, spread as it is across many different academic areas, together with the unwillingness of many to discuss research in anything other than specific terms, masks the crisis waiting to happen. That crisis comes from the contests which are hidden within different discourses. We have entered contested space and we will need to resolve many dilemmas and tensions if we are to feel at home in this world and know how to move forward in it. In the remainder of this chapter I want to look at some of the tensions within the academic community in relation to research which give the questions about the nature of research the urgency to which I have already alluded. As the argument of the book unfolds we shall see that it is in the interests of the powerful to stifle discussion. My hope, however, is that being aware of the multiple tensions directing our thoughts and actions provides us with a basis for choosing to take different routes. New thinking is required but it is in comparatively short supply.

WHAT IS RESEARCH?

What is research? The question demands an answer. It suggests that there is something which is research. Some of the definitions I have come across recently include the following:

- Research is finding out something and making it public.
- Research provides a means of generating, testing and validating knowledge.
- Research is a systematic process of investigation, the general purpose of which is to contribute to the body of knowledge that shapes and guides academic and/or practice disciplines (Powers and Knapp 1995: 148).
- Research is about advancing knowledge and understanding (Oliver 1997: 3).

These are all definitions designed to be read by people who already understand quite a bit about the nature of research. To the inexperienced researcher or the new academic, however, they raise more questions than they answer. For example, the idea of a 'body of knowledge' contains a number of assumptions about what knowledge is and how we come to know it. If research is about finding out and then broadcasting it, what is special about academic research? If research is 'the means' of generating knowledge, then it equates to the methods. But what about the social aspects of research: things like grants and funding and the role of publication? We will return to more definitions of research in Chapter Three when we consider research in relation to scholarship. But for the moment, let us be clear. There is no one thing, nor even a set of things, which research *is*. It is obviously a complex phenomenon. It cannot be reduced to any kind of essential quality. Indeed, some academic researchers and managers would argue that any attempt to discuss research in general is at worst impossible and at best foolhardy. Surely, so the argument goes, research has to be discussed in relation to its disciplinary context.

DISCIPLINES

When individuals and groups of people do research in academic contexts they learn from each other and from various areas of literature about what it is they are doing. The nature of research is, for many, unproblematic. It is something to just get on with, not to spend time agonizing about. In talking to academics I have found that a general question about what the main interests and concerns in the university about research are, has often been interpreted as being a question about what is happening in a particular discipline. Researchers have their ideas about how the research they are engaged in in their own discipline is similar to and different from the research in a neighbouring discipline.

Research activities do of course differ in different areas of the university in a number of important ways. Disciplinary differences provide a rationale for this and the work of Becher (1989) is frequently quoted to support such ideas. If, like Becher, you start by assuming that there are separate disciplines, then this can provide the rationale for differences in activities and focus. It is inevitable, from this disciplinary starting point, that Becher's analysis should have focused on the interplay between epistemology, culture, politics and values and that his work should focus on the actions and ideas of groups (academic tribes), not the ideas of individuals. Becher argues that 'the ideals and practices of academic communities are intimately bound up with the nature of the knowledge they pursue' (Becher 1989: 169). Nevertheless, Becher constantly struggles with the finding that disciplines do not provide the primary way in which people think of their research. For example, he found that academics had less of a tendency to stay in one discipline than expected and also that they differ in the extent to which the external climate or their personal concerns influence their perceptions of research. Many academics hold tenaciously to the idea that what determines differences in research is the discipline, even though their ideas about what people do and think in disciplines other than their own are often naïve and outdated (Brew, submitted for publication). In some areas of study they do not even conceptualize themselves in disciplinary terms (see e.g. Usher *et al.* 1997). There is also the problem of shifting disciplinary boundaries: 'the boundaries between disciplines are dissolving and giving way to a more open structure where varieties of knowledge and competence are combined and recombined in novel configurations' (Gibbons *et al.* 1994: 48–9).

Mourad (1997b), in summarizing the critiques of the notion of disciplinary knowledge of four postmodern philosophers (Foucault, Lyotard, Derrida and Rorty) argues that the postmodern critique of the disciplines liberates inquiry, expanding the possibilities of what counts as a scholarly activity. The purpose of eschewing disciplines, he says, is not simply for the sake of it, but rather to pursue the kinds of intellectual inquiry which result. This might be a fundamentally different understanding of 'intellect, reality and the pursuit of knowledge' (Mourad 1997b: 72). Indeed we are witnessing growing specialization, competing methods of inquiry within disciplines and the growth of interdisciplinarity as well as the growth in professional areas of study where the concept of a discipline is alien. All of this now means that the emphasis on describing the nature of research from a disciplinary perspective is somewhat outdated. Even Becher's much-quoted analysis demonstrates that individuals' conceptions of research are a function of a complex set of factors of which disciplinary allegiance is only one. Indeed, in my research, many academics had extreme difficulty in consigning themselves to a specific single discipline (Brew, submitted for publication).

With the information explosion, new knowledge frameworks are needed. Traditional conceptions of disciplines do not enable us to describe them and they restrict possibilities for growth. A greater depth and a greater breadth of expertise is frequently required within research teams and research degrees are not able to continue to preserve a status quo which is rapidly becoming outdated. New methods and new standards are required which take account of the emergence of new discipline areas, interdisciplinary and multidisciplinary work. Yet alternative structures for cross-disciplinary work lack resources and will do so while we hold erroneously to the notion that it is disciplines which drive research activity. Indeed there are acute tensions between the realities of shifting areas of discourse and investigation and government funding mechanisms which are rooted in what are fast becoming outdated disciplinary practices. It is therefore no longer appropriate to base explanations about differences in the experience of research primarily on disciplinary distinctions.

As new researchers, how are we to make sense of the different ways in which our colleagues are talking about research in this shifting disciplinary context? I am not denying that people from different disciplinary cultures may do research in different ways (Becher 1989); that they may do different kinds of research and that ideas about the nature of research are, by and large, learned within university departments and are the result of individuals' experiences and discussions with immediate colleagues. The institutional and historical and social and political contexts are implicated in the concept and must be taken into account. Disciplines are historically hierarchical and related to communities of practice. As such, they exist as an heuristic device to explain differences in research activities. But they do not explain why people think of research in the ways they do and they are not as static and stable as many would have us believe. So we need to find some alternative frameworks.

It is difficult to enter the contested space inhabited by the traditional disciplinary areas – science, social sciences, humanities – without taking sides. As a person whose background is broadly in the humanities and social sciences, I am already located on one side of this battlefield. I have to weather the assumption that non-scientists cannot speak about science (Stove 1998; Sokal and Bricmont 1999), even though, as Mary Midgley (1992) elegantly demonstrates, scientists have no such hesitations about attempting to enter philosophical domains.

HOW RESEARCH IS EXPERIENCED

When we are aware of a phenomenon or use a particular concept, there are some aspects that are in the forefront of our minds and other aspects that recede to the background. As in those puzzling pictures where we see the two shapes of the vase, or the faces of the old or young woman, different aspects are more or less important for us. In my research among senior academic researchers I have found that, while for some academics research is defined by the methodology of the discipline and by their status as experts within that discipline, the ways most think about research transcend disciplinary differences. There are some qualitatively different ways in which researchers think about research. In describing the different ways academic researchers speak about their research, the focus is on what they perceive, how the elements of what they perceive are related to each other, and then on what meaning they give to what they perceive. Remember, we are talking here about the same concept, i.e. 'research'. What I am describing is the variation I found in my study in the ways that senior academic researchers think about that concept.

My work identified four distinct variations. These ideas are researchers' attempts to make sense of the conventions of research and the context in which they are working and living. They provide ways to understand the different perspectives on research encountered in committees, groups, the world outside the academy as well as the different orientations of academics meeting in cross-disciplinary groups. In addition, these ways that researchers think about their research reflect the changes as well as the dilemmas posed by old and new ideas about research and by the fact that academics are increasingly being asked to give an account of themselves. They get us away from tired disciplinary debates and a focus on methodology, providing a fresh perspective to look at research in new ways. The different aspects academic researchers focus on when they think about research which were identified in my investigation among experienced researchers, provide a language for understanding the debates and point to new ways to think about them. So in the remainder of this chapter, before going on to discuss researchers' ideas about whether and how research is changing, I will explain these variations.

First, research is talked about as if it were a series of separate tasks, events, activities, problems, experiments, ideas or questions, each of which is viewed as distinct. The aim of research is then seen as being to solve distinct practical problems or answer specific questions. I call this the *domino variation*, for just as in the game, dominoes are separate but can be combined in a number of patterns, so too, separate elements of research are viewed as illuminating other elements. Research may be talked about in terms of first identifying a problem or question and breaking it down into a number of sub-problems and then working on these. Solving one problem or finding an answer to one question can set up a chain reaction in regard to other problems or further questions, as in a *domino effect* where dominoes are lined up and each falls in turn. This can be a very complex process, involving reactions in different directions and levels. Intuitively this makes sense when I think of scientific research. It is important, though, to remember that it can equally well be found in the social sciences and humanities and that not all scientists think of their research in this way. So in the foreground are sets (lists) of atomistic things: techniques, problems, etc. These separate elements are viewed as linking together in a linear fashion. Research is interpreted as a process of synthesizing separate elements so that things fall into place or questions open up.

The second way of experiencing research is essentially as a social phenomenon, i.e. as located in a social context. There is an emphasis on the idea of the finished product and how the researcher is going to be seen at the end of it. I call this the *trading variation*. The trading idea can be thought of as being like a village fair where research outputs and ideas are commodities which are exchanged. Research outcomes (publications, research grants or products) provide a constant reference point for those who experience this variation. What is also notable here is that when such researchers describe the processes of research they only talk of the work which other people are doing, of the meetings they are having or, alternatively, they talk of writing. The importance of belonging to and being valued by an international community is strongly stressed. In the foreground here, then, are products, end points, publications, grants and social networks. These are linked together in relationships of recognition and reward. Research is interpreted as a kind of marketplace where the exchange of research products takes place.

It is helpful to think of the third variation as describing two or more layers. The researchers view themselves dipping through the top layer to reveal what lies beneath. There is a sense of illuminating the darkness by looking beneath the surface. I call this the *layer variation*. Reality is presented as a surface and the researcher is investigating or uncovering the phenomena, descriptions, explanations or meaning lying beneath that surface. There may be a sense that what is being sought is a correct description of a reality that exists, in which case research has a sense of discovery about it. Alternatively, the task of examining the layer underneath may rest on the idea that there actually is no correct explanation. What is being sought is simply a better explanation. And finally there may be the idea of research as an artistic process; in which meaning is created, not discovered. So in the foreground here are data containing ideas together with (linked to) hidden meanings. Research is interpreted as a process of discovering, uncovering or creating underlying meanings.

Finally in the fourth variation, research is experienced holistically as personally transformative. The emphasis is on the life issues which underpin the research questions. Research is assimilated into the researcher's own life and understanding. In the *journey variation*, intellectual activities in which the researcher engages, whether or not they appear to have a direct bearing, are viewed as relevant to the research because they inform the underlying issues. There may be the idea that the issues have been explored over a long period of time and are intimately bound up with a person's career and, indeed, life. What is in the foreground here are the personal existential issues and dilemmas. They are linked through an awareness of the career of the researcher and viewed as having been explored for a long time. Research is interpreted as a personal journey of discovery, possibly leading to transformation.

The investigation on which these ideas are based was a qualitative study of variations in ideas about research held by academics. Following an initial pilot stage to explore, trial and then refine open-ended questions, in Phase I of the study thirty researchers from a large Australian 'research' university were interviewed. These were all holders of large Australian Research Council (ARC) grants. These grants are highly competitive and there is evidence that seniority is required to acquire them (Bazeley *et al.* 1996). The researchers were chosen to represent three disciplinary groupings: sciences and technology, social sciences, and the humanities. There were ten researchers in each group. In Phase II of the study, twenty-seven experienced researchers from four Australian universities were interviewed. These were again chosen to represent the three disciplinary groupings. All had a track record in obtaining research grants and/or a substantial record of publication. In this group eleven were in scientific and technical areas, seven were from the social sciences and nine were from the humanities. Although strenuous efforts were made to ensure gender balance, only one-quarter of the respondents were women. This, however, represents a greater proportion than those in the target group (see: Bazeley *et al.* 1996). Interviews sought information concerning the nature of the research participants were pursuing and their experiences of research. Interviewees were encouraged to reflect upon their research, learning and teaching, and there were some background questions to check that the researchers were in the target groups. (For a fuller discussion of the study and the phenomenographic approach used for the analysis of data see Brew 1998a, Brew in press). We will return to these different conceptions of research as we proceed. I shall use some of the things researchers said to illustrate my argument at different stages of the book. (The references given after quotations will anonymously indicate the phases of the research, 1–30 indicating researchers from Phase I and 31–57 from Phase II.)

EVIDENCE OF CHANGES?

When you are in the middle of a landscape it is hard to see it as a whole. Similarly, while the trends within a particular field of study may be obvious, the parochial nature of much academic activity, confined as it is to particular departments, precludes the bird's eye view. The artist shows us what the landscape looks like to an eagle. When we take a broader perspective we can see discrepancies between theory and practice; between theoretical ideas which suggest that research had substantially changed over the course of the twentieth century, including an awareness of the factors, personal and social, which influence how knowledge is pursued, and research activity which is largely unaffected. Research is self-reflexive. The ideas it generates about knowledge and how we come to know apply to the process of research itself. This provides the means of transformation. For it is in the freeing of old ideas and old rigidities that the hope for the future lies. However, there is a time lag and an important tension between rigidity and creativity. We shall see later that there has been a breakdown in traditional rules of research and dramatic changes in what we understand knowledge to be which have run like an earthquake through the academy. Yet there is an uneasy tension between a tenacious pull to hold on to traditional practices on the one hand and attempts to break free on the other. In my study, the researchers were asked whether they thought research had changed during the course of their careers, or was changing in any way. When we come to look at the ways in which research was seen to be changing for these researchers what we find is somewhat surprising. Indeed, there is a discrepancy between common views about the ways in which research is changing and the ways in which these changes are perceived by successful researchers in traditional disciplines. It suggests we must be cautious in translating into practice ideas about research which have been generated from this theoretical work. Indeed, these intellectual challenges have not amounted to significant changes in research practices, except at the margins.

Particularly surprising is the fact that some researchers conceptualized research as being essentially unchanged from the eighteenth and nineteenth centuries. By and large, the changes to research were conceptualized as being a result of pressures coming from outside the discipline in which the research was being conducted. Several researchers mentioned increased pressure to find funding. Mounting demands on other areas of academic life, they said, add to the pressure, for example, increased teaching loads, popularity of collaboration with industry and applied research, doing more managing of research projects and less 'hands on stuff'. Research was becoming more demanding and more competitive. The underlying idea behind all the ideas about funding is that the government was dictating the research agenda, not the academics. The pressure to publish articles was a cause of concern. It meant that there was not always time to do what they wanted to do. However, there were some more serious reservations, including scepticism, about what people were publishing. Counting publications contributes to research being more oriented towards outcomes. This had led to researchers having to change the way they conceptualized their research and this was affecting the character of research. It has now, they said, to be conceptualized in terms of projects. A trading conception of research was being forced on them by the funding agencies. This is unfortunate, particularly since some researchers, as we have seen, conceptualized their life as one long research project. Some were seriously worried by the tendency to publish shorter articles which did not allow for ideas to develop over time, and which relied on having a number of good ideas. We will pursue the implications of these ideas in Chapter Eight.

A number of researchers mentioned the way in which information technology had changed research. Perhaps surprisingly, many were anxious to point out that changes brought about by computers were superficial, rather than fundamental. Having material in a database means that the researcher is able to concentrate on higher level activities. In the natural sciences there are gadgets which enable you to do things you could not do before but you still have to do the work; it is just that the machinery costs more. One researcher said the computer is used less in his field than it was a decade ago. The computer can speed things up but it has increased the expectations:

> [N]ow research has to be so detailed. You have to have huge footnotes with umpteen references because people expect you to have access to all those references . . . that's made it a bit more of a challenge. (04)

In some subject areas the existence of databases was considered to have transformed the discipline, as there is information available which was not available before. 'You don't have to clutter up the brain with all that information' (27).

We shall examine later the major intellectual shifts that took place during the twentieth century to which I have already alluded. It is perhaps surprising that research was seen by these successful researchers as changing in response to external pressures rather than in response to the intellectual climate. Such changes appear to have affected the emphasis of the research – its content – but do not appear to have had significant effects on research methodology. The ways in which people do research are perceived as largely unaffected. Indeed, changes brought about by pressures of government funding appear to have done more to change research methodology in traditional discipline areas than shifts in intellectual climate. It may be that the climate of funding in Australian universities contributed to the dominance of views about extrinsic pressures. However, in view of the extensive intellectual debates which have been going on over the course of almost a century, it is perhaps surprising how funding decisions taken only a couple of years ago have become so much more dominant influences. There was a conception that paradigms are changing all the time but that essentially this was concerned with the intellectual context. The actual activities researchers engage in are unchanged. There was an idea that disciplines change but that researchers continue doing the same thing: researching the same issues.

The ways in which postmodern ideas were influencing research were conceptualized, by and large, as being unrelated to what researchers personally were doing. For example even though it was recognized that 'the bottom has dropped out of English literature' and that the questions which are asked had changed, this had not really changed the methodology. Content in a few disciplines (e.g. English and history) had radically changed including the introduction of cultural studies. Theory was reported to have changed in some disciplines e.g. philosophy and sociology with the inclusion of critical theory and postmodern writers, and the use of theory from other cultures (e.g. black writing, feminist ideas, etc.). This suggests that changes in how research is approached in practice are less radical than the large volume of theory would suggest. The extent to which traditional research boundaries are being broken appears to be dependent, not upon the level of familiarity of researchers with new ideas, but on their views of the ways in which the overall intellectual climate influences their research.

So we are witnessing changes to our ideas about knowledge and knowing while the implications of these in terms of research practice are only just now being felt on the margins. In the next chapter we shall see how a freeing of the rules of research is finding expression in new ways of doing research. We shall also see that this is in acute tension with traditional rules and ways of researching. To understand the nature of research is to live these tensions. If research is to avert a crisis and teach us how to live in a complex, confusing and uncertain world, it has to find a new justification for its existence. This means it has to free itself from the old rigidities and give expression to its creativity. It has to bring its practice in line with its theory.

Chapter 3

Research and scholarship

'Then you should say what you mean,' said Alice.

(Lewis Carroll)

Dust, like a velvet blanket, lay silently over the piles of decaying documents. In the dark, musty room, the air felt heavy. All life had long ago left or been stifled. Charles waited for what seemed like a century, taking in the rows of ancient books on the dreary dark brown shelves. They had obviously remained unread for many a long year. In one corner, rolls of what looked like decaying maps had been bundled, and a stepladder to match the shelves, with rungs worn, stood covered in dust like everything else.

Charles wondered when anyone last came into the room. He sat down on a relatively modern chair resting his wrists on the large, dusty oak table. Told to wear white cotton gloves to look at ancient manuscripts, his hands waited like a surgeon ready to operate. Light, thrown by a small casement window high in the wall to his right, threw a triangle of particles of dust in the air. He watched as the dust flurried, but it never seemed to settle. His nostrils felt itchy and for a while Charles thought he was going to sneeze. Silence. Silence and dust and books. Charles wondered when the room had last been used. He read the backs of some of the books: lots of volumes of the *Observer*, *The Reasonableness and Certainty of the Christian Religion*, *Lectures on Natural and Experimental Philosophy*. Others would have meant getting to his feet but he felt unable to rise. The claustrophobic atmosphere of the room was making him feel drowsy and he thought for a moment that he might fall asleep.

Distracted by the dust in the light of the window, and in this state of somnambulant reverie, Charles had failed to notice that someone had entered the room. Yet in a small dark alcove someone was reading.

As his eyes alighted on the man, Charles was startled. How could he not have noticed him earlier? Dressed in the habit of a Franciscan friar, the man read, mouthing the words, silently. Charles blinked. Here was an apparition. He couldn't remember which order of monks it was that lived in silence and the man was so engrossed that Charles did not know whether to make his own presence known or not. The friar in any case seemed totally oblivious to Charles' presence.

There was something not quite right. In this little micro-world of stale books, of dust and of brown-ness, no other universe seemed to exist. Time had stopped. Or so, to Charles, it seemed. He was ready with his clean, gloved hands and dared not move. If anyone had asked how much time he spent trying to make out what was strange about the man in the alcove he could not have said. Yet eventually, when he was beginning to tire of wondering where he had come from and how often he sat in the alcove and what his name was, the man arose, closing the book as he did so. Holding the book in two hands across his chest he walked to the other side of the room and disappeared. Charles just felt sad.

The door clicked and the librarian entered. 'I've found what you wanted,' he said.

Some eight or nine years ago, I was talking to a colleague about how academics spend their time and he said: 'I don't think I've read a book for ages. I can't remember the last time I read a book.' Then he added that he had not read any articles either: 'We just don't have time for reading these days.' The statement profoundly disturbed me and I have thought about it a great deal since. 'What', I thought, 'are the long-term consequences of academics not reading?' We used to talk about students going up to university to 'read' a particular subject. I can remember a sense of pride when someone in my social circle, knowing I was a university undergraduate, would ask me: 'What are you *reading*?' Nowadays, in our systems of mass higher education, the language has changed. 'What are you studying?' is much more likely to be asked and I am often surprised at how little time the students of today have for reading outside classroom hours.

Watching what was happening to reading in the academic community was one of the major concerns leading me to examine the nature of academic work and hence to explore the nature of research in academic contexts and then to write this book. In empirical studies of academics' ideas about the nature of academic work we can see that scholarship has been the term used to refer to a wide variety of academic activities. Indeed, if we look at how academic work is described in the academic literature about higher education it is frequently in terms of different varieties or forms of scholarship.

In universities you might hear talk of someone's work as 'mere scholarship', by which the person might refer to the fact that the work had not added anything new to the discipline and was just going over old ground. On the other hand you might hear the term used as a form of praise to refer to someone eminent as in the phrase, 'he's a true scholar'. So scholarship is central to academic life, but its meaning is far from unambiguous. In this chapter we shall be concerned to see what we can learn about the nature of research in academic contexts by looking at the concept of scholarship. For scholarship is frequently spoken of in the same breath as research. 'Research and scholarship' sounds as if it were a meaningful phrase, yet nowhere is the contested space which research must occupy more evident than in debates about the nature of research vis-à-vis scholarship. So we shall see that there is a wide range of things scholarship may be said to encompass, some of which are contradictory.

The image which has been with me in thinking about these issues is Picasso's painting *Guernica*. This large monochrome oil painting was painted just after the bombing of the Spanish town of Guernica in 1937. I have always found this painting disturbing. It seems to present a number of disparate elements tied together in different ways. To make sense of the whole picture is to feel its anguish, but I find it hard to focus in a rational way on it as a whole. Every person seeing the painting must have their own conception of it, of its relationship to events in the Spanish Civil War in general and Guernica in particular, and to Picasso's intentions, subconscious and otherwise, which led him to complete this work of art. Ideas about scholarship and its relationship to research are similarly confusing, sometimes disjointed and likewise often disturbing.

We should acknowledge at the outset that some of the confusion concerning different ideas about scholarship might relate to some disciplinary differences. As one researcher in my study said:

> You're trying to get into that debate we have with the scientists, who don't regard reading . . . what historians call – primary sources. They don't call that scholarship. I don't know what they call it actually. [It seems] you've got to make some kind of new discovery in a test-tube or something. I have this argument with scientists all the time. (05)

Boyer (1990) argues that each discipline or professional area has to define scholarship for itself. In some disciplines, however, scholarship is less relevant than others, for example professional areas which do not have a tradition of scholarship. So how are we to understand the relationship with research in these areas of investigation? What does it mean in nursing or in physiotherapy, for example? Barnett (1997a) goes as far as to argue that scientists do not do scholarship. They do not read books. There are few books in science because the rate of publication is too slow. However, as I have indicated earlier, my concern in this book is to take a bird's-eye view and examine the nature of research in broad brush terms. In any case, as we have seen, disciplinary distinctions are problematic. So I shall not be concerned with disciplinary differences here, only with elements of scholarship in so far as they help in understanding the nature of research.

HOW SCHOLARSHIP IS EXPERIENCED

In a study on the nature of academic work, Pellino, Blackburn and Boberg (1984) asked academics, of the time spent on activities they thought of as scholarly, what proportion of it was used for research leading to publications. This investigation found that although many academics outside research universities were not carrying out research leading to publications, over 90 per cent of them reported that they were engaging in activities they considered to be scholarly. In this study academics also indicated how frequently they engaged in each of thirty-two different activities which were listed for them and how central the activity was in their conception of scholarship. Analysis of this data led to six factors being identified:

- scholarship as professional activity
- scholarship as research/publication
- scholarship as artistic endeavour
- scholarship as engagement in the novel
- scholarship as community service
- scholarship as pedagogy.

(Pellino, Blackburn and Boberg 1984: 107–10)

Sundre (1992), in contrast, carried out a qualitative study seeking to clarify the nature and form of scholarship by identifying the dimensions and components from the point of view of academics at a large US public doctoral granting institution. Attributes of scholarship were defined by the academics and weighted in relation to their importance. The activities were then grouped into four domains of the conception:

- activities in which academics engage
- academics' professional characteristics and orientations
- academics' skills, tools and techniques
- the influence academics have on their field and others.

(Sundre 1992: 310–14)

These different domains include the activities mentioned by Pellino and colleagues. However, Sundre (1992) argues that they go beyond them, suggesting that the concept of scholarship is much more complex than previous studies had suggested.

These studies examine elements which go to make up the concept of scholarship in general. However, individuals in higher education and in society each have their own ideas about what constitutes academic work in general and scholarship in particular, i.e. they focus on different aspects. In my study of academic researchers' conceptions of research that we looked at in the last chapter, the senior researchers who participated were also asked for their ideas about the relationship of research to scholarship. The data were analysed in the same way as the data on conceptions of research, namely, phenomenographically (see Brew 1999a for a fuller discussion of this). Five qualitatively different variations were identified. By illustrating the ways in which different people focus on different aspects of scholarship, these tell us different things about the nature of research. Using our analogy with Picasso's painting, it is not possible to focus on the picture as a whole without particular elements coming into focus at different times.

Preparation, new knowledge and dissemination

Three of the conceptions of scholarship I identified held as fundamental the idea that scholarship involved detailed preparation as a basis for the development of new knowledge. Indeed, at its most basic level, scholarship was perceived solely as the background work done as a foundation for research. Here the concept of scholarship was equated with reading and then understanding the field of study through a knowledge and critical evaluation of what is known. In the foreground were the literature and the activities of reading and learning. They were viewed as being linked through the idea of providing a context for the research. Scholarship was thus interpreted as the preparation for research.

> I've always been keen on insisting . . . that the research is new and the scholarship is the background into which it fits. (28)

> [Y]ou have to know what has been done, what has been written, you can't publish without putting it in the context of the existing literature, so . . . the scholarship is an essential preparation for the research. (32)

Interestingly, Elton (1986, 1992) in using the concept of scholarship to link research and teaching, similarly defines scholarship as the interpretation of what is already known; the primary work that feeds into everything else academics are supposed to do. Some researchers pointed to the fact that university research offices defined the difference between research and scholarship in terms of scholarship being about the synthesis or evaluation of what is known while research concerns the generation of new ideas that are publishable. This expresses the sense of this preparation conception of scholarship.

In contrast, some academics in my study saw scholarship not just as a preparatory activity but also as adding something to what has already been done. What was in the foreground for them was the preparatory work plus the addition of new ideas and discoveries. The new knowledge had to be contextualized in the existing knowledge. Scholarship was interpreted as the process of adding new knowledge to that existing literature.

> [M]y understanding of scholarship means bringing new knowledge into the arena of academia. If I discover a new compound and interaction, it's some-thing new that hasn't been found before, then that's bringing new knowledge

in, and other people can learn from that so I assume that creating new molecules, finding out and investigating about them . . . is a scholarly activity. (40)

I think of scholarship as something that's breaking new ground . . . and I think . . . even though we are . . . starting off with a particular set of hypotheses, structure and so forth, . . . we are trying to treat this as a bit of a voyage of discovery. (13)

The third way of viewing scholarship included the idea of dissemination. Having carried out the reading and preparation and added new knowledge, the work is then disseminated through, for example, publication and teaching. Scholarship was interpreted as the process of making a contribution to society through the integration and dissemination of ideas and knowledge. I called this the *integrating variation* because here scholarship means bringing together everything you have done and disseminating it. Teaching was seen as not essentially any different from the process of dissemination. Interacting with colleagues, giving seminars, engaging in correspondence are all scholarship in this variation.

[T]o me scholarship is . . . getting on top of the literature. It's doing your research. It's writing it up. It's the correspondence that you enter into. It's . . . the way it informs your teaching, the way you bring students into an appreciation of that area of our history and the way you interact with research students and encourage them – if they are interested – to be part of it. And all of that I would regard as scholarship and I think that's what I do, yes. (54)

Writing papers and presenting papers and disseminating the results of the papers is scholarship I think . . . I suppose to a certain extent the degree to which you go there and engage in the society and get a sense of what's happening can also be seen as a part of scholarship. Interacting with colleagues is a scholarly activity. (11)

Some researchers focused on the end product, which invariably included the production of texts again for use by others.

I would normally associate scholarship more with writing, so . . . either writing papers or books or some way disseminating the knowledge perhaps . . . even teaching. (03)

I suppose scholarship to me is ultimately captured by the end product, which is the research you put out and disseminate . . . through discussions with your colleagues, through presentation of research workshops at other universities, through presenting papers at conferences and ultimately through the publication of those papers. (39)

These three variations in ideas about scholarship build on each other. They share a basic orientation to the concept of scholarship, with increasing complexity as one moves from reading to creating to integrating. Each variation incorporates the activities foregrounded in the previous less complex one.

CONTESTED SPACE

If these three conceptions of scholarship were all there were or if scholarship merely described the set of academic activities outlined in the studies mentioned earlier, I doubt whether it would be contentious. It would certainly not be the focus of such intense debate as it is in higher education today. However, the situation is clearly more complex and at this point we enter the contested territory.

Some responses in my study were characterized by a simple assertion that research and scholarship are the same thing and that any attempt to separate them is impossible. The distinction between research and scholarship was viewed as confusing and problematic.

> The first time I heard people actually talking scholarship as opposed to research was in the context of whether you publish what you were doing in research . . . and so it was used in the kind of discourse when you talk about teaching as involving lots of scholarship, and . . . research is something – well obviously – [that] feeds into your teaching but it's something that you're publishing. Whereas teaching . . . I mean I find it very hard to . . . I mean I can't make that distinction . . . I mean that's . . . ridiculous, I mean that's just manipulating this vocabulary and saying . . . research and scholarship have . . . applications to this, that and the other, promotion. It didn't make much sense to me, because . . . often when you're teaching . . . It happens to me frequently when I'm involved in teaching a course on such and such and I work on a particular area that I mightn't have necessarily worked on because . . . in a French department . . . there aren't students battering the doors down wanting to do esoteric types of subjects on 17th Century French. Phew! in fact, so . . . I teach lots of things. I teach contemporary French literature and things like that and . . . so I work in . . . French authors that . . . I know very well because I've worked on them a lot and often that results in an article. I suppose the work I did was research but . . . if I hadn't published, it would've been called scholarship, would it? And then it's research because I published it. So . . . I just don't make a distinction, I don't really understand the distinction. (02)

The confusion expressed here reflects a much more complex scenario than we have so far encountered in this chapter. Several researchers in the study attributed the confusion to policy documents on research.

I find the term 'scholarship' really problematic . . . the way the university uses it, especially in promotions committees and stuff, I always find it very problematic. (09)

Both research and scholarship are hard to define. They're slippery terms . . . what constitutes research, what constitutes scholarship? I think research offices do make a distinction. . . . Research has to be something that is original, scholarship tends to be more synthesis of work that other people have done. I guess I'm happy with that definition, although I think any work of writing is in a sense research, since you're always saying something new or putting things together in new ways. And in a sense nothing is completely original, because we are always working on materials that are used. But accepting that distinction, even if it is artificial . . . of course all research is scholarship, I think scholarship embraces research. . . . I don't believe in making enemies by saying 'I can't make the distinction'. If I have to make the distinction I'll make it in a way that seems logical to me. (46)

It is not surprising there is such confusion. If you look at promotions policies and procedures for academic appointments in many universities you will see as criteria statements such as these from four major Australian universities:

1   Evaluation of academic performance . . . is based, at each level of appointment, on four categories of activity: teaching; research/scholarship/ creative work; service and leadership within the University; service and leadership to the profession, wider community and the development of Australian society.
2   An academic at this level (senior lecturer) is also expected to play a major role in scholarship, research and/or professional activities.
3   Three key criteria for promotion – namely, advancement of the discipline, contribution to teaching and service to the University.
4   Teaching; research, scholarship and creative activity; service.

It is clear that promotions criteria are driven by some unwritten and unstated assumptions about the nature of these activities even though, by and large, university policies leave open the interpretation of terms. This makes things particularly difficult for the new academic trying to make sense of them.

As we shall increasingly come to recognize in our quest to understand the nature of research, and as Part II will amply testify, the pursuit of knowledge has clearly been recognized as being deeply embedded within the political and economic contexts of society (Lenoir 1997). Thus in recent years some attempts to spell out the meanings of the terms research and scholarship have been made in some countries by government bodies wishing to be able to measure research 'output'. For example, consider the New Zealand Government's definitions:

> Research – includes the creation of new knowledge through the discovery and codification of new information, and the development of further understanding about existing information and practice. May include scholarship.

> Scholarship – either ongoing learning and erudition that signifies a full command of a subject or discipline; or a grant to assist a student undertaking study.
>
> (New Zealand Government 1997)

In contrast, the UK Government's definition of research states:

> 'Research' for the purpose of the RAE (Research Assessment Exercise) is to be understood as original investigation undertaken in order to gain knowledge and understanding. It includes work of direct relevance to the needs of commerce and industry, as well as to the public and voluntary sectors; scholarship*; the invention and generation of ideas, images, performances and artefacts including design, where these lead to new or substantially improved insights; and the use of existing knowledge in experimental development to produce new or substantially improved materials, devices, products and processes, including design and construction. It excludes routine testing and analysis of materials, components and processes, e.g. for the maintenance of national standards, as distinct from the development of new analytical techniques. It also excludes the development of teaching materials that do not embody original research.
>
> (HEFCE 1999: 6)

There is a recognition here (indicated by the asterisk) that the term 'scholarship' needs to be defined. In the 1997 draft version of this document the explanation of scholarship given was:

> *Scholarship embraces a spectrum of activities including the development of teaching material; the latter is excluded from the RAE.
>
> (HEFCE 1997: 17)

The difficulty with this definition, as with that given by the New Zealand Government presented above, is that scholarship in these terms is impossible to measure. It is interesting to note therefore that the definition of scholarship was rephrased in the UK's final version of the document as:

> *Scholarship is defined for the RAE as the creation, development and maintenance of the intellectual infrastructure of subjects and disciplines, in

forms such as dictionaries, scholarly editions, catalogues and contributions to major research databases.

(HEFCE 1999)

The shift towards defining scholarship in terms of output such as dictionaries, scholarly editions, catalogues and contributions to databases, illustrates a fundamental dilemma of governments in regard to research and scholarship. Ideas of research which I described earlier in terms of a number of academic activities, many of which are based in scholarly reading, cannot be quantified. There is a saying in some universities that trying to make academics do anything is like trying to herd cats. This is the task which governmental agencies, with a brief to make higher education more accountable, have set themselves. One of the ways they have endeavoured to do this is by defining fundamental activities of academic life such as teaching and research in measurable terms. Research assessment exercises are an attempt to tame academic work; to make it manageable in financial terms and to make academics demonstrably accountable for what they do. This is a theme to which we return in Chapter Eight.

REDEFINING SCHOLARSHIP

Thus a tension exists between narrow views of research and scholarship as measurable activities producing quantitative outcomes, and wide definitions of research and scholarship as essentially facets of the nature of scholarly work grounded in a scholarly background of reading. However, this is not just a contested space but also a shifting one. In order to explore notions of scholarship further and to examine what these say about the nature of research we have to take a historical perspective. For as one of my interviewees said:

> Scholarship isn't just a static category. It's developing and evolving along with people's interests. So what people thought scholarship was in the 19th Century or the early 20th Century is not what people think scholarship is today, and of course there are lots of fights amongst scholars as to what good scholarship might be, so it's very much a political domain in which you try to make your own vision of scholarship be the one that most people will adopt in the future . . . For example in performance studies, which is very much a developing field, it's a very recent discipline . . . nobody really knows what performance studies is, so everyone who writes about it is in a sense putting out a charter for how they think it should be, and I'm one of those, I'm fighting for a certain line, a certain position about what I think people should be doing under the rubric of performance studies. (38)

A number of writers have argued, like the researcher quoted here, that definitions of scholarship have changed over time and that this follows the historical development of universities. Indeed, even in 1837, the American poet, Ralph Waldo Emerson, in an address to the Harvard Phi Beta Kappa Society, suggested that a new definition of scholarship was needed (Rice 1992). It seems one is needed every few years. It has been suggested that changes in how research and scholarship are perceived resulted, in the late nineteenth and early twentieth centuries, in an emphasis on research viewed in narrow terms as referring to publication of fundamental knowledge based on technical rationality (Rice 1992; Schön 1995; Scott and Awbrey 1993).

> The modern research-focused university emerged in the nineteenth century in Germany. Its key strengths were the establishment of the research laboratory which concentrated the critical resources necessary for forefront research; the organisation of research around a powerful professor with his team; and the strong attention given to the rigorous training of new researchers.
>
> (Sutherland 1994: 40)

In the early years of the nineteenth century under the bold visionary leadership of Alexander Von Humbolt, state-funded universities grew up within different German states. Humbolt's vision included introducing a reform of the high school system and university entrance based on a matriculation examination. In the German university, teaching and research were perceived to go hand in hand.

> During the nineteenth century, the philosophy faculty grew out of all proportion to the other faculties and within it the proportion of students taking sciences almost trebled. If to this growing number of scientists at the universities who underwent a specialized training to a very high level are added the large number of engineers and applied physicists who were studying at her technical institutions, it is not surprising that Germany forged ahead in almost every field of scientific endeavour.
>
> (Simpson 1983: 15)

For our purposes there are several things to note in this. First, there is the influence of state funding on research and teaching. Notions of scholarship and research are intimately connected with the uses to which governments wish to put it. Second, there is the extent of state control which was considerable in Germany but neither customary nor desired in, for example, Britain or America. University teaching and research were also related to the levels and types of school education which in Germany was, as indicated, similarly under state control. Thus it was possible for Germany to turn the universities, and university research in particular, to the service of the state whether for the development of industry or for the purposes of war, which, in the event, had ultimately disastrous consequences during the first half of the twentieth century.

Nonetheless, the nineteenth-century German universities, with their emphasis on the unity of knowledge, well-funded laboratories and practical seminars, attracted scholars from countries with less well-organized provision for advanced study, including Britain and the US. In the latter years of the nineteenth century growing concern was expressed in Britain, for example, about the 'majesty of German knowledge' and the paucity of its own university education and research training (Haines 1969: 99; Simpson 1983). Yet given that there was no history of state control in Britain and university autonomy was a well-established principle, and given the highly individualistic character of British society, the government found it harder to accept responsibility for publicly funding universities and, therefore, to turn the activities of institutions of higher education towards its own purposes. This only happened for the service of industry to a small extent in the latter part of the nineteenth century and then again more substantially during the war years.

> Although there had been much debated on the subject from the middle of the nineteenth century and a modest beginning in the national physical laboratory for example, it was war – the first and second World Wars – which brought home the need for public investment in research in the UK. And such public investment was always linked to the need to underpin industry and the economy.
>
> (Sutherland 1994: 40)

Research, when the government needed it, was well funded and encouraged. Scholarship in this scenario was the poor relation. It has been in the large and diverse system of American higher education, however, that concern with the concept of scholarship has been most prevalent.

Boyer (1990), tracing the development of American scholarship, highlights three phases. First, there was, he suggests, the colonial college where the focus was on the student and the task of the academy was viewed as developing character and leadership. The founding of Harvard College in 1636 was, he points out, designed to educate the clergy. For both teachers and students, scholarly achievement was not a high priority; indeed teaching was central. But, Boyer argues, this was soon to change in the latter half of the nineteenth century. Professors became viewed as having a duty to disseminate knowledge which could benefit industry and agriculture. Service to the community became part of the academic enterprise. In the growing context of industrialization, knowledge was to be applied to practical problems. Influenced by the German system of higher education where research was pursued as a primary goal, the Ph.D. and research training began to be seen as a key to university life and universities developed a commitment to the scholarship of science. So by the end of the nineteenth century the idea of advancing knowledge through research had taken hold on academic life in the US. Compared to traditional ideas of scholarship, research, it seems, is a relatively recent phenomenon (Van Ginkel 1994).

The idea of research as a primary activity in the US, Boyer suggests, gained ground in the early part of the twentieth century. It was fuelled by the usefulness of scientific research to the government, particularly with the establishment of the Office of Scientific Research and Development during the Second World War. 'Being a scholar was now virtually synonymous with being an academic professional' (Boyer 1990: 10). Even so, the image of the academic professional prior to the Second World War was that of the teacher-scholar.

However, in the mid-1950s, following the launch of Sputnik by the USSR and the introduction of the GI Bill of Rights, what it meant to be an academic professional changed in the US. In the expansionist period in higher education in the 1960s scholarship was equated with research at the cutting edge of the discipline. The academic professional image of that time assumed that research sustained by peer review and professional autonomy was the central professional endeavour of academic life; that knowledge in the form of cognitive truth was pursued for its own sake in discipline-based departments. National and international professional associations established reputations and advancement of specializations was rewarded (Rice 1992).

Although the research mission noted above was appropriate for some universities, it cast a shadow over those institutions for whom it was not appropriate, such as in institutional contexts focused more on teaching or which were less research intensive (Boyer 1990; Rice 1992). This has led more recently to growing unease about universities' role and mission, which has coalesced around calls to redefine or to expand the concept of scholarship (see for example Boyer 1990; Rice 1992; Scott and Awbrey 1993).

> Not only do our institutions have diverse missions – commitments to serving a wide range of scholarly needs within region, states and action – but also there is the special commitment to the education of an increasingly diverse population, to the intellectual preparation of the educated citizen necessary for making a genuinely democratic society possible. Scholarship in this context takes on broader meaning.
>
> (Rice 1992: 128)

Calls to redefine or to extend the nature of scholarship have arisen from the changing context and climate of universities and their changed relationship to society. First, there was concern about the way in which academic work was rewarded; in particular, about the status of teaching vis-à-vis research and the rewarding of achievements in research publications vis-à-vis teaching performance (Leatherman 1990; Mooney 1990; Ruscio 1987). Second, there was a concern to give conceptions of scholarship contemporary relevance. This highlighted the need for scholarship to result in a greater connection between the university and outside and for there to be a greater sense of connectivity within the university community (Scott and Awbrey 1993). It meant taking account of the closer integration of universities and society as well as accepting the increasing focus on applied work and the integration of theory and practice, as well as the need to educate previously unimagined numbers of students and to integrate new intellectual challenges (Rice

1992). Third, Schön (1995) argues that new definitions point to the need to change institutional epistemology to take account of the requirements of professional practice. Finally, there is a desire simply to sort out the confusion surrounding the concept of scholarship and its relation to research.

Boyer (1990: xii) suggests that 'the most important obligation now confronting colleges and universities is to break out of the tired old teaching versus research debate and define, in more creative ways what it means to be a scholar'. The response of the Carnegie Foundation for the Advancement of Teaching has been widely quoted and has gained popularity particularly where there has been a desire to reward teaching. The ideas of Boyer (1990) and colleagues conceptualize research, scholarship, academic teaching, and learning as all part of the same academic enterprise, since they are all implicated in the pursuit or development of knowledge, personal and social.

Following investigations into undergraduate education, the Boyer framework suggests a fourfold definition which, it is argued, corresponds to different approaches to the ways knowledge is perceived and approached: the advancement of knowledge, its application, representation and integration in society. The scholarship of discovery, Boyer (1990: 17) suggests, comes closest to the idea of 'research'. It contributes to the 'stock of human knowledge' and also to the intellectual climate of the institution. The scholarship of integration is concerned with making interdisciplinary connections. 'In calling for a scholarship of integration, . . . what we mean is serious, disciplined work that seeks to interpret, draw together, and bring new insight to bear on original research' (Boyer 1990: 19).

The third type of scholarship defined by Boyer and his colleagues is the scholarship of application. By this they draw attention to the application of knowledge in the wider community. There is a caution against seeing theory and practice separately, for what is envisaged is a dynamic interaction where the 'one renews the other' (Boyer 1990: 23). Finally there is the scholarship of teaching. This involves well-informed teachers; teaching which is carefully planned, continuously evaluated and related to the subject taught; teaching which promotes active learning and encourages students to be critical creative thinkers with the capacity to go on learning after their university days are over; and a recognition that teachers are also learners (Boyer 1990: 24).

What we notice about the attempts at redefinition that Boyer and colleagues present is that theirs is a normative framework (Davis *et al.* 1998). In other words, it is concerned with conceptions of scholarship which Boyer and colleagues believe *ought* to prevail, not the conceptions which *do* prevail, which were the concern of the empirical studies we looked at earlier. Nevertheless, the Boyer categories have had enormous influence, particularly in leading to expanded definitions embodied in policy documents of individual institutions such as those quoted earlier. In respect of academic promotions, widespread acceptance of teaching as a component owes much to the work of the Carnegie Foundation in spelling out the idea of the scholarship of teaching.

Integrating conceptions of scholarship

While the Boyer framework has been influential in raising the status of teaching, it accepts a narrow view of research as 'discovery'. I cannot help feeling that what characterizes scholarship are those elements which integrate Boyer's four categories, not the categories themselves. The way in which different elements of scholarship relate to each other is clearly important to the academic community and it is vital in our understanding of the nature of research. Activities spanning all four conceptions, such as the role of careful reading and preparatory work, begin to provide an integrating context. But I do not think this goes quite far enough.

Endeavouring to provide an integrating framework, Paulsen and Feldman (1995) examined scholarship in terms of Talcott Parsons's four-function analysis. The scholarship of research and graduate training, they argue, performs the function of pattern maintenance in the 'scholarship action system' (Paulsen and Feldman 1995: 623). The scholarship of teaching performs the function of adaptation. The scholarship of service performs the goal attainment function, and the scholarship of academic citizenship performs the function of integration for the overall scholarship action system. They suggest:

> The conventional awareness of the importance of research as scholarship, combined with a current understanding that the scholarship action system has four functions that, in different ways, are just as important, helps explain the conflict surrounding scholarship as well as the impetus to reconceptualize the construct.
>
> (Paulsen and Feldman 1995: 631).

Comparing these four functions of scholarship with Boyer's (1990) framework, Paulsen and Feldman (1995) admit that three of the categories are similar. However, they suggest that Boyer's scholarship of integration properly belongs within the scholarship of discovery, or, in their terms, the scholarship of research and graduate training. The function of integration is performed, in their view, not by disciplinary integration. If the overall scholarship action system is to survive and remain effective, they argue, then the scholarship of academic citizenship is required to perform the integrating function. This, they suggest, is missing from Boyer's framework (Paulsen and Feldman 1995).

Paulsen and Feldman (1995) suggest that empirical studies have consistently identified a wide range of traditional teaching, research and community service activities as important elements of university scholarship. For example, they attribute Sundre's (1992) categories to their four-function framework, arguing that some academics will be seen to divide their time between all four kinds of scholarship while others will specialize. However, as we have seen, academics have qualitatively different understandings of the concept of scholarship and may engage in some activities without calling them scholarship. Moreover, while both Paulsen and Feldman and Boyer include four of Pellino, Blackburn and Boberg's (1984) categories, they leave out scholarship as artistic endeavour and scholarship as engagement in the novel.

SCHOLARSHIP AS THE QUALITY OF ACADEMIC WORK

However, there is something much more significant which is left out of these analyses and which is truly an integrating component. The fifth variation identified in my study is a vital clue to understanding the nature of research. A critical element in the idea of scholarship is that it describes *the way* in which academics work. It refers to the qualities of meticulousness and rigour associated with academic inquiry and reporting. This includes, for example, making sure all statements can be substantiated. This is a neglected but very useful aspect of scholarship particularly in relation to our quest to understand more fully the nature of research. As one researcher said:

> Scholarship is the description of a calling or profession, research is the technical name for an activity. (24)

This idea of scholarship (which I call the *quality variation*) emphasizes the role of a professional approach to whatever academic activities are engaged in. There is some overlap with activities Sundre (1992: 311) grouped as 'faculty members' professional characteristics and orientations'. For the idea of professionalism is central to this way of thinking about scholarship. Neumann (1993) has also suggested that the concept of scholarship includes the idea of a quality describing the way in which inquiry should be done.

Among the researchers in my study, similar aspects were mentioned: 'techniques of critical thought' (09); 'reflective, scholarly process' (55). This variation also describes the possession of relevant professional skills and knowledge needed to carry out the work.

> The word 'scholarship' for me means being precise, being absolutely clear what you are doing, what categories you are working in. Making sure that you're consistent . . . (27)

> When you say scholarship, in my mind, that puts it on a bit of a higher plane and . . . makes it sound as though we are . . . really trying to be very thorough and very careful . . . (13)

There is also some overlap here with Sundre's (1992: 312) group of 'faculty members' skills, tools and techniques', because there is the idea that being professional means bringing specialist knowledge and skills to bear in doing the work:

> You have to make scholarly decisions about which reading you think is most likely in a given case. So you have to understand a lot about the genre of the poems. . . . You have to know a fair bit about the language . . . in order to know what's most likely. . . . If you've got a number of variant readings, how are you going to decide between them? It's usually on the basis of metre or on the basis of a common image that occurs elsewhere in the body of poems . . . you've got to know quite a lot about it in order to make those kinds of editorial decisions. It's very scholarly, very specialized . . . [There is] obviously knowledge of the field . . . there's a huge body of knowledge there that I've acquired. Also knowledge in terms of understanding [and] dealing with manuscript culture rather than print books . . . The skills I have . . . are mostly to do with language, translating, interpreting, reading a particular language . . . paleographical skills, interpreting manuscripts, being able to read abbreviations, other kinds of paleographical skills . . . It's really the difference between amateurism and professionalism, that's the only way I can describe it. Being scholarly is being professional. It's treating your work professionally. Thinking about it as something that needs to be done well, that needs to stand up to the scrutiny of other scholars. (04)

The importance of delineating this conception of scholarship should not be underestimated. In the context of changing ideas of knowledge and knowing, and in the face of challenges to traditional notions of objectivity and rationality brought about by critical perspectives, it suggests an alternative basis for judging the quality of academic work. While at a basic level it draws attention to the idea of professionalism embodied in an emphasis on giving attention to detail, including logic, use of evidence, making sure work is properly referenced, etc., the idea goes further. For the conception sees academic rigour as an aspect of professionalism, not as a rule-bound pursuit of objectivity. In a postmodern context where the idea of truth as a function of the view of a detached observer is terminally challenged, as we shall see, new conceptions of rigour are important. The quality conception of scholarship provides the basis for defining rigour in terms which are uncluttered by questionable traditional notions of objectivity.

Yet this too is contested space. For the quality conception of scholarship has been all but forgotten in the context of governments taking on the role of defining the nature of academic research and scholarship. This conception of scholarship provides an important backdrop to concerns about accountability and performativity which have characterized so much of the debate about research in recent years. Emphasizing the measurable instead of the ways in which what is measurable has been achieved operates at the expense of academic professionalism and integrity. Emphasizing that academics value, advocate and practise professionalism – expressed on the one hand in the attention to detail and meticulousness of their working methods, and on the other in the possession of a set of specialist and general skills and knowledge which enables them to carry out that work – pulls against the idea that all that academics do should be demonstrable and measurable.

The nature of research is informed by the quality conception of scholarship and embedded in the idea that new work has to be contextualized within existing knowledge. This is in stark contrast to ideas of knowledge simply as a quantity of measurable outcomes. There is an important contest going on which we must remember as we continue.

Chapter 4

Following rules

Anything goes.
(Cole Porter)

Mustak is a society where there is a heightened sense of anxiety that people will not obey the rules. It's not that there ever was a time when lawlessness was rife; just that there is a fear of things getting out of control. It is madness which is feared, not deliberate acts of disobedience. Yg had set up an investigation she wanted to carry out. But all studies had to be approved and Sealed by Grand Master. Yg thought it would be a good idea to involve a group of Mustakians in deciding the questions she would ask all of them and in making sense of what she found.

Grand Master said: 'Let me see your Questions.'

Yg was taken aback. She had carefully explained in her Document that these were to be negotiated. 'Er . . . I am going to discuss and agree them with the Mustakians,' she hesitantly replied.

'You cannot enter the House of Studies before I approve them,' said Grand Master pompously.

'So does that mean I can't meet with my Mustakian group until I get The Seal?'

'Of course.' Grand Master gave no hint that he understood this was a problem. He added: 'You must let me approve your Questions before you can get The Seal and you must get The Seal before you can go into the House of Studies.'

Yg felt defeated. Yet she had an idea it was important to pursue this. After all, her friend Sy had experienced difficulties. Grand Master had approved his Questions. Having got The Seal Sy had entered the House of Studies. But the Mustakians had beaten him because he asked them to give him a snippet of their hair for inspection. Yg did not want that to happen to her. She decided to try another tack.

'Grand Master,' she began, respectfully bowing, 'I appreciate you are concerned that I should not exploit nor ask inappropriate Questions of the Mustakians. I also understand that if I ask them Questions I have to be careful how I interpret the responses.'

'Of course,' said Grand Master patronizingly.

'So,' Yg continued, 'I have decided to involve the Mustakians in designing the investigation. I don't want to ask them Questions they would not find useful to have answered or that they would find offensive. Therefore, er . . . would it not be appropriate . . . er . . . I need The Seal to enter the House of Studies before I can give you my Questions.'

Showing signs of impatience, Grand Master replied: 'I well understand the nature of your investigation. I have read your Document. However, you must tell me your Questions.'

'And so how can I do that?'

'You must make some up, of course!'

'So if I make up some Questions, er . . . any Questions, and you approve them, you will give me The Seal? Is that what you are saying?'

'Yes, before you enter the House of Studies you must have The Seal, and before you can get The Seal you must give me your Questions.'

'But isn't that dishonest? Suppose I go in and talk to the Mustakians and they object to my Questions?'

'Those are the Rules,' Grand Master said, closing the interview.

The ways research is conducted, the requirements for reporting on it and how the wider academic community evaluates it, all depend on a framework of rules. A process of inquiry is a *process* of inquiry precisely because it follows certain rules of procedure. Rules define standards of acceptable and unacceptable research behaviour. So if we want to understand the nature of academic research, we need to look at its rules. The rules and norms of behaviour tell us something about the underlying values of the research. They also reflect the values prevalent in the societal context and the concerns of the community at large. The rules and values embody underlying assumptions about the nature of reality, the nature of knowledge and the relationship between the two; and they determine what counts as valid knowledge. They also determine what counts as a valid method of investigation. The methods used and the theories about which methods should be used (methodologies) are intimately related to and reflect the rules of research. Yet the rules go much further. Research includes not only the investigation, but also how that investigation is communicated through publication and other forms of dissemination, how the research is funded and evaluated, and indeed whether the research takes place at all. All of these are founded on the rules of research behaviour. So fundamental to any understanding of the nature of research is an understanding of the rules of research.

Talk of rules is unfashionable nowadays. So to say that doing research means following rules is rather provocative. When I see a café called 'The Slug and Lettuce' something inside me jars and I think: 'You can't have a café called that! It's a contradiction. A café should have a name which . . .'. I have an internal set of rules for what is acceptable and not acceptable as a name for a café. Similarly, those who set out to do some research have in mind a number of things which they think they should and should not do. They have an idea about what research is and what it is not. As we saw in the previous chapter, some people have clear notions of the rules of professionalism. When I have conducted workshops for academics who do not have a conventional research training, perhaps because they have come into academic life through a profession, I find that even though many have never engaged in a sustained piece of research before, they still have in mind some of the things which they believe they must strive to do and things they must endeavour to avoid. These ideas can sometimes have an oppressive quality. Of course we do not consciously think: 'Oh, I'd better follow this rule or that rule.' What I am referring to as the rules of how to do research are our ideas about what constitutes professional academic practice. Where the new researcher enters a laboratory or joins a research team, the rules will define the ways in which their colleagues behave, and the newcomer learns to imitate their behaviour. In an area where the new researcher is essentially working alone, the rules may appear somewhat mysterious. However, stated or not, the rules provide the etiquette of research behaviour.

So I talk of rules recognizing that this is a rather strict word for what are both implicit and explicit, vague and precise ideas which we try to adhere to when we engage in activities we call research. In this chapter I want to look at what these are. To do this we will also have to look at some of the problems associated with them, for to talk of the rules of research is again to define a contested space, as we shall see. I will look first at the role of rules in the research process, i.e. what they do for us. New forms of research are now coming into being and there has been critical questioning of traditional rules in many academic areas, so we consider how conventional rules are changing and giving way to a more diffuse pattern. We shall see that there are tensions in academic research between adhering to the old rules on the one hand and breaking them on the other. Using our picture analogy, this chapter is about how we decide what kinds of research pictures are appropriate; how we decide on appropriate methods and techniques and with what criteria we evaluate them. But the chapter is also concerned with what makes the picture a coherent whole. I shall look at the conventional picture and then examine some unconventional ones, noting the tensions as researchers attempt to create new pictures while still based in a culture which values the old.

WHAT DO RULES DO?

When we talk about the rules which govern how a research project proceeds, we are talking at one level about what particular researchers feel they should do to make their work acceptable to the research community to which they belong. There are many different kinds of rules. There are the formal rules and the informal rules. There are straightforward procedural rules. There are rules about appropriate content, rules about method and rules about how to behave as a researcher. There are specific rules for different kinds of research, for example rules about safety in the laboratory, rules about confidentiality, etc. There are rules about which rules are to be followed and when. The process of research can be conceptualized as intimately bound up with layers and series of rules, all of which define its character. For any particular system of rules means that certain kinds of research are sustained and nurtured, and other kinds hindered or excluded. As we shall see in the remainder of the section, there are some research areas which are outside the boundaries of acceptability, perhaps because it is inconceivable that they could be investigated without breaking key rules. The rules 'preserve the status quo of intellectual life' (Feyerabend 1975: 45). They are a vehicle for recognizing order in people's behaviour. Indeed, the tacit and embedded nature of many of the rules means that the activity of research and the following of rules of procedure may be considered one and the same thing.

Some of the same rules apply to a much wider enterprise than simply academic research. An inquiry into which car I should buy follows some of the same rules (look at the literature, gather data about cars, make judgements, test out in practice, draw logical conclusions). So are there general rules which apply to all processes of inquiry and special ones which apply to academic research? I believe that the rules of academic research define for society what counts as an inquiry. The extent to which its rules are adhered to depends on the system of evaluation. Different kinds of inquiries are evaluated in different ways by different people, e.g. public inquiry, market research, personal purchasing inquiry, industrial research. Academic research is characterized by being evaluated by academics through a peer review process.

Not that researchers always follow the rules. Latour and Woolgar (1986), in their study of what happens in a biological laboratory, show the way in which, under the guise of epistemological or logical arguments, social negotiation and evaluations of individual researchers take place. They suggest that logic may be misused in discussions between researchers, but these illogicalities are forgotten when the resulting fact is accepted. Feyerabend (1975) suggested that scientific methods were successful precisely because people ignored the rules. In addition, the work of postmodern writers appears intentionally to break many rules (see for example the work of Derrida). Yet even in the most radical traditions, going against the evidence, plagiarizing and using unsubstantiated speculation or illogical argument amount to breaking with the tradition and risking non-acceptance. There is a constant tension between rule-based procedures on the one hand and freedom and creativity attempting to break away on the other.

TRADITIONAL RULES

Let us turn now to some of the ideas people have about how they should go about their academic research. Here is a list of rules which a group of new researchers in the field of education came up with. They had these rules in their heads. Some of them were causing problems in their efforts to get their research going.

1   You must be impartial.
2   You must publish in a refereed journal.
3   You must have lots of references.
4   It must be an academic discourse.
5   No spelling mistakes.
6   You must sound like you have read the book.
7   You must be systematic.
8   You must not intervene in the lives of your 'subjects'.
9   Research must be an original contribution to the field.
10 You must publish.
11 You must be aware of the social and political context.
12 You must be 'objective'.
13 You must find the description of reality/the 'truth'.
14 You must use an 'acceptable' methodology.
15 You must be detached.

Similar lists have been compiled in numerous workshops with beginning researchers. Even the newest academic researcher may start with some belief that research must be objective and that their own opinions have to be eliminated. There might be an implicit assumption that, if research is done systematically and in accordance with the rules of objectivity, one researcher could be substituted for another because there will be agreement on what the facts are. In other words, everyone who looks at the data will see the same thing. Findings are reproducible because nature is assumed to be consistent. The aim is commonly thought to be to arrive at knowledge which looks as if it has not been touched by human hands. Our new researcher may also have the idea that facts must be grounded in evidence, and that the task of research is to find such facts and combine them to form some kind of theory. The goal of research may be seen as the progressive accumulation of truths or facts, and an increase in ability to predict or control. This is likely to be viewed as progress.

The new researcher is likely to have picked up the idea that when they write about their research they have to do so as if it were detached impersonal knowledge. Where people are the 'subjects' of the research they have to be treated as if they are objects. Wolff (quoted in Bauman 1992: 72) describes this as a 'puppet view' of research. Assuming there is a world outside of and separate from ourselves as the focus of study, the new researcher learns to see separate objects, just as, when we look down a microscope we learn to differentiate the different things we are seeing.

Another rule which the new researcher may have internalized is the rule of rationality. The belief is that truth can be established by logic based on or supported by empirical evidence. Logical argument is a fundamental rule of research.

The rules of research, and therefore the criteria for judging it, which many have internalized, concern the extent to which rules of logic, consistency, objectivity and so on, have been followed. These are perhaps the commonest and the most prevalent rules for academic research behaviour. In some form or another they enter into every conversation about research activities. Some would say they define the nature of research.

But these rules are not an ad hoc aggregate. They form the basis of a self-consistent whole, a coherent system based on a set of assumptions about the nature of reality (ontology) and the nature of knowledge (epistemology). They represent the tradition of inquiry which has been characteristic of Western thought for some considerable time. This tradition enshrines a view of the nature of reality, assumptions about the logical and empirical requirements for studying it and about the relationship of theories to one another, as well as ideas about the relationship of research findings to reality. The most common term used to describe this set of rules is 'positivism'. Originally used by Compte (1971) in the 1850s in the context of social thought, positivism arose as an attempt by the then newly emerging social sciences to emulate the physical sciences. It is not a unitary idea but refers to a network of interrelated ideas with 'family resemblances' (Reese 1980). What I refer to as positivism has variously been called 'logical empiricism' (Harré 1981), 'the standard empiricist account' (Hesse 1980), 'the philosophy of knowledge', 'standard empiricism' (Maxwell 1984), 'Enlightenment thinking' (Usher *et al.* 1997), 'conventional inquiry' (Lincoln and Guba 1985), 'objectivism', 'scientific method', 'foundationalism' (Norris 1997), 'modern inquiry' (Mourad 1997a) or 'traditional methodology' (Brew 1999b).

The positivist/objectivist rules of detachment, objectivity and logicality operate on a number of different levels and they are logically related. These have traditionally defined and bounded areas of investigation which the academic community and society at large considered useful or acceptable. It is this system of rules which defines standards of rigour. The validity of an investigation is determined by the extent to which it has adhered to this self-consistent set of rules.

These rules, and the values which underlie them, however, also serve to limit what is found out. For example, the requirement to be objective means that only a certain area of the total possible knowledge available to the individual researcher or team of researchers can be accepted as legitimate and an even more limited range presented to a wider audience. In Chapter Five we explore further what this means in terms of the knowledge which is generated, and look at some of the research questions this tradition leaves out. In Chapter Six we shall see ways we need to break the rules if research is to move us forward in learning how to live in a context of uncertainty and super-complexity.

Traditional rules are pervasive in the norms and values of the community of academic researchers as well as in the activities of research. If we look, for example, at the ideas of objectivity and detachment mentioned earlier, we see that these not only characterize encounters with the data; they also affect the way academic work is organized in different disciplinary domains as well as ideas about how research should be evaluated, what should be taught and how research is reported. There is no inevitability about this. It is a matter of choice:

> Scientific education . . . simplifies 'science' by simplifying its participants: first, a domain of research is defined. The domain is separated from the rest of history (physics, for example, is separated from metaphysics and from theology) and given a 'logic' of its own. . . . Stable 'facts' arise and persevere despite the vicissitudes of history. An essential part of the training that makes such facts appear consists in the attempt to inhibit intuitions that might lead to a blurring of boundaries. A person's religion, for example, or his metaphysics, or his sense of humour . . . must not have the slightest connection with his scientific activity. His imagination is restrained, and even his language ceases to be his own. This is again reflected in the nature of scientific 'facts' which are experienced as being independent of opinion, belief, and cultural background.
>
> (Feyerabend 1975: 19–20)

CHALLENGES TO TRADITIONAL RULES

It is doubtful if there ever was a time when traditional methodology was un-challenged, and, as I have already indicated, following its rules to the letter was never possible. Nonetheless, the rules of objectivity, consistency, rationality and detachment are still the major way in which research outcomes are judged in the peer review process. But today, however, there is growing confidence in questioning their adequacy. Research now draws on a wider range of rules, some of which are inconsistent with the empiricist framework. The coherence of the system of rules used to guide research behaviour is breaking down. Indeed, the consistency of method and content which neatly characterized the positivist philosophy has become extremely problematic. Research can no longer be eval-uated simply in terms of additions to the general store of knowledge for, as we shall see in Chapter Five, this idea has now been discredited. This loss of consistency has enabled a widening of the subjects and questions available for investigation. Research has been freed from a restrictive view of its purpose and focus and straitjacketed methodology, to include consideration of important human questions which were previously outside its range. This means there are not just new rules, but new kinds of rules.

Theoretical arguments against the knowledge and reality claims of traditional research have been advanced from an increasing number of directions. This is true in general terms but it also characterizes debates in specific disciplines. Challenges to the practice of research are also growing. For example, whatever one does during the research process, however the ideas are derived, whether from the deepest personal insight, from close examination of evidence, from rigorous or non-rigorous experimentation or from deep imaginings and hopeful wish-fulfilling dreams, in traditional research the work had to be reported (and in many areas still has to be reported) as if it were the product of a detached, logical mind. The findings had to be presented in the form of a logical statement or argument, whether in mathematical or verbal form, and assertions had to be backed up by evidence. This means separating the process of doing the research and its product. The researcher's learning that took place in the process of doing the research was almost forgotten. Indeed strict rules about how to present scientific papers not only forbid personal statements of learning outcomes and insist that new work is related to old, they specify the stylized way this has to be done. Researchers are increasingly challenging this by researching topics which are of personal significance to them and including personal journals, etc. in their writings. We see in new forms of research a move away from externally imposed subjective denial and detachment of the subject who is doing the research from the object of study, to a reclaiming of the role and involvement of the self, particularly where the self is personally involved.

Usher and colleagues (1997) suggest that in traditional research, the idea of validity is tied to the idea of closure. Conventionally, validity is determined at the point where the work can be viewed as a whole. Because it was based on a coherent fabric of rules, traditional research was rigorous because of its consistency as a whole. Coherence was assured through its system of rules. What we are now seeing is a move away from a closed and coherent (positivist) system of general rules governing research behaviour towards open, pluralistic and particularistic systems of rules. These amount to a move towards emphasis on the exploration of how to operate in a complex, uncertain world. Yet if rules define standards of rigour, what happens when the rules change? How can we tell whether the research is valid? We need some mechanisms to insure against self-deception. 'Standards', says Feyerabend (1978: 99), 'are developed and examined by the very same process of research they are supposed to judge.' Criteria of validity are tied to a particular tradition. New kinds of research require new standards. Traditionally the externally imposed rules of logicality, detachment and objectivity supplied such standards. New forms of research cannot be judged in terms of the extent to which they have kept to traditional rules for they may deliberately set out to flout or to critically question them. Since we can no longer fall back on traditional rules, the research must develop and contain new kinds of rules.

Any piece of research, in so far as it is a quest to make sense of a phenomenon or phenomena, has to work towards coherence. The search for understanding is the search for order in our world view. So we cannot do without coherence. Since it can no longer be achieved in general terms through positivist rules, it is problematic: it becomes a matter for investigation. Recognizing we are never going to find coherence on a general level, how we search for it, I think, must become a local, context-dependent activity. Coherence in the issues of the research and the way in which these develop should arise from the material, not from externally imposed rules. They are a matter for investigation in each context. For example, when I was engaged on my doctoral research, I became aware during the early stages that I was breaking the rules in order to find out what the boundaries were and what lay beyond them. This included a refusal to narrowly define a topic to be studied and an open-mindedness about what was relevant to the research. In many ways it could be said that I let the research openly define itself rather than pre-judging and constraining it artificially. I had to find out how to do it in the course of doing it. I had to be open to the process as it proceeded (Brew 1988). Through research, a conceptual framework is built up: a set of ideas which describes an aspect of our experience. Whether one conceptual framework agrees with some kind of reality 'out there' is no longer the point. Coherence not based on traditional methodology takes on aesthetic quality. Its 'truth' lies in its interweaving cohesiveness. For the mathematician this is the notion of elegance; for the physicist, the idea of simplicity.

Reason and Rowan (1981) suggest that validity in research has something to do with the relationship between the knower and what is known. All research in every academic domain depends upon the consciousness of the researcher. Valid research depends on valid consciousness (Reason 1988). The quality of the knower is important. Traditionally, research, as we have seen, has relied upon the development of a detached consciousness where the aim is to minimize the effects of subjective interpretation (Usher *et al.* 1997). Detached consciousness was assured by the rules of objectivity and rationality. But with the breakdown of traditional rules, research increasingly depends upon an involved, aware consciousness, which Reason (1988) has called 'critical subjectivity'. Reflecting on the material means being aware of subjective inputs and seeking to minimize them. Postmodernism, Usher and colleagues (1997: 208) suggest, is 'an injunction to be constantly vigilant'. We are talking about the shift away from an externally imposed set of rules concerning personal involvement towards the development of the habits of self-discipline. In Skolimowski's (1984) terms we give up the 'yoga of objectivity' and develop 'the yoga of participation'.

NEW RULES

From numerous surveys of guidelines from university promotion committees, granting agents, scholarly journals, university presses, and teaching evaluations, Glassick, Huber and Maeroff (1997) identified six basic criteria that were being used in the US to judge academic work:

1 Clear goals, well defined, significant and feasible.
2 Adequate up to date preparation with a clear understanding and capacity to realize the goals, i.e. competence of staff carrying out the work.
3 Choice of appropriate methods.

4   Significance of the results: that what has been accomplished adds something to the field.
5   Effective communication: sharing scholarly work with others (including teaching) with a plan for reporting and dissemination.
6   Accompanied by reflective critique in which one's own learning is developed, i.e. learning to do it better.

(Glassick *et al.* 1997: 22–36)

These standards, they argue, define the core of scholarly work. They embody rules for rigorous research. Noticeably, the criteria are all based on an evaluation related to goals. While many of the new forms of research, ways out of tired dilemmas and responses to the conditions of postmodernity welcome the idea of a reflective critique, more often than not they fairly and squarely reject the idea of goal directedness. Not only are such studies on the increase (Brew 1998b) and are supported by numerous theoretical and methodological arguments, they are an inevitable consequence of the breakdown in traditional rules. In the newer disciplines, for example the health sciences such as nursing, occupational therapy or physiotherapy, and in other professional areas and the creative arts, traditional ideas about how to do academic research are being questioned.

For some time now I have been tracking innovative, or as someone once called them, 'exotic' theses. I started a database building on suggestions made to me. Subsequently, I searched *Dissertation Abstracts* for theses which were unusual. Clearly such work represents only a small proportion of the 1.5 million or so theses presented in universities around the world since 1861. However, it is clear that there has been an exponential growth in such work. A significant number of the (approximately) 1,000 theses I found are different in style and challenge notions of what constitutes a thesis (Brew 1998b). Even taking out those which focus on the creative arts, we are left with a number of examples in many disciplines which challenge the foundations of the academic enterprise and provide inspiration and encouragement to those for whom conventional approaches are inappropriate. The growth of such work is reflected in the expansion of what is referred to as qualitative research, where significant shifts in methodology are taking place. I like to use the term 'experiential research' to refer to methodologies which endeavour to put into practice the critiques contained in postmodernism, seeking to free themselves from the straitjacket of traditional research.

Earlier I developed three new rules to guide this kind of research methodology (see for example Brew 1993). I called them 'guidelines' to avoid the sense of imposition that the term 'rules' invokes. They were an attempt to suggest how rigour in research could be established when the old rules were broken down and when criteria for validity for research have to be established anew in every project. I am not suggesting that these are the only rules or these are *the* rules. I present them here to illustrate what I mean when I say we need to define new rules for research. I shall illustrate them by means of some examples.

Looking again

The German phenomenologist, Edmund Husserl (1973) said that when you think you know you should look again. Looking again and again is a way of minimizing self-deception. It means we are always in the process of coming to know. There is always the journey, never the destination. In looking again, we do not take our impressions as 'true' or 'the way things are'. We continually go round the experiential research cycle, progressively deepening our understanding. This is my first guideline: look again.

Alex Nelson's (1995) doctoral study of the role of imagination in how individuals construct their own personal autobiography illustrates this. Looking again means, for Nelson, reconstructing one's personal autobiography, particularly when what he calls a 'remarkable' change in one's life occurs. Nelson looks again and again at his own experiences and encourages five other Roman Catholic priests who decided to marry to do the same. One device he used was to encourage each to tell their life story in the form of a parable. Here is an extract which illustrates both the personal nature of the thesis and its unconventional presentation.

> The Knight worked hard. As time passed, he became tired and sick. Some of his fellow Knights gathered around to lend him their strength, but he seemed to become sicker and more tired. He liked being a Knight, but he seemed to be losing the ability to draw strength from the signs of the Society. While everyone still saw him as a Knight, he felt as though he was slipping away from the Society – being drawn into a chasm of fear and pain.
>
> A brief holiday in 1985 did little to revive the Knight.
>
> He was still a Knight and could not run away, and so he returned to his people after a short while. A cloud came over him. Others – Knights of the Table, his people, his family – tried to return gifts to him, but he needed something different. He felt his heart slowly turn to stone.
>
> One day over a meal, he looked up to see a peasant girl he had known for some time, but she was no longer a peasant. Rather, she shone as a Princess. This was new in many ways. The Society of the Table had many Princes but no Princesses. Why had he mistaken this Princess for a peasant? What was the nature of her Royalty?
>
> The Princess showed the Knight her heart. Her Royalty was of the Heart, not of Proclamation. She could show him this Royalty of the Heart. She could lead him to discover his own heart. The Knight discovered what he had suspected – a heart of stone. The Princess brought her own gifts to the Knight, and he started a journey of discovery. His heart was thawed; he learned to love; he learned to live; he learned to receive as well as to give. He had become a Prince of the Heart.
>
> The peasant's son had become a Prince – his castle is smaller than before and his people are fewer than before, but he still gives of his gifts. And yes, his Princess keeps his heart from turning to stone.
>
> (Nelson 1995: 167)

Nelson comments: 'The prospect of leaving behind the role of the priesthood was daunting for him. Having constructed his identity in terms of his performing a role to gain acceptance, he feared what a future without that role might mean' (Nelson 1995: 168). For many innovators it has seemed important to keep a sense of the different voices. Alex Nelson says:

> In writing this thesis as a story about life stories, I employ a variety of voices. At one time or another in this account, my own voice as narrator, interpreter, theory-builder and practitioner may occupy centre stage. Sometimes my voice is that of a participant; at other times I am taking the stance of the principal researcher. The voices which speak from the various positions which I have occupied in this research, are to be expected in a cooperative inquiry. They reflect the movement I experienced from being in connection with, and distant from the other participants.
>
> (Nelson 1995:13)

Using different voices is a device for demonstrating that the author has engaged in 'critically reflective research' (Jones 1992). It is research where the author is continually looking again. This can be accomplished either separately or in collaboration with other people or both, as in participatory inquiries or cooperative research.

Relevance

My second guideline is to act on the hypothesis that everything is relevant. In the inquiry process we have traditionally prejudged relevance and drawn narrow boundaries around a field of study. Yet, as Usher *et al.* (1997) point out, any understanding of human actions based on this kind of closure is necessarily incomplete. Subsequent looking again from different viewpoints can often illuminate connections which were previously obscured. An example of this was the obsession I had during my doctoral research with cutting garden hedges. It was not until much later that I was able to see this came at a time when boundary maintenance and the breaking of rules in traditional research was a major intellectual concern. I was living my research on a practical (gardening) level! Such connections became a major part of the research as it proceeded, since the events of my life, in what then seemed like an uncanny way, paralleled my research concerns. The way I lived my personal life and coped with its problems informed and was informed by the issues with which my research was also concerned. By treating everything as relevant, the interconnections were inescapable.

In a remarkable thesis, Marge Denis describes how she started learning to do tapestry at the same time as she began her Ed.D. research into intuitive learning in adults (Denis 1979). As she progressed with her study, first observing and then interviewing sixteen people about their experiences of intuition, she became aware that her own experience of weaving a tapestry was itself an expression of intuitive learning. She then applied the conceptual framework she had developed to an interpretation of the tapestry. Her supervisor commented: 'Marge says she wove her thesis' (Griffin 1996). In my view, even more remarkable than her amazing tapestry was the way in which the tapestry was itself woven into the fabric of the thesis. She did this by not only including the tapestry as part of the thesis, but also included plates depicting it overlaid with interpretation related to her interview study, as well as poetry describing the ideas contained in the tapestry.

There is the idea here that whatever methodology is used or developed dictates the structure and content of the inquiry. The precise medium through which the inquiry process is pursued can vary. I used writing to explore issues as they arose. Marge Denis used weaving. Someone recently asked me whether a design exhibition could count as research output. What is important, in my view, is that there is a way of capturing the research in action. Neither the content nor the structure, nor again the product can always be narrowly decided in advance. Acting on the assumption that everything is relevant means having an openness to new insights from wherever they come, and it relies on scrupulous honesty in recording material. Feeling stuck or confused are viewed as opportunities for moving on in the research, not for closure and avoidance.

Unbending intent

My third guideline is that the researcher should proceed with 'unbending intent'. I borrowed this phrase from Casteneda (1968). 'Unbending intent' carries the sense of diligence with it, but it is much more than that. In treating everything as relevant, there may be times when one is submerged in personal material and unable to see how it fits in with research. But what makes the process research is the standing back to reflect on the issues perhaps from a different perspective. Sometimes the immersion and reflection are intertwined and difficult to distinguish. Reflection takes place on many different levels. If research is pursued with unbending intent, it means not shirking its difficulties. The research process is part of the individual's process of becoming. Learning to discriminate pathological manifestations of our own material as reflected in our own lives, in the lives of others and in the academic community leads us to understand the world in which we live in new ways. As Reason and Rowan (1981) point out, delving into our own subjectivity usually means getting more than we bargained for. Unbending intent means carrying on even when the going gets tough.

An example of this is provided by the thesis of Judy Lumby (1994). This is an account of the relationship between two women, one of whom is suffering a life-threatening illness. The method used consisted in reflection and story-telling:

> Critical conversation was a key element of the method, since it was through the use of this process that the two women were able to develop a critical awareness, both of their personal and professional lives, enabling meaning to be constructed out of the relationship and the illness.
>
> (Lumby 1994: 1)

The thesis is told in the form of a story. Here are the two women reflecting on the methodology:

> Maree admits that she enjoyed the time but *'I was pleased to get away from you.'* This was partly to do with the method I chose – that of Critical Conversation. For Maree:
>> *'The time was . . . very, very exposing. One of the revelations that weekend was about sin . . . From one of the questions you asked me I was able to open up and gain understanding about my marriage situation . . . From there I was able to look at my situation . . . It was so releasing for me.'*
>
> We both found it a very confronting time. Once more I faced ethical concerns about the method. Was this too confronting – did I have the right, even though Maree agreed that the process was the only way to go? I found the process exhausting, painful, and, at times, frightening, as it led us down our own paths. While I shared my own life to a certain extent, it was not the same. I was involved in watching another human being pull her life apart and put it back together again. She depended on my support and expertise in all this. But despite the pain, upon reflection, Maree said:
>> 'I have *shared things with you that I have not shared with anyone else . . . I was not going to get anything out of this unless I was willing to expose myself . . .'*
>
> (Lumby 1994: 236. Italics in the original)

By the application, with 'unbending intent', of the principle to 'look again' and by treating everything as if it were relevant, we are led to examine the deepest assumptions behind what we are doing. We are led to examine the psychological and cultural impulses which direct our actions. And we are led to examine again and again, our findings. One of the strengths of the methodological guidelines I have suggested is that they move us to explore new issues and questions, a theme to which we return in Chapter Seven.

ENFORCING THE RULES

We have seen in this chapter a relaxation of traditional rules and an idea of what new research guidelines could begin to look like. I hope that through the examples of new kinds of research presented here, the new researcher may be encouraged to be creative. Such work moves away from externally imposed rules such as detachment to a reclaiming of a sense and presence of the self in research. Such work begins to redefine rigour in terms of the development of rules of research as an integral part of each research process.

Critical questioning of the old rules has reduced their power and made it possible to define new ones and these are being developed particularly in doctoral thesis work. But there are drawbacks and these put a brake on the extent to which research practices have been able to change and the speed at which they change. Rules, as I said, define not only the methods of research and standards of behaviour of researchers; they also reflect the values and concerns of society and embody underlying ideas about reality and knowledge. However, they go much further, determining how investigations are communicated through publication and other forms of dissemination, how the research is funded and evaluated, and even whether the research takes place at all. The process of peer review is fundamental to this process. Traditional rules are currently enshrined in it. The examples of breaking the rules I have given are of highly innovative thesis work. While this work, as I have argued, is growing, there are many hurdles if researchers attempt to publish it in academic journals. Milton (1994) uses the term 'paradigm police' to describe the ways in which journal editors can suppress research which does not fit conventional views. These include stalling, labelling the researcher as a crank, sending an article to someone who has already exposed fraudulent claims to scientific theories, publishing the article alongside a counter-claim, and commenting on the weakness in research design in an editorial. Collins and Pinch (1998: 111) argue that a 'no-nonsense way of dealing with troublesome ideas' is to turn a blind eye to them. Other ways in which the establishment maintains the status quo are to question the skill or competence of the researcher, or to establish controversial status for the ideas so that other researchers then feel they have to reject them. They suggest that when controversial findings or methods are afoot then processes, which are normally invisible, start to become visible (Collins and Pinch 1998).

Yet the rules of traditional methodology have proved to be constraining and we urgently need to find new ways of doing research if we are to thrive within the uncertain super-complex world. We shall see in the next chapter ways in which turbulence in ideas about knowledge underlines this imperative.

Chapter 5

Knowledge

We did the devil's work.
(Robert Oppenheimer)

It was one of those clear, fresh, Spring days. You could see for miles. They climbed steadily to the top of the down, winding first through fields and then cutting across the heather. As they reached the summit, Rosie noticed the strange way the land undulated. To the left were steep slopes and to the right was a small ridge. Rosie wondered if it had been earthworks for an iron age settlement. She examined the evidence: a small mound, perhaps a burial chamber; a flat piece of ground just about the size to have a building on it; and then another. She thought of what she knew of similar settlements found in nearby locations. As she walked, Rosie imagined the houses and the people: how they were dressed, their children running around. She asked herself: 'How did they eke out a living in that spot? On cold and misty nights, how did they keep warm?' Knowing what she knew of the wind in that area, Rosie thought: 'Surely it would have been better to have settled down in the valley?'

They were reaching the top of the little ridge. Aloud Rosie said: 'Isn't it curious, the way the land lies here?'

'Yes,' Ben replied, 'perhaps it's the result of aliens coming. See that building there?' He pointed to the landmark which was their destination. 'It looks just like a child's painting of a spaceship. Perhaps the ancient people built it there because of what they had seen.'

'Oh yes, and that must be where the spaceship landed,' Rosie said, abandoning the iron age theory and pointing to a large flat surface near the area they had just traversed. 'Look. You can see the different vegetation there, suggesting – '

Ben took up the idea: ' – suggesting they had grown a different kind of crop?'

'No, no. Suggesting that something has happened to the earth to change the chemical composition so that different things now grow on it.'

They continued to speculate on how the aliens had arrived: what kind of spaceship, what they looked like and how they lived.

Walking on up the hill, Rosie reflected on how curious she was about everything. She wanted to know. She tried out another hypothesis, saying: 'Perhaps it's the result of quarrying. You know, in the Victorian era.' She picked up a stone. It was a piece of flint. 'Perhaps it was a flint quarry.'

'So are there lots of houses built of flint around here?' Ben asked.

'Well, no, not really. Not around here anyway. But perhaps there are some and we don't know them.'

Rosie thought about her three communities and how each might have lived. She wondered how she could find out more about the area. 'I could go to the library and look,' she reflected. In the core of her being there was the desire to know. Yet she was also aware of not really wanting to know. After all, she liked the idea of different histories of the place. She thought of another idea: 'Perhaps it's just the way the land has weathered. Here's another suggestion.'

As they descended, Rosie's attention was focused on the view. Stunning!

Since research is a systematic process of developing our knowledge of the world and our relationship to it, ideas about knowledge are fundamental to an understanding of its nature. Academic research is carried out according to conventions defining what counts as knowledge, what counts as an appropriate method for looking and what counts as evidence. But this, as we are now aware, is by no means a static process. Ideas about knowledge have been changing alongside ideas about rules and methods. There is now a widely held view that knowledge is in crisis (see, for example, Barnett and Griffin 1997). The ownership and creation of knowledge have become contested. In undertaking research in any academic context nowadays we have to negotiate our way through this space. We have to find new ways through and out of it.

University research has traditionally defined for society what knowledge is and has also, of course, been the major contributor to it. We sometimes say we are in an era of a knowledge society. But knowledge is now produced as much outside universities as within them. The generation of knowledge is no longer the preserve of university academics (Barnett 1997c). Gibbons *et al.* (1994) make a distinction between what they call Mode 1 and Mode 2 knowledge. They conceptualize Mode 1 knowledge as the usual disciplinary knowledge generated in universities. Mode 2 knowledge, which they argue has now become a significant force in society, is generated in practice within society. Such knowledge is transdisciplinary and socially distributed (i.e. over many sites of knowledge production and different contexts of its application). It is intrinsically related to commercial interests going beyond academics into business and industry. There is an emphasis on knowledge that can be of use in practice and a questioning of theoretical knowledge, traditionally the preserve of universities. Mode 2 knowledge arises, Gibbons and colleagues argue, from scientists adopting a strategic approach to their careers and recognizing the social applications of their work. What this adds up to is a dynamic and intimate interplay between knowledge generated inside and that produced outside the academy.

The crisis in ideas about knowledge, however, goes even deeper. For it is not just where knowledge is generated that has undergone transformation. Ideas about what knowledge is were seriously questioned over the course of the twentieth century. If, as McNair (1997) suggests, there is a crisis of legitimacy for universities in terms of their role in managing and disseminating knowledge, if universities can no longer claim ownership of particular forms of knowledge based on a linear notion of the creation, ownership and transmission of knowledge, then they have a problem on their hands. I am not suggesting that there is a solution to this problem. It is a scenario which each researcher, research team and manager has to resolve in each context, as we shall see.

In this book I have chosen to focus on academic research. Some will argue that in view of these difficulties in relation to the generation of knowledge, it is inadvisable to limit discussion to the academic sphere. In pointing to the problematic nature of knowledge, my concern is what is happening back at the ranch, as it were. I am interested in the kinds of research that are conducted in universities and, more especially, how they can develop and grow. However, before we can examine the dimensions of the crisis more fully and look at its implications, we have to see what it is a crisis about. In this chapter therefore, with new researchers in mind, I am concerned with traditional ideas about knowledge. Although such ideas have been critically questioned, they nonetheless still influence research practice. So I will examine some of the theories purporting to provide a rational basis for ideas about knowledge and then, drawing on my study of senior researchers, I shall look at an example of how these are manifested in practice. Critical perspectives that draw attention to other factors defining what counts as knowledge will be pursued in the next chapter.

ORDER THROUGH RATIONALITY

Mary Midgley (1992) suggests that our conception of order in the universe is fundamental to all that we endeavour to know, and how we think of that order determines the way in which we arrange our concepts. This conception of order, she argues, affects the questions we ask and what we conceive to be problems worthy of study.

One of the ways in which order has conventionally been maintained has been by using rationality as a criterion for deciding whether knowledge is acceptable. It used to be thought that research proceeded in a wholly rational manner and that therefore the problems and questions research attempted to address, and the knowledge which resulted, were determined by rational means. For example, one way of distinguishing academic, or as he saw it, scientific from non-scientific, knowledge was Popper's (1980) criterion of falsifiability. Popper said a theory has to be potentially falsifiable. Any scientific system must be capable of being refuted by empirical means, i.e. through experience. Otherwise it is either meaningless or metaphysical. There is, he argued, an asymmetry between verifiability and falsifiability. No instances of a phenomenon will not prove it does not exist; a single instance proves it does. Lakatos (1981), building on Popper's ideas, claimed one cannot immediately say whether a research question is falsifiable. He saw scientific progress as the proliferation of rival research programmes and progressive and degenerative problem shifts. Lakatos thus pointed to the interlinking of research programmes. Lakatos held that criticism does not kill theories as fast as Popper supposed. Research, he says, is a 'battleground' of research programmes rather than isolated theories.

> Purely negative, destructive criticism like 'refutation' or demonstration of an inconsistency does not eliminate a programme. Criticism of a programme is a long and often frustrating process and one must treat budding programmes leniently. One may of course show up the degeneration of a research programme, but it is only constructive criticism which, with the help of rival research programmes, can achieve real successes; and dramatic spectacular results become visible only with hindsight and rational reconstruction.
>
> (Lakatos 1981: 179)

Popper's and Lakatos's ideas are examples of philosophical attempts to find a wholly rational explanation of how knowledge is generated. Popper's falsifiability criterion of demarcation was a rational way to determine what knowledge was acceptable and therefore what issues were to be addressed. This was a way of trying to ensure that order would be maintained. Only problems and questions which were capable of conforming to the principle of falsifiability were researchable. Consider the following topics:

- The alchemist's search for gold
- Inquiry into the existence of God
- Inquiry into the causes of cancer
- Investigations of patient non-compliance
- Investigation of the behaviour of complex systems
- Inquiry into what happens when two black holes collide
- Inquiry into the causes of the industrial revolution
- The search for gravitational waves
- Investigation of morphogenetic fields

- Cold fusion experiments
- The relationship between human character and the positions of the stars and planets
- Investigation of the life of Chaucer
- Inquiry into the behaviour of sub-atomic particles
- Inquiry into the behaviour of football hooligans
- Investigation as to whether crop circles are made by extraterrestrial beings
- Inquiry into the way students experience their courses of study
- Investigation of the markings on the Turin Shroud
- Investigation of the form of a symphony.

Some of these topics immediately seem far-fetched and it would be laughable to see a research grant application focused on them. Others are obviously subjects of research and command large resources. Still others are questionable and have had difficulties in acquiring acceptance. Popper's and Lakatos's ideas do not explain why we are attached to many theories which are not falsifiable (for example, theories of evolution, Marxist theory, etc.), nor the many which have already been falsified. As we saw at the end of Chapter Four, there are a number of non-rational ways in which findings can be considered 'falsified', and we shall see in Chapters Six and Seven that there are other important determining factors. However, these theories still exert an influence on the way knowledge is viewed in universities. The difference between those issues which are subjects of research, and those which are outside of it in the above list, largely corresponds to those which conform or potentially conform to Popper's demarcation criterion. Though the logic of this very criterion has been questioned (the demarcation criterion does not itself conform to the principle of falsifiability!), and though the use of rationality as a criterion has itself been critically questioned, Popper's criterion is deeply embedded in our research culture whether we can name it or not.

Though the ways researchers behave are not necessarily based on rationality, the assumption of a rational universe determines what kind of knowledge we consider improbable and what we think is reasonable and worth pursuing. In other words, we superstitiously assume a rational universe, when really it is our way of viewing the universe in which the rationality resides (Milton 1994). We can see what this means by looking at how in the past, or in other cultures, people's preoccupations have been different. For example, in a fascinating study of the way Western cultures progressively fixed on the idea of quantification, Crosby (1997) portrays in graphic detail what it was like when there was no conception of measurable time and when space was viewed in qualitative terms. This was not just a question of people not having watches or clocks, but more fundamentally, in the Middle Ages, he argues, there was simply no idea of accurately measuring time. The length of hours (the smallest unit) varied depending on the time of year. In those days:

> How did Christians look at the Ebstorf map, the latest thing in world maps of
> the thirteenth century? We note its distortions, omissions and outright mistakes

and find them forgivable, considering how little firsthand data or training in geometry the mapmakers had. But we do not know what to make of the map as a whole. It is drawn on a background of Christ crucified, with his head in the Far East, pierced hands at the extreme north and south and wounded feet off the shore of Portugal. What were the mapmakers trying to say . . . ? Their map was a nonquantificational, nongeometrical attempt to supply information about what was near and what was far and what was important and what unimportant. . . . It was for sinners not navigators.

(Crosby 1997: 40)

Crosby links the development of ideas of quantification with the development of trade and specifically book-keeping in the thirteenth to sixteenth centuries. Many preoccupations in the Middle Ages were similar to those of today. Like then, we are constantly asking questions such as 'why we are here and where we came from' (Hawking 1988: 13). Indeed, Horgan (1998: 3) asks: 'What other purpose is worthy of us?' The universe has turned out to be larger and older than people in the Middle Ages imagined, and the idea of God as a causal factor has ceased to be invoked. Our era is now obsessed with quantification and with logic. This is not inevitable, neither is it simply a historical development. It is both the reason for and a product of our way of viewing the world. It fits with our need to provide order without invoking God.

It is useful in this context to employ the concept of a paradigm. The concept has been around for a long time but it was Kuhn (1970) who popularized it. A paradigm broadly refers to a set of beliefs, axioms or assumptions which provide order and coherence to our picture of what exists and how it works. The use of this term is now a little out of fashion owing to the number of criticisms which have been levelled at it. Kuhn's original analysis was criticized because it called into question the rational explanation of the demarcation between science and non-science, suggesting instead that knowledge was determined by convention. But that is another story. For our purposes, it is useful in drawing some kind of boundary around a range of issues which we must consider here. The concept of a paradigm has been used to refer to subject areas within a particular discipline, to disciplines themselves, to groups of disciplines and to historical traditions. Here, I am using it in Kuhn's first sense of standing for the entire constellation of beliefs, knowledge, values, techniques, and so on shared by the members of a given community (Kuhn 1970).

Ceruti argues that at the root of the beliefs, knowledge and values enshrined in traditional research is the idea of a 'movement towards both a truth and a point of view of all-encompassing total knowledge':

The discovery of a law gives access to the Archimedean point, a necessary and sufficient condition for the control and exhaustive understanding of phenomena. It allows for both the dissolving of the particular into the general, the predicting of the past and future course of events, and allows us to conceive of time as the simple unfolding of an atemporal necessity.

(Ceruti 1994: 17–18).

One assumption related to these ideas about knowledge and knowing is that an increase in information and an increase in skills can provide a complete description of the universe. This means we are in a position to control or manipulate aspects of our world, that we are better able to predict a course of events. There was then, in traditional ideas of research, an 'overriding requirement for empirical science to exhibit increasingly successful prediction and hence the possibility of instrumental control of the external world' (Hesse 1980: xviii).

Cole (1998), in an intriguing little book about mathematics, says that the nature of prediction in science is frequently misunderstood. Prediction, she argues, is about pattern recognition, a guide to tell scientists if they are on the right track. If a correct pattern is discerned, certain consequences will follow. Despite much current speculation among scientists about how the universe will come to an end, prediction is not, she argues, a matter of foretelling the future.

> Chemists can 'predict' the outcome of reactions based on their knowledge of the periodic table and quantum mechanics; they predict what will happen if certain elements are brought together under certain conditions, not what will happen next week.
>
> (Cole 1998: 70)

A focus on prediction, in any case, means that we focus on a limited range of questions. Control is illusory. In terms of control and prediction, what we have accomplished can be interpreted as relatively trivial. The universe pursues her course in spite of us and not because of us. But this does not adequately explain the boundaries of acceptable knowledge. Intellectually interesting ideas, whether or not they lead to prediction or control, are pursued in research programmes. But what about research that confirms our inability to predict or control, or research that confirms we do not or cannot know, or research that suggests we are ignorant? These are an altogether different matter, for they are outside the conventional paradigm.

If you are fixed on measurement, the idea of the movement towards all-encompassing total knowledge implies that knowledge consists of a quantity which is added to. Knowledge was seen in this traditional paradigm as something we acquire. What this tended to do was to emphasize knowledge as a product; as an end result of our searching. It was seen as a store of more or less useful information, an accumulation of skills, a product of our study or experience, etc. We acquire it through our epistemological acquisitiveness.

Popper believed that there is a distinction between the world of physical objects and the world of consciousness. But he added a third dimension: a world of 'objective contents of thought'. He called this an 'epistemology without a knowing subject'. In this world he located theoretical systems, problems, problem situations and critical arguments, and suggested that this world of knowledge can exist independently of knowers (Popper 1972: 106). This reflects the view, held both in the academic community and society more widely, that research accumulates a quantity of knowledge separable from those who know it. For example, research reports, theses, publications, etc. add to the store of knowledge located in a library and much of it is not visited by anyone. It remains unread. It has been suggested that the amount of knowledge we are acquiring is increasing exponentially but that the 'shelf life' of any specific fact is getting shorter (Van Ginkel 1994). Ideas are treated as if they were objects that can be added to, taken away, and stored for future use, like shopping put in a larder. (We shall return to this in Chapter Eight when we consider research as a commodity.)

KNOWLEDGE CREATION IN PRACTICE

What we think knowledge is and how we come to define it are tied to our ideas about reality and our relationship to it. We saw in Chapter Four that enshrined in research practice is the rule of objectivity and the requirement to look at reality as if it were on a stage: the 'puppet' view of research. Let us now look at how this idea manifests itself in practice. For while we have difficulty in grasping theories of the nature of knowledge grounded in attempts to provide rational explanations, the application of these theories to research practice may be conceptualized by researchers as quite unproblematic.

Lincoln and Guba (1985) have identified four variations in ideas about the nature of reality, all of which presuppose the idea of reality as independent of the researcher: objective reality (there is a tangible reality that is knowable and will be known); perceived reality (there is a tangible reality that is objectively separate from the observer; it is doubtful whether anyone could ever 'know' it, so instead it has to be appreciated from one's current vantage point); constructed reality (each person constructs reality from their experience of it); created reality (there is no objective reality, only a web of potential realities whose actual existence is triggered by the observer) (Lincoln and Guba 1985). Some of the ideas within the *layer variation* described in Chapter Two (p. 25) demonstrate clearly how these different ideas reverberate in research practice.

A mirror to reality

For example, some researchers in my study of senior researchers had the idea that if they get all the facts or data, or if they look meticulously enough, they will end up with a description of a reality which exists. There is a true sense of discovery about this view. Through doing research, the idea is that you get the right answer or the true picture as opposed to the erroneous ideas which existed before. This may involve going back to the starting point and putting together explanations in different ways from those of people who have previously looked at the topic. Here is how some researchers expressed it:

Often theoreticians will come up with some mathematics that says that a certain phenomenon should exist under certain conditions, but no one has necessarily observed it before or at least been aware that they've observed it so you can do experiments to go and try and set up those conditions and observe the phenomenon that they've predicted. And if it exists then you can say 'okay, this theory has some validity' and if it doesn't exist or if something else occurs then you can say 'the theory perhaps needs to be modified'. Or the experiment wasn't correct. (03)

In this book . . . I relied rather heavily on secondary sources and official sources pushing a certain line. And I came out with an interpretation which – how shall I put it? – was better than any other interpretation but still wrong. And . . . it was only later as I got into the party history materials and interviewing people that I began to realize just how wrong it was. I was finally able – last year – to publish a book re-examining the whole case. And it is simply a case where everything else that had been written, including this old thing of my own, was . . . really 180 degrees wrong . . . We had just missed the point because we didn't have access to sufficient data. (29)

Anyway . . . what we did was, we were looking at the conduction of oxygen through those [mangrove] roots and we discovered that we couldn't account for the conduction of oxygen by the number of known conducting structures that were on them. And as a result of that we discovered a new conducting structure that hadn't been described before, and so we did electron microscopy there and we showed by experiment in the lab by oxygen electrode that that was indeed doing the conducting. . . . We thought that we would have different structures and . . . even different physiology related to the oxygen needs . . . but, as it turned out, the mangrove appears to be preprogrammed, at least in its first few years of life, so they know they are going to form that much root, that much air space, that many peg roots, and that's it. So that was unexpected. (08)

The language in these extracts is illuminating. The use of the words 'right' and 'wrong'; the emphasis on what 'actually' happens. Sufficient data and of the right kind, perhaps combined with appropriate experiments, mean researchers end up with the correct interpretation. Consciousness is separated from objects because, for these researchers, truth lies in statements which mirror states of affairs in a world that is viewed as external to the researcher. Pre-existent phenomena are explained (Mourad 1997a). Hypothesized phenomena are found to exist. There is the idea that true propositions are in a one-to-one relation with, or correspond to, the facts. There is a belief in one true reality, the task of research being to find it.

Knowledge as interpretation

Other researchers had the view that what they are doing is putting ideas together in different or novel ways to find new patterns, new interpretations. There is a sense that if you get the right bits you can see the pattern. The idea that this mirrors a state of affairs in the world is, however, missing here. The task of examining the data, or interpreting it, rests on the idea that there is not a correct explanation and that it is not possible to find one. What is being sought is simply a better explanation. Research here can exhibit a kind of jigsaw puzzle quality. By synthesis or integration, new perceptions or patterns are to be discerned. These researchers describe the process of coming to such an understanding:

> [Research is] understanding the way securities markets work . . . collecting observations about the world and analyzing them . . . forming judgements about . . . the underlying trends or the underlying systematic patterns that exist within observed phenomena. A lot of what I do is concerned with trying to explain previously documented anomalies. (21)

> We've tried to look at some key journals . . . magazines that were published in the period up to about 1914, like the *Australian Pastoral Review*, . . . the *Town and Country Journal*. We've also tried to look at every account written about rural Australia in the nineteenth and early twentieth century. . . . These have been used extensively before by historians but I wanted to go back over them to see if you could actually . . . read them in different ways and interpret them in different ways. (05)

> There's a major theme in the nineteenth century of woman as water . . . particularly in body and in the landscape . . . there's a huge range of figures in which the tree or forest emerges. . . . So, (the research) takes up that . . . centuries-old notion of the identity of humans and nature, as expressed in myth and so on; but pushing that against the reality of what was happening in the nineteenth century, which was of course urbanization, industrialization, and modernity. And it's turning out pretty interesting I think. So what I wanted to do was to establish . . . how to start working with this . . . through looking at images and the ideas that come from them. . . . The medical treatises of the nineteenth century see woman as a kind of watery substance. She's a biological body that's rather prone to dissolve. . . . And some of these medical treatises are just revolting, quite repulsive, but . . . there is a huge range of images of women bathing nude, either mythological or actually modern, contemporary women. Plus, there's a relatively new theme in the high arts [of] women . . . washing themselves in tubs of the period. And the critics will . . . almost invariably see those as . . . prostitutes . . . essentially dirty women; contaminated water. There are medical and sociological reasons for understanding that reaction. . . . But what about the women who are depicted rather . . .

unrealistically naked near rivers. Now it's unlikely to see naked women near rivers in the nineteenth century, even less likely than today. . . . But there are dozens of images . . . what does that association mean? So my objective . . . evidence would be looking at things like . . . how the nineteenth century thought of water and washing. For example, certainly not how we think of it. You know, washing the body was not thought well of at all until about the 1890s, 1880s . . . and a direct cause of that was Pasteur's discovery of microbes. Suddenly people started washing . . . So water wasn't regarded as the neutral thing that we see it; something that cleans you in a way that you get up in the morning and wash yourself and don't think about it. It was a loaded . . . element. So when I say objective I would look at . . . trying [to] push my reading of the themes against the knowledge of contemporary sociology and my beliefs, as far as one can get. (22)

Knowledge here is seen as a process of interpretation. There is an emphasis on the researcher's use of judgement and on comparing different interpretations. Research is about making meaning; about making sense of chaos and translating this into culturally accepted explanations. It is the process of constructing knowledge. This then becomes the way in which the academic discipline or the wider culture subsequently makes sense of phenomena. Individuals, by engaging with the data, make sense of a random or chaotic range of events, phenomena, understandings and the like. This becomes their reality and their meaning. There is nothing deterministic in this. Meanings may be culturally influenced but they cannot be culturally determined. This 'interpretive' view is generally assumed to be characteristic of social sciences and humanities although Feyerabend (1978) suggested that research has always operated in an interpretive mode: making sense of phenomena hitherto unexplored; creating socially recognized knowledge. My findings also suggest different views of knowledge are not tied to specific discipline areas. Indeed, it is likely that even in close-knit research teams different conceptions are to be found.

Knowledge as a creative process

For other researchers demonstrating the *layer variation* in the study, the process of illumination is conceptualized as a process of gathering data from a wide variety of sources and then creating or 'shaping' it, rather like an artist creates a painting or sculpture or a musician composes a piece of music. Research is described as an artistic process; meaning being created, not discovered. You 'imbue the data with meaning' (01) or as another researcher said: 'I am creating a new vision' (28).

Once [I was] reading something about the difference between Mozart and Beethoven, how Mozart composed everything in his head and then wrote it all down perfectly, and Beethoven could never re-copy a manuscript of his own without making changes all the time. And that was put up as totally different diametrically opposed ways of composition, and I definitely fall into the Beethoven category, because I can't sit down and read something I write without . . . introducing changes all the time and I think . . . for me it's a constant process of getting new ideas and . . . seeing things in a different way . . . I think of it sometimes like painting where you're working with a palette knife and you're constantly touching it up, jumping back into earlier parts of what you've written, adding new data. It's a constant . . . creative process . . . It's like painting or it's like sculpting or it's like composing . . . Really in a way you are composing and all of your notes are all the bits of data you have gathered coming from a lot of different sources and you are really putting it together into the equivalent of a painting or a piece of music. (01)

the amount of information, knowledge, and the fact that you've read so much . . . really does enable you to put it all together sometimes in a creative way that depends both on a very close knowledge of the material and on serendipitous insights that you get because of your long acquaintance with the material and the fact that you're continuing to amass information about it. (14)

For these researchers the theories that are created do not simply illuminate the surface reality: they define it. In this conception, we have no sense that there is a correct or even a better explanation: knowledge has an aesthetic quality. Reality is created through knowledge.

TRADITION AND CHANGE

These ideas of how knowledge is generated in the research process are all consistent with our traditional paradigm and begin to exemplify how traditional ideas about knowledge and how we come to know manifest themselves in practice. They are also consistent with the traditional rules for how to obtain it considered in Chapter Four. This is not surprising, for all the statements were made by researchers who have extremely successful research careers within the current system. In all of the examples, knowledge was seen as separate from knowers. This is the Archimedean point I referred to earlier. The idea is that you can substitute one researcher for another and no one would be any the wiser. Also, there is the 'puppet' idea mentioned in Chapter Four, that the researcher is detached from what they are researching as if they were seeing it on a stage. Even so, there are some crucial differences in these ideas about the relationship of ideas to reality, and we shall see their significance as we proceed.

As we continue our exploration of the kinds of problems and questions research addresses in the next two chapters we shall see that much of it is predicated on these traditional views of knowledge. For although its logic has been questioned from many quarters, and although, as we shall also see, there are many other reasons why academic research focuses on the issues it does, academic research practice is still imbued through and through with the rational view presented here. We could say that research is still trapped by what Habermas (1987) termed the 'methodological noose' of rationalism and objectivism.

However, it is difficult to present these 'rational' ideas these days without being struck by the sense of barrenness in the ways they limit ideas of knowledge and knowing. A number of critical perspectives have pointed to such things as the irrationality of the idea of research as an accumulation of knowledge. Feyerabend, for example, suggested that any attempt to draw a boundary between the scientific and the non-scientific is not only artificial, it also gets in the way of advancing knowledge. All attempts to find a rational demarcation criterion have failed, says Barnes (1982). Non-scientific theories, practices and traditions can both rival science and display its weaknesses, if they are given the chance. As we have seen in earlier chapters, there are movements gathering momentum that are challenging the traditional boundaries. Falsification is meaningless in much education, social scientific and person-centred research. For example, it does not make any sense to falsify findings concerning conceptions of dying among patients undergoing euthanasia (Street 1999) or how childless women redefine their sense of self (Kirkman 1999). It is always possible to offer an alternative construction of reality if you can think of one (Bannister 1981). Feyerabend made a similar point when he said, 'no single theory ever agrees with all the known facts in its domain' (Feyerabend 1975: 55). There are always alternative theories that fit the data.

In Chapter Six we shall see how these views of the nature of knowledge and the traditional rules for how to develop it have been sustained and how they have limited the range of problems and questions considered. Chapter Seven will then examine some of the ways in which research is now moving into new domains of knowing. These are important in our quest to avert the crisis in research because within the ideas and explorations of bold researchers we can see the germ of intellectual transformation. In Part II we shall see traditional ideas about knowledge and reality reverberating in other aspects of higher education research culture to put a limit on the domains of future knowledge, in ways that support the interests of funding bodies and powerful institutions and individuals.

Chapter 6

Problems and questions

Don't you see how useless it is to know the answer to the wrong question?
(Ursula Le Guin)

And the old King set out on a journey through all his kingdom. Taking with him just a small entourage, he took leave of the castle on horseback. The air smelt good and feeling the rhythm of the horse beneath him gave the King a sense of freedom. Once they were out of the thicket surrounding the castle, they all stopped to take in the view. For here they could see to the farthest reaches of the land.

But instead of the green of summer they had expected to see, much of the land appeared barren and the trees were bare. The King felt sad. He had heard reports of drought and hardship but it had been difficult to take them seriously in the high towers and luxurious apartments of the castle. His advisers had assured him that all was well and he had lived a life of idleness unconcerned by these reports. Yet he was not an uncaring King and now that his days were numbered, he had wished to see for himself the state of his Kingdom and to ensure that everything was in order for his Son, the next king, to take over.

'I am surprised', he said to the Lord Chamberlain, 'to see bare trees in the height of summer.'

'Ah, yes,' the Lord Chamberlain replied. He offered no explanation and simply suggested they continue. And so the regal party pressed on, wondering as they crossed dried river beds and passed through leafless forests what made the land like this.

Late in the afternoon, when it was time to rest and refresh the horses, they stopped at a village. The people were lining the streets to welcome their King because they had heard he was coming and were curious to see him. The King thought they looked poor but happy.

They stopped for the night at the inn and the King enquired of the innkeeper about the people who lived nearby and how they spent their time.

'They have jewels,' the innkeeper said.

'Jewels?'

'Yes. They polish their jewels, blue, red and green jewels, and make them bright and shiny.'

'But the people all look so poor,' the King said.

'Oh yes,' replied the innkeeper. 'They are very poor.'

'Do they not sell the jewels?' asked the King.

'Oh no. They are too precious for that!'

The next day the King and his company continued their journey until they came to a town. There was no one about and the King wondered where everyone was. They made for the Town Hall where there was to be a Grand Reception. The Mayor greeted the King and his entourage and led them into the Mayoral Chamber where a few dignitaries were waiting to welcome them. The King enquired about the people of the town and the Mayor explained that they were working. He led the King to some maps laid out on a long table at the side of the grand room. 'This is what we are searching for,' he proudly said; 'the lost city of Jesmiraldo. We know it is near and we are close to finding it, but it is taking much labour and many years of work.' The Mayor then explained that they had thought the King would like to visit some of the places where they were searching and that after lunch they were to set out in the Mayoral Carriage to go and see. The King said that he would be very pleased to see what his people were doing. So at last, after too much lunch and a lot of long speeches, they set off.

By this time the day was far advanced and long shadows were cast across the barren landscape, giving everything an eerie glow. Still no one was in sight and no birds sang.

'And where shall you find Jesmiraldo?' the King enquired of his host.

'Well we know it is somewhere beneath the earth,' the Mayor explained. 'There have been reports that it is one mile down. Most reports, however, seem to suggest that five is much more likely. When we have found it,' he added thoughtfully, 'the people of the town will be able to move there and they will be happy.'

'But if it is beneath the earth . . .' The King was hesitant in his question for he did not want to appear ignorant. 'If it is beneath the earth, how will you be able to live there?'

'Ah, there are many issues still to be resolved,' the Mayor said.

'However, we do know that there is water there for on the other side of that mountain we have reached one mile down and we have discovered a great river. There are caverns where people used to live so that gives us hope that one day we will discover a world that we too can live in.'

'But why do you want to do that?' The Lord Chamberlain was less worried about appearing stupid.

The Mayor, sadly shaking his head, said: 'You have seen the state of the land. We do not know why it is now barren and we do not know if this will continue or whether there will be abundance again as there was in the time when His Majesty was a boy. So we have to be prepared. We are seeking another world we can live in and we have heard that it is to be found under our feet.'

'But it is a lot of work,' the King observed.

'Yes it is,' the Mayor agreed. 'And we have to do it before it is too late.'

The Lord Chamberlain was growing impatient. He asked: 'Has anyone investigated why the land is barren and what can be done about it?'

'Oh no,' the Mayor replied. 'We are too busy looking for Jesmiraldo.'

Many would say that the purpose of research is to solve important problems or answer important questions. But what makes a problem important? Why is it, for example, that so much money is spent on astrophysics, which is concerned with looking at deep space, and proportionately so little is spent on solving social or educational problems? Ernest Boyer (1996), in an article published after his death, argued that scholarship must be engaged in solving fundamental problems of society; that scholars must work with society in addressing its concerns. He called this the scholarship of engagement. Whatever we take research and scholarship to be, that, surely, must be our greatest endeavour. Yet we will see in this chapter that research has an ambiguous relationship with what is of value to people. In discussing the problems and questions research addresses, I shall argue that research sometimes avoids attempting to solve society's closest and most pressing problems, instead choosing to escape from the world to pursue knowledge of that which is distant and socially unproblematic.

It is abundantly clear that research is not driven simply by a desire to solve problems. Neither is it simply a matter of people asking questions and providing answers. On one level it has to consist of solving or asking the 'right' kinds of problems or questions and that means solving certain kinds of problems and asking certain types of questions. Later, we shall consider some of the issues of power determining which questions are posed and examine some ways in which problems get distorted through dominant ideologies (Spanier 1995). However, there are those who argue that research is not about solving problems at all, but rather is about

answering interesting questions or is concerned with identifying, posing, illuminating, or just investigating problems. Perhaps we have to do as Midgley (1992)
suggests and give up the metaphor of problem-solving, seeing research as more
about addressing a range of different dilemmas operating at different levels. I like
Mourad's (1997a) description of research as the pursuit of intellectually challenging
ideas because, while it does not explain why some areas of activity command more
funding than others, it does explain why researchers become so intently engrossed
in their work even when there is no likelihood of any kind of practical outcome.
However, once again, not all intellectually challenging ideas are considered
acceptable as research topics. So how do you differentiate between problems and
questions considered researchable, and problems and questions considered less
important or even taboo?

We shall see in this chapter that our research picture is determined not just by
rational but also by historical, social and political factors. A combination of factors
competes to decide whether or not a particular issue is considered researchable.
I am not framing the chapter around specific problems and questions within any
single discipline; I use examples from a range of academic areas to elucidate general
issues. So why is the picture like it is? What is it that determines the picture of
our world that academic research has created, indeed, that it is creating? It is
clear that our picture is confusing, incoherent and at times contradictory. So can
we make sense of the problems and questions as a whole? Is there any coherence
and why do we accept some topics and reject others?

Increasingly, as we have already seen, new researchers, including many research
students, are wanting to challenge the boundaries of what is considered acceptable
academic practice. So a key question we are concerned with here is what is left out
of our research picture and why? In the next chapter we shall consider whether
research is perhaps concerned with avoiding solving particular problems or
avoiding answering certain questions. We shall see there are also psychological
factors influencing the issues we choose to research, and look at some new ideas
which extend the boundaries of the picture. These issues are important to our quest
to explore how research might open up new understandings of the world around
us and move us towards the fundamentally important task of learning how to live
in an age of super-complexity and uncertainty.

SHOULDERS OF GIANTS

Let us begin by considering how someone beginning research makes a choice about
what they are going to investigate. When, in my research, I have interviewed
experienced researchers, I have always been struck by the amazing variety of
problems and questions they are interested in. When you hear researchers talk
about their work, there is frequently a passion; an intense personal interest in the
issues, problems and questions. Research can have an obsessive quality. So what
makes people fascinated by particular issues or topics? There are clearly many

personal, psychological and situational factors which contribute to the choice. One of the things that is going to determine what people research is simply personal preference, the ideas that interest them. For example, the broad area of study may already have been chosen through their initial training and this may have followed interests developed at school or early in their career. In many subject areas, research is dependent on industrial support or government funding and this to a considerable extent determines the research individuals do. So other factors may include who is going to fund them.

It is clear from my investigation among experienced researchers that they have different foci of attention in thinking about research. It does not seem unreasonable to suppose therefore that the topics people choose to research are related to their ideas about what research is and what it is for. For example, in the *journey variation* the research questions were intimately related to the researchers' existential life concerns, things that had puzzled them throughout their lives. On the other hand, in the *domino variation*, problems and questions were viewed as being quite unrelated to the researchers' lives (see Chapter Two).

By and large, the topics which our new researchers choose are going to be ones which are acceptable to the people around them. We have seen that it used to be thought that what makes a topic acceptable was determined, at least to some extent, by a desire to create order backed up by notions of rationality. We have also seen that this does not provide a satisfactory or a sufficient explanation and that although these ideas used to be popular, they have been seriously questioned in recent times. So we still need to explore why it is that we collectively pursue the particular issues that we do and who or what determines that. We also need to look at what kinds of topics are left not addressed.

A key element in explaining why some ideas are researched and not others lies in their interrelationships. This is allied to the idea of research as a rational enterprise we considered in Chapter Five. It is also related to the historical development of fields of investigation and to the researcher's personal history of investigation. This researcher expresses the sense of history:

> I don't know how many people feel this very strongly, but I'm sure in most fields there is a very strong sense of . . . those people who have worked before you. It's . . . [a] very powerful sense of great personalities and . . . giants of scholarship, certainly in my field and I suppose that's true in most people's fields. Because I think . . . that all . . . academic fields are very much stamped by these great personalities, and by the examples which they set personally for their students and by what they wrote. So there's a great feeling that you're actually up there with them and you have come up with something that none of them have ever done. (01)

Answers raise new questions. Solutions lead to more problems. Research is a never-ending quest. Our picture can never be finished. Every question is related to every other question in a network of relations in the same research programme or academic area and each academic area is related to every other. As Kant wrote in the *Prolegomena*, 'however we go about it, every answer according to fundamental laws of experience always gives birth to a new question, which also demands an answer and thus clearly shows the inadequacy of all physical kinds of explanation to satisfy reason' (Kant 1953: 118).

Let us look at this more closely. In my investigation of senior researchers' ideas about research, in the *domino variation* the idea of linking separate elements in the effort to solve problems or answer questions was in the foreground. Here is how one researcher conceived research as first identifying a problem and perhaps breaking it down into a number of sub-problems, and then working on these:

> the process is basically . . . identifying a problem . . . and then you compose the problem into smaller pieces, basically trying to isolate or reduce the complexity involved in the problem and then breaking that into achievable goals . . . and then trying to achieve these goals while at the same time saying how progress in one particular goal can affect others. (23)

Other researchers described the process of applying different techniques and synthesizing new information. There was the idea that solving problems of a practical nature in this way can illuminate wider areas of understanding. Solving one problem can have spin-offs in regard to other problems.

Sometimes hundreds of sets of dominos are all meticulously lined up in a big hall (probably for a charity event). Then someone pushes just one which is at the end of the line and this causes the next to fall and that causes the next one and so on until all of the dominos have fallen. From this we get the idea of a domino effect. A view of research as consisting of separate problems or questions that are viewed as being linearly or hierarchically linked so that one affects the others in turn is rather like this. That is why I call this the *domino variation*. As in a domino effect, finding an answer to one question may illuminate a range of further questions. Alternatively, answering one particular question may raise a number of further questions. Problems or questions may be arranged in different ways to form patterns that make sense, provide an explanation or solve a problem or answer a question. In the following extract separate questions are hierarchically arranged:

> If you find an answer then there are subsidiary questions that stem from that and then eventually you find questions that don't have a good answer in the literature and those are the ones that we tend to pursue . . . if you use a particular style of questioning as . . . I try to encourage in my lab, you tend to discover the most basic questions that don't have answers and those are the most valuable because they are right at the root. . . . The more basic a question is that is unanswered the more valuable it is. I enjoy questions that [are] . . . almost an obvious question, but then when you explore it you find no answer, then it becomes extremely potent, because it then determines the behaviour of things downstream from that which is, you know, when you think about

it it's just . . . amazing . . . That sort of stuff I really find extremely exciting. And those are the good questions. . . . If you look at it as a tree, here's one question and answer, then off that comes various understandings that pin on that one. Then as you go up that dendrogram . . . the number of possible questions is proliferating as you go up from those levels. So if you answer a basic question then you essentially open doors in a whole series of other directions . . . (19)

In talking with academics in a variety of areas I am frequently struck by the ways in which questions and topics of research are worked on; one new piece of research building on the next. This is the case both with individuals and with teams. The work can seem quite alien to those who are not familiar with the historical development of the subject.

I have been concerned – really throughout my career – to study mythological concepts and their realisation in texts both poetic and prose . . . the record of the pre-Christian beliefs of the Germanic peoples are . . . captured in medieval Scandinavian literature of various kinds. My research thesis was an edition of an early Norse poem, which is rich in mythological and other allusions . . . and, since then I really have written a great deal about myths and the way . . . they are presented in literary texts. . . . I have been interested throughout my life in the way in which oral cultures – cultures that do not use writing . . . or use it only to a very limited extent . . . represent . . . important cultural concepts. . . . Ideas that I have had in a . . . germinal form . . . early in my career, which probably then I couldn't have articulated in the way that I can now, have come back into play, so that . . . things that I'm writing now . . . I have been thinking about off and on for a long time and sometimes I surprise myself and think 'Oh yes, I was thinking about that when I was a graduate student.' (14)

So I, in the last five years, have shifted my research interest – about half of it – into this area, as you can see it has enormous potential. So I'm doing some of the basic science and looking for applications and there is a small company involved with trying to commercially exploit it. And the other area is largely at the moment part of the chemistry of the periodic table called 'conditioned metals': copper, nickel, platinum, palladium and so forth. And I've done that all my life, worked in that area. In . . . reactions in which they change oxidations in which they take up and give off electrons. But the particular area that I'm playing with now involves industrial catalysts, where a number of these complexes that are corrugated complex with carbocyclic acid, like acetate and so forth and become active catalysts. And so we're looking at the structure of these things and the properties. That's a life-long interest. That's called oxidation reduction chemistry of metal complexes. And again that's an evolutionary thing which has been in increasing focus over the last four to five years. (32)

What we have here are snapshots illustrating how researchers explain the linking of ideas in research. Each snapshot is like one of those separate television screens making up a giant one. You cannot see what the picture is just by looking at the individual screens. You have to step back to look at the whole matrix of screens. If you try to do this, if it were in any way possible for you to do this, then the question which needs to be asked is: why this picture? What is it that gives coherence and legitimacy to this knowledge picture? This is similar to the question Lyotard (1984) asked. He suggested that as with the laws of a society, what counts as scientific is determined by scientists who practise science according to specific rules of procedure. Authorization to do this is claimed on the basis of a fictional story or epic which provides the legitimation. He argued that in the modern period there were two meta-narratives: a political one and a more philosophical one. In the first, knowledge is linked to ideas of freedom and democracy. In the second, legitimation is provided through reason: scientific knowledge is given credibility because it represents the logical unfolding of the pursuit of truth, a view we looked at in the last chapter. Lyotard discusses the ways in which the epic or narrative is changing in Western thought. With the recognition that logical systems cannot be both complete and consistent, a shift has now occurred, he said, and we have moved to a recognition of the unpredictability and instability of truths. Lyotard defines this state as 'incredulity toward Grand Narratives' (Blake 1997:157). This characterizes the postmodern condition.

Returning to our TV picture we can say that what we thought was the whole picture turns out to be just another screen within a bigger picture. Once we step back and recognize other ways of viewing the world we find there are no grand theories which explain everything. Every picture is contained within another. Ideas of Western knowledge are seen to be contained within a 'grand narrative' which has given it a gloss of coherence.

Scott suggests that what characterizes postmodernism is a distaste for meta-discourses; an awareness of indeterminacy of knowledge and eclecticism and variety (Scott 1991:18). Scott criticizes postmodernism, arguing that 'in most human and many social sciences it has always been recognized that experience, knowledge, culture are rich, complex, variable, unsystematic, even indeterminate' (1991:18). Moreover, postmodernism, he suggests, rejects the idea of authority of some ideas over others. Yet some ideas do have, he argues, more authority than others, so postmodernists are naïve about power. Indeed, Scott suggests that postmodernism has taken on an anti-meta-discourse which is difficult to distinguish from its opposite. So not only can we never see the whole picture, there is no whole picture to see. We have to take into account that both ideas are located in a context and that there are a myriad of contexts and ideas-systems. Pluralism is endemic. Fact may be juxtaposed with fiction. Research findings are permeated with metaphors. The medium through which we come to know, and the discourse within which that knowledge is framed, influence what we see.

In postmodernity this is true of our life as much as our research. We are located between a growing range of competing knowledge systems. For example, many people now go to their general practitioner for certain ailments and their acupuncturist for different ones. When people live in cultures where there are competing knowledge claims, such as in South Africa under apartheid or Germany under Nazism, different knowledge systems are not a matter of polite choice. But with examples such as these in the world, we cannot escape the recognition of the ways in which our knowledge is shaped by our cultural experiences. We have to account for different knowledge and different ways of knowing. For: 'the view from nowhere is generated by those who can afford the luxury of the dream of everywhere' (Harding 1991: 276). In this postmodern condition, in the absence of any alternative way out, an emphasis on performance (Lyotard calls it performativity) is establishing itself. In this there is an emphasis on the use of research to maximize profitability and economic power, as we shall see in Chapter Eight.

HUMAN INTERESTS

Notwithstanding the indeterminacy of knowledge and knowledge systems, we still need to address the question of why particular issues are pursued and others not; why some questions are considered acceptable or researchable questions and others unacceptable and outside the domain of the academy. Habermas (1987) argued that inquiry proceeds through the knowledge-constitutive interests of the human species. However, this raises the question of precisely whose interests he is talking about. For whoever defines what counts as a problem or question for research has a powerful role in defining the pictures of reality which result (Harding 1991). Whoever's interests are upheld in the meta-narrative is in a position of power. For knowledge systems sustain the interests of the rich and powerful. Issues of knowledge are intimately related to questions of power. This is not just a question of who is deciding what counts as valid knowledge or who the powerful and powerless people are. Rather, for Foucault (1972) for example, the concept of power is an integral part of the concept of knowledge. The assertion of a truth is itself an exercise of power. This means that even within our concepts and the way we frame the discourse, the kinds of questions we ask and how we ask them, we exercise power. For Foucault there are two kinds of such knowledge: historical researches which are surplus to intellectual requirements; and bodies of popular knowledge, for example, patients' and nurses' knowledge being considered minor in comparison with doctors' medical scientific knowledge. Traditional academic knowledge subjugates knowledge which it defines as outside its range.

If questions about knowledge cannot be divorced from questions of power, we have to ask not just what counts as knowledge, but who the knower is. As long as knowledge was described in terms of being separate from those who know it and presented as if it existed independently of them, provided that the knower was known to be detached and objective, the whole enterprise could be characterized by a policy of non-involvement. Academic research in general and science in particular was simply charged with the task of explaining everything. Methods and rules of research are now recognized to be bound up with social questions not just about what is defined as knowledge but by *who* decides what counts as knowledge. Research shows itself to be by no means neutral.

Once you begin to ask who the knowers are and what gives them the right to determine what counts as knowledge, a number of problems present themselves. Code (1991), for example, has argued that the sex of the knower is epistemologically significant. That much academic literature is traditionally written in an impersonal mode hides the particular characteristics of knowers such as their sex, ethnicity, sexual orientation and so on. These personal factors, feminists and others have argued, significantly affect what is known and how it is known. Impartial, rational knowledge is seen by feminists as a construction of patriarchal knowledge. Feminists have argued that the interests which are dominant in research are those of Western, middle class, white, heterosexual males, at the expense of females, people from other races, the lower classes and homosexuals. It is a sobering thought that, not being in the category, 'white, middle aged, middle class, Western male' our ideas may never, however insightful, achieve the recognition they deserve. Fortunately this is now beginning to change.

However, the implications go deeper. Spanier (1995), for example, argues that patriarchal knowledge presents a partial and distorted view of humanity and the world. Her field of molecular biology endeavours to provide answers to a number of major problems in society. In focusing on 'life', genetics is held as a key to the elimination of disease and famine. It therefore has high status within the scientific community and more widely in society, notwithstanding growing concern about genetically engineered foods. However, Spanier argues, the emphasis on the problems and questions which are the preoccupations of white males in molecular biology, has led to the systematic skewing of descriptions of nature. This in turn, she suggests, has consequences for scientific knowledge and society's uses of that knowledge. It has fed back to create a distorted world view of the meanings of social relations.

> From the point of view of science – its accuracy in representing nature and its directions of development – prior commitments to limited and repeated themes promote partial and distorted knowledge and narrow research agendas. The distortions that result from ideological bias in biology feed back into society to reinforce a view of 'difference' as inherently asymmetrical and naturally hierarchical, with consequences for subordinated groups. From the point of view of the struggle against societal inequities based on race, class and gender, we must systematically reassess recurrent conceptual patterns and revise our paradigms.
>
> (Spanier 1995: 94)

Or, as Harding notes more generally: 'androcentric explanations emerge from the testing, by men only, of hypotheses generated by what men find problematic in the world around them' (Harding 1991: 116). Women want to know, Harding suggests, but the questions they bring are differently oriented:

> Women want to know about how their bodies really work, just which social forces are most responsible for keeping women in poverty, why men rape, how imperialism specifically acts on women, how women can gain the power to improve their condition – and we want to know these things now, or at least as soon as possible.
>
> (Harding 1991: 173)

Add women of colour, she suggests, and even more radical questions result. Rationalists have argued that we can eliminate these biases through the rational use of research methods. Spanier argues that you cannot. Biases enter in at the very stage of problem definition. Harding suggests that the combination of rational and social elements which have defined research have both liberating and oppressive consequences. Rather than eliminating values and biases, the application of a rational framework to research activity does away only with those social values which differ from the dominant values in the academic community (Harding 1991: 41).

Harding agrees that the picture of the world resulting from research activity is determined in part by individual researchers' interests and ideas about what constitutes a research problem. But what counts as a problem is linked to the purposes of research. This in turn is related to its funding. Agendas for the extra-ordinarily expensive research in physics, chemistry and much of biology are set in international councils and are heavily dependent on state and industrial funding (Harding 1991). Using the word 'science' to refer also to the social sciences, human-ities and arts, Harding argues that doing science has 'been part of the apparatus of ruling'. She continues: 'science generates capital in the form of information, ideas, and technologies that are used to administer, manage and control the physical world and social relations' (Harding 1991: 95). Harding says we need to ask how the dominant ideology of society becomes expressed in patterns of funding and in political decision-making and argues that this permeates at all levels the research questions and the explanations which flow from the research activity. Maxwell (1984), coming from a different theoretical orientation, also suggests that political considerations are important. He points to what he calls the:

> scandal of the priorities of world scientific research, around one quarter of the world's budget for scientific and technological research being devoted to military research, some 95 per cent being spent in, and devoted to the interests of, the developed world.
>
> (Maxwell 1984: 41)

Maxwell, like Boyer whom I mentioned at the start of this chapter, argues that the outcome of academic inquiry should be: 'our enhanced capacity to solve our fundamental problems of living' (Maxwell 1984: 73). However, traditionally research has given 'sustained attention to subordinate, peripheral problems (of knowledge and technology), while discussion of the primary problems (of personal and social action) are excluded from the intellectual domain of inquiry altogether'. He describes this as a 'disastrous intellectual mistake' (1984: 48).

OUTSIDE THE PICTURE

Once we acknowledge that there are different ideas concerning what knowledge is; that there are different narratives, then we can acknowledge that it is a matter of choice what knowledge academics choose to pursue. We have seen that there are cultural and political reasons preventing deviations from accepted practice, and we have seen that accepted practice represents the interests of a particular group or groups. The practical choices we make about what knowledge to pursue, the methods we choose to use, how we analyse our findings, how and what we communicate to others, are all caught up in the tension between, on the one hand, adherence to the traditional idea of knowledge separate from knowers, and on the other, an awareness that we are culturally and historically located and that this is affecting what we look for and what we see. For – notwithstanding critical questioning, notwithstanding theoretical recognition of the indeterminacy of knowledge, notwithstanding acknowledgement of the unsystematic kaleidoscopic pictures research creates – as we saw in Chapter Two, academic research practice has been less affected by critical questioning than the large volume of theory would suggest. Where there has been a widening of areas of investigation these have tended to be confined to particular academic domains. For example, feminist and gay literature is still relatively isolated from what has been called the 'malestream' (see for instance Code 1991).

Despite shifts in the margins, it is clear that some research which could be of enormous social benefit is not given priority. Indeed it can be actively suppressed. For the topics which are left out are not only topics and issues which are not researched, they are also left out of discussions about research. In order to examine what these might be, we have to go outside the boundaries of what is considered acceptable knowledge, or what are considered acceptable topics for discussion. So for the moment let us gird our loins, put our academic armour on and boldly talk about the unknown and the unknowable. What I am doing here is focusing on those aspects which are behind the picture so to speak, like the dinosaurs which can only be seen by those who look in a particular way through the computer-generated pattern.

Some of the areas not researched include topics which have, or are thought to have, perhaps dubious commercial implications (e.g. cold fusion research, research into the effects of nicotine addiction, etc). There may be political and social factors preventing some research (e.g. research on inherited characteristics of humans). Ethical considerations may prevent other topics being researched (e.g.

research on human cloning) or the topic may be simply too outlandish or difficult (time travel). However, there are other areas which are precluded because they do not fit our traditional frameworks. For example, the emphasis on rationality in theories of knowledge means we cannot yet explain how ideas may be thought up at different parts of the globe simultaneously even though physicists have discovered that, in the subatomic world, seemingly unconnected events may occur simultaneously. Sheldrake's (1987) notion of morphic resonance attempts to do so, but this is still a taboo subject. Gauquelin's work on the relationship between professions and positions of planets (quoted in Milton 1994) is also precluded because of its non-rational basis; Lovelock's (1979) Gaia hypothesis is a further example. All of these question powerful metaphors and break the Enlightenment idea of the separation of mind and matter.

It is clear that attempts to broaden the range of questions research addresses are fraught with difficulties. Milton (1994) describes a number of mechanisms for keeping some questions taboo. We have already noted some of the ways in which our current scientific paradigm is sustained by the 'paradigm police'.

> At its simplest and most direct, tabooism is manifested as derision and rejection by scientists (and non-scientists) of those new discoveries or new inventions that cannot be fitted into the existing framework of knowledge. The reaction is . . . strong enough to cause a more widespread adoption in the community of the rejection and disbelief, the whipping up of opposition, and the putting down of anyone unwise enough to step out of line by publicly embracing taboo ideas.
>
> (Milton 1994: 83)

The rejection is then supported by the peer review process because it places the subject 'out of bounds' to any rational investigation. Milton argues that this means that whole areas of investigation are 'fenced off'. Lakatos (1970: 175), putting a positive slant on it, calls these 'protective belts'.

The emphasis on detachment and objectivity in the rational model of inquiry means that coming to know aspects of ourselves has not been part of the academic agenda and this is perhaps most worrying of all. Indeed, the value of human subjective experience is consistently devalued and denied when we separate the knower and the known and choose to pursue 'objective' knowledge. Increasingly, researchers in the human sciences are involving themselves in their research. (Some examples were presented in Chapter Four.) Fortunately, in recent years there has been a growth in studies of this nature, particularly in newer disciplines such as nursing, social work and in the field of adult education, as well as in newer traditions such as feminist, post-colonialist and gay research. However, alchemy, in which investigations into the relationship between the self of the alchemist and the physical world were systematically conducted, is still taboo. Yet until the eighteenth century it was a respected tradition of knowing. Indeed Newton, considered to be one of the founders of modern science, engaged in it and wrote alchemical texts. However, because alchemy postulated a relation-ship between the self and the world, which is inconsistent with the grand theory of mind as separate from matter, it does not fit into today's paradigm; not because its findings have been found to be false but because its view of knowledge is alien to the Enlightenment view of knowledge.

Similarly, if we look at different kinds of intuitive knowing, we enter uncharted waters. Not only is there no academic discipline to study them, the mention of other kinds of knowing is taboo in academic circles. Yet if we ask people about their deepest knowing, we find the concept is not alien. Such questions cannot be researched within traditional boundaries according to conventional ideas of knowledge and knowing. Some bold researchers are beginning to ask questions about different kinds of intuition, consciousness and spiritual experience (see Lorimer 1998). Indeed, the emphasis on separation of knower and known can be viewed as a defence against knowledge of the self, including intuition. This means that questions about the effectiveness of holistic treatment of cancer or heart disease, or about the role of spiritual influences in the treatment of illness, or the mapping of energy meridians in the body, or the use of personality factors to predict death are all excluded. There is even evidence that such work is routinely suppressed (Milton 1994). Another example is Bob Johnson's research to cure psychopaths (Johnson 1996). His work in a top security prison demonstrated clearly that some of the worst criminals, serial rapists and murderers, were curable. By leading them to examine their own terrors, he was able to free them from essentially childlike anger. They came to appreciate what they had done and feel remorse. Indeed, they began to feel again and to act as they then were: mature adult human beings. Attempts to fund research into this, indeed to disseminate information about his findings, met with amazing resistance, including a threat of court action (Johnson forthcoming). Yet, this work could have enormous implications in the context of large amounts of public expenditure on overcrowded prisons, not to mention on the offenders themselves and their otherwise potential future victims. It would therefore have enormous social benefits. Society, it seems, does not want to know that it is possible to cure psychopaths.

The question which these few examples raise is why there is such a gap between the recognition of the indeterminacy of knowledge on the one hand and the vigour with which the academy holds on to its taboos on the other. Rather than being stifled by prejudice, we need to examine what must happen if the taboos are to be broken. Once research committees, including funding bodies, have a conception of research as being historically and culturally located, and are aware of the power and control issues which this implies, it would be encouraging to think there was the possibility of opening up to a wider range of studies. Yet such studies are currently met with hostility and prejudice. Once the implications of a truly multi-perspectival academic discourse are realized, we should expect that criteria for their evaluation would be developed. However, this seems a long way off.

Since research knowledge is no longer able to be justified by its rational relationship to a self-consistent set of externally defined rules, which as we saw in Chapter Four was traditionally the case, those rules are being relaxed. Many new methods are being tried. There has been an opening up of the narratives of inquiry. In the next chapter we shall look at some of the ways this is being done and why it has to happen. For just as the gardener needs to sow lots of seeds to be sure that some germinate and bear fruit, so much research has to take place as an act of faith. We do not know what research will bear fruit. We do not know what particular investigation will solve a major world problem, but the pursuit of intellectually interesting ideas by the most able people in society is perhaps the best way we have to solve humanity's problems; to answer the questions we have about the universe around us and to enrich our lives through intellectual stimulation and ingenuity. There is still much about our ideas and knowledge that we do not understand, nor do we have any clue as to how to find out. What we do know is that knowledge is gained as much by undoing what we thought we knew as by accumulating new findings or facts. The unexpected result is a vital part of the research scenario. This is little recognized in the setting of research agendas by funding bodies and governments, where there is an emphasis on defined objectives. Research is full of surprises. Knowledge ends up being what it is, not just what we would like it to be.

Chapter 7

New knowing

We are caught in an inescapable network of mutuality, tied in a single garment of destiny. Whatever affects one directly, affects all indirectly.

(Martin Luther King Jnr)

The train waited petulantly in the station. It was time to get a move on. Dora sat impatiently looking out of the window, staring at the people on the platform; at the flower stall and the young woman who was trying to balance umbrella, parcel and the newly acquired bunch of flowers as she rummaged in her bag for a purse; at the small boy swinging his legs vigorously as he sat on an uncomfortable-looking seat. In the midst of the bustle of those who came and went too fast for Dora to do more than register their presence, a man stood quite still, staring in front of him as if in another world.

Dora noted his brown suede shoes, his gabardine, beige-coloured trousers. 'Nothing out of the ordinary in that,' she thought. His suede jacket matched his shoes and Dora thought he looked like an architect or designer; someone with a bit of flair, anyway. She concentrated her attention on his ear. She imagined the soft down of the left lobe. He was too far away for her to actually see it. But for a few minutes she imagined what she would see if she was much closer. Cautiously, yet deliberately, just as Dora's attention was waning, the stranger's hand, which up until this point had remained in his trouser pocket, moved. He pulled the very ear lobe which had been the subject of her attention. She stared incredulously. Then reason set in. 'No, no, you can't infer that just because you were thinking of his ear that your thoughts could in any way affect his actions. Things like that just don't happen.'

The train gave a jolt and began to move. Dora shook her head slowly from side to side. 'If only I could find out,' she said to herself. Suppose it were possible to influence people's actions like that. It was not an isolated incident. Train stations were good places to carry out such experiments. The trouble is, you never know. The train always leaves the station. The stranger always remains a stranger. Sometimes people don't respond. Anyway Dora had already discovered that trying to make someone move didn't work. Any connection there was between her thoughts and the person's actions was much more subtle than that.

Dora sighed. She imagined what her academic friends would say if she told them that she wanted to do research on telepathy. They'd say it was impossible; that she wouldn't get funding. They'd say that it didn't exist. They'd say it wasn't important anyway; that she was crazy to even think of it. 'Yes, that's it,' she reflected. 'They would just laugh!'

In her reverie, Dora reflected on how many times she had had similar experiences. 'How many times has this happened? Lots. Suppose I were to record each occasion. Then I could work out whether it was greater than chance.' She thought about the difficulties of carrying out this little experiment. 'Anyway, even if I could, just supposing I could show it was greater than chance, would that change anything?' Dora suspected her friends would just laugh even more. It would clearly demonstrate she was out of her mind. Later as she walked from her station home she was still thinking about the problem. 'Yet it's an important question, isn't it? What about those physicists and all those non-local events and stuff?' The voice of reason intervened again: 'No it's not.' Dora wasn't convinced. 'People just don't want to know. It's too scary. The implications are just too scary. You can't do scientific experiments on things that science is deliberately set up to avoid.'

Although at first sight research appears to be based on the idea that there is nothing we would not want to know, we now know that is not the case. We have seen there are a number of topics and issues within the boundaries of acceptability, but there are others on the margins and some which the established academic community considers taboo. In addition, we have looked at some of the rational as well as social, cultural and political factors determining what issues are researched. At a time when the world has a desperate need to solve major problems and find a way through what Barnett (2000) describes as super-complexity and uncertainty, and when society is hungry for information, university research, as we have seen, is steeped in dogmatism. Ideas about the nature of knowledge and how we come to know, together with critical questioning of who defines what counts as knowledge and where it is produced, mean that academic research is faced with a crisis waiting to happen. This crisis is eating at its heart. I am not denying much useful work is being done by many dedicated researchers across a broad spectrum of fields of investigation. But, as we have seen, we have moved from a situation where the philosophical basis of this work, its status as knowledge and its relationship to reality, were assured. We now have no agreed ideas about what truth is, nor how ideas about knowledge relate to ideas about the nature of reality. We used to believe in one self-consistent set of ideas to explain this. But we now know that this was just a belief and we also know that we have no agreed criteria for deciding what would constitute an explanation. In this contested context, the only option new researchers have is to do what many of their more experienced colleagues are doing and deny it is happening.

Yet the crisis creates a situation where possibilities for the future are potentially open. We need to find new meaning in an activity designed to improve society's knowledge, meaning that can coexist with attempts to redefine the nature of that knowledge. Universities need to find new rationales for doing research and to embrace new ideas about knowledge and new ways of coming to know. The positive side of the crisis is that there is a wider range of choices available to researchers than is available within traditional ways of researching. New ideas about what we consider knowledge to be are proliferating. New forms of academic research are coming to know the world in new and exciting ways. Yet such ideas have to struggle for survival in a context which, as we have seen, is dogged by conservatism.

When I write of taboo subjects as I did in the last chapter, I do so in trepidation. I know that the very mention of subjects such as alchemy, morphic resonance and spirituality instantly casts me as a heretic. The questioning of traditional positivist views is a red rag to a bull and likely to engender a tirade of abuse from some academic quarters. In a tradition which prides itself on rationality and on the importance of critique, this is a contradiction. It suggests there is something we have not yet explored which is powerfully at work to limit creativity, academic freedom and criticism. It suggests we need to look at the relationship between views of what is knowable and the psychology which drives research activity.

THE PSYCHOLOGY OF KNOWING

Organizations reflect the personality of powerful individuals and groups past and present. For example, if they are fearful of their emotions, people are likely to create and sustain institutional structures that can contain that fear and those emotions. So we need to consider to which psychological impulses the institution of academic research gives expression. This is a vitally important question in our quest to understand more about the nature of research. For like a disturbed individual, unless we are aware of the psychopathology which drives our actions, we have no possibility for transformation. Unless we understand the psychopathological impulses to which our quests for knowledge give expression, we cannot see ways for it to move us forward in teaching a society faced with super-complexity and uncertainty how to live.

So what do I mean by psychopathology? Let me make it clear, I am not suggesting that every researcher is psychologically unbalanced! However, academic research, like any other human phenomenon, can be seen as a response to, or a reflection of, a number of psychological impulses. So imagine the rules 'of traditional research as applying to an individual person. Such a person would tend to assert that what they did was good merely by the fact of their doing it (science is a 'good thing'); to assert their view as true over and above anyone else's (science produces truths expressed in laws); to be emotionally cut off from the world (policy of non-involvement i.e. objectivity); to justify all actions with irrefutable logic (rule of rationality). In its adherence to these norms as ways of proceeding, traditional research values such a person. Its products, some of which take on the form of technological achievements, embody these values. This is frightening. Think about it. The most logical people you know are probably the ones least in touch with their feelings. The use of logic can provide a way of cutting ourselves off from those things we do not want to know. It can be seen to have a similar use in research.

So research gives expression to particular psychopathological patterns and protects us from facing particular truths about our place in the cosmos. Midgley (1992: 65) argues that central to the questions we ask and to the importance that academic inquiry has for us is 'the fear of lostness, the desire for connection and meaning'. Research protects us, for example, from acknowledging our insignificance; it protects us from getting involved; it preserves our separateness. Indeed we could not find a better method of inquiry which more effectively denied our individual subjectivity. Code (1991: 119) talks of 'a remarkable coincidence between stereotypical notions of masculinity and the characteristics of the rational knowledge producing enterprise'. Fox Keller (1985) suggests that science tends to attract people for whom objectivism and detachment provide emotional comfort and that usually these are men. While I am highly sceptical of an argument that equates psychological inadequacy with men, it does seem to me that there is something psychologically odd about objectivity.

If we wanted to produce a method of inquiry which would most effectively protect us from ideas we do not want to know, which would also effectively prevent us from coming to know ourselves, we could do no better than dream up traditional positivist thinking. It is emotionally comforting because the person is left quite out of the picture. Reason and Marshall (1987) suggest we frequently choose topics for research which are central to our life concerns. By leaving out the subject who is conducting the research and the processes they have gone through in doing it, traditional research leads to a containment of what is problematic in life. When we look more closely at the issues and topics which are the subject of research and the ways in which this is done, we find there are many things academic research is set up to avoid knowing. So research can be a defence against knowing what we fear to know and a way of avoiding that which we do not want to acknowledge (Brew 1988). Although things are fortunately now changing, we should not underestimate the power of the establishment to hold on to this pathology. The implications of critiques advanced by, for example, postmodernist, post-colonial, post-structuralist and feminist arguments, however logically valid, are psychologically difficult to accept, particularly by people who feel threatened by them.

Midgley (1992) suggests that science is a matter of dealing with things that can seriously affect the way we see human life. This is an interesting criterion for examining which research questions should command the most funding. In the 1980s, farmers in the southern counties of England were becoming increasingly worried about a curious phenomenon which kept occurring in their fields of grown wheat. The phenomenon of crop circles was widely talked about and people travelled long distances when it was reported that yet another of these indentations had appeared. It was argued that the crop circles were made by spaceships or some non-human energy sources. Many people testified to strange lights, unusual energy fields, the brief length of time taken to make them, the effects on dowsing rods and so on. The circles began to take on a bizarre character, with protruding antennae. Farmers became increasingly worried because crops were being destroyed.

This example is interesting in relation to our present discussion for several reasons. First, everyone wants to know whether there is extraterrestrial life. It is an important question. To find that crop circles were made by extraterrestrial beings would require fundamental shifts in the ways we live our lives. Funding for research into these phenomena is almost non-existent. It will be argued that this is because they are improbable. Why, then, is so much money put into the somewhat impractical search for extraterrestrial life in deep space? To find it would indeed change the way in which we viewed ourselves. But since, supposing some was found, it is likely to be many millions of light years away, we probably would not have to change our political systems much to accommodate it! But how much more improbable is it that the deep space research will find something of use to us? As we saw, Popper had said that a theory is scientific if it is potentially falsifiable (Popper 1980). How do you falsify the assumption that crop circles are made by spaceships? Rupert Sheldrake solved the problem with no government funding, and the way he did it is explained in his book *Seven Experiments that Could Change the World.* He set up a crop circle competition. There was a prize for the person or persons who could create the best crop circle. A secret destination was chosen. It was found that the circles could be replicated and the mystery was solved (Sheldrake 1994). We have to entertain the idea that there are fears behind what we want and do not want to know, as much as there were fears behind what medieval people wanted and did not want to know even though, as we noted in Chapter Five, the frame of understanding of people in that other era was quite different.

Going back to traditional ideas of knowledge and knowing, the quest was not simply to know, but to know for certain. It is a quest which has occupied philosophers over the centuries. Many rules governing research procedures are, as we have seen, concerned with the criteria for deciding whether something is true: logical consistency, coherence of data, inter-subjective agreement, integrity of research procedure, objectivity, and so on. But even if all of these criteria are satisfied, the question of certainty still remains. In traditional epistemologies certainty is always problematic. We can never know that the next instance will not result in refutation (the problem of induction). Academia abhors the idea that there may be no way of deciding between truths (relativism) and even though postmodern critiques have opened up debate so that relativism is no longer a taboo subject for discussion, nevertheless this does nothing to overcome the psychological need for certainty. The quest for certain knowledge supports a need for security. Descartes was said to have sat in a large stove when he wondered if, because he was sometimes mistaken, he might always be so. I like that image of one of the founding fathers of so-called Enlightenment thinking. There is a kind of symbolism in the idea of daring to think the unthinkable while sitting in a safe womb-like atmosphere.

It is interesting to note in this psychological context that in the face of arguments showing that there are no grand meta-narratives which are true across the universe, there have been a number of recent attempts to claim a theory of everything, demonstrating a refusal to accept that we cannot be all-knowing (see e.g. Wilson 1998). Mary Midgley suggests physicists have a remarkably high opinion of themselves in believing they can know everything and that one day we will be in a position to change aspects of the universe:

> Most of us have begun to see that the party is over. The planet is in deep trouble; we had better concentrate on bailing it out. At this point, to keep up one's spirits by further orgies of self-congratulation may be a natural reaction, but it is a dead end. Paranoia, if further encouraged, is liable finally to undermine all wish to get back in touch with reality. The discrepancy between image and fact is growing too wide to be tolerated. For the general sanity, we need all the help we can get from our scientists in reaching a more realistic attitude to the physical world we live in.
>
> (Midgley 1992: 224)

The same is true of empirical findings in scientific studies which demonstrate alternative descriptions of reality (e.g. light is both waves and particles). We have difficulty dealing with what philosophers call the 'excluded middle', i.e. the idea that something can be one thing and also its opposite.

> The idea that things are well defined and that we do not live in a paradoxical world leads to the standard that our knowledge must be self consistent. Theories that contain contradictions cannot be part of science. This apparently quite fundamental standard which many philosophers accept as unhesitatingly as Catholics once accepted the dogma of the immaculate conception of the Virgin loses its authority the moment we find that there are facts whose only adequate description is inconsistent and that inconsistent theories may be fruitful and easy to handle while the attempt to make them conform to the demands of consistency creates useless and unwieldy monsters.
>
> (Feyerabend 1978: 36)

The description of light as both waves and particles is such a case. Allowing the possibility of contradiction in research opens up a wide range of possibilities.

For once something (event, action, etc.) is seen as contradictory, the number of contradictions appears to multiply. Chaos ensues. The world becomes more complex than we had hitherto imagined. The standard response to this is to disallow contradictions and so keep everything in research neat and orderly. But in doing this, it is notable that we lose control. Knowledge turns out to be what it is, not what we would like it to be. Being open to the possibility of contradiction means allowing the natural mechanisms and processes of the research to cohere in their own way. It means being open to the possibility that reality is contradictory and non-contradictory at the same time. This is the ultimate paradox! But it is very scary. The quest to know for certain has to be seen to be rooted in psychological needs. It is asked in the face of a vast universe of not-knowing.

BREAKING DOWN THE PATHOLOGY

I have argued that research is in a crisis waiting to happen. Failure to acknowledge the psychological factors driving our research agendas is a central issue in this crisis. Wertheim (1995: 7) argues that our conception of the universe has been filtered through physics, which has shaped the imagination. This has replaced theology 'at the helm of epistemological power' such that senior researchers in physics have become high priests. The enormous prestige associated with science has given them a view of themselves as saviours. Science has become the new religion (Midgley 1992). Yet Heron (1992) describes this charismatic personality as pathological.

Fortunately, there is now a critical questioning of the role of research in providing explanations of the universe:

> I think it is very significant that we still seek some unifying and ennobling vision. We live in an age that is supposed to be post-ideological, yet all around one can see attempts to re-construct old meta-narratives or to fashion new ones. In the United States especially, no quarter passes without somebody producing a book on the modern mind or the condition of society, etc., and although these are often pessimistic in outlook they are also struggling to try and answer the questions of who we are, of what we have become and where we ought to be heading. The issue therefore is whether such efforts are in vain.
>
> (Haldane 1997: 57)

This kind of questioning is captured by the science journalist John Horgan (1998), in his book *The End of Science*. Many scientists he interviewed

> seemed gripped by a profound unease. . . . *If one believes in science*, one must accept the possibility – even the probability – that the great era of scientific discovery is over. By *science* I mean not applied science, but science at its purest and grandest, the primordial human quest to understand the universe and our

place in it. Further research may yield no more great revelations or revolutions, but only incremental diminishing returns.

(Horgan 1998: 6, italics in the original)

There is an admission here of the concerns of scientists that the days when they are centre stage are numbered. The idea is that science is reaching its limits. One of Horgan's interviewees, the mathematician Richard Feynman, said we already know the physics of almost everything in everyday life and anything that is left over is not going to be relevant. This view rests on the idea that the things which are currently being worked on are basically not testable, or require huge expenditure to build equipment which may not work; for example, detectors for gravity waves or the search for solar nutrinos. The question is whether the expenditure on research which may result only in adding one more decimal place on issues which have already been investigated is justified or whether it is too great for the public purse to bear. Science, the physicist Per Bak argues in the same volume, has to be useful for something, not pursued for its own sake. This, he suggests, is becoming increasingly difficult from a practical political point of view. Increasingly governments are baulking at paying the high cost of scientific research. Horgan argues that only specialists care about the precise mass of the 'top quark, the existence of which was finally confirmed in 1994 after research costing billions of dollars' (Horgan 1998: 30). So the research we do is limited by the funds we have available to do it. But there is a curious irony. Gregory Chaitin, a mathematician, said that people who did good scientific work were always a small group of lunatics. 'Everyone else is concerned with surviving, paying their mortgage. . . . Chaitin pointed out that quantum mechanics was initally done by people as a hobby in the 1920s when there was no funding' (Horgan 1998: 240).

The line between the activities of scientists who Chaitin describes as 'lunatics' and those of people who the establishment describes as 'cranks' is a thin one. The consequences for the people concerned and for society are hugely different. Research is dependent on small groups of enthusiasts being obsessed with solving particular problems or exploring particular phenomena. The psychology of obsession is bound up with Western ideas of knowledge and knowing.

Yet some have questioned whether the important questions have been solved (see also Collins and Pinch 1998, for example). There is the idea that as humans we actually have the ability to invent profound but unanswerable questions. This clearly goes against any notion of the completion of science. Horgan argues there are some kinds of problems which are beyond the scope of research. Because rational language is linear it cannot explain a number of complex systems. These are more than the sum of the parts and relations: something research cannot readily cope with. Chaos and complexity researchers have found that, when pushed too far, explanations always result in incoherence (Horgan 1998). Prigogine and Stengers (1984) suggested that the major discoveries of science in the twentieth century have proscribed the limits of science. Nature, they argue, cannot be described from the outside as if by a spectator. While Casti (1997) in his book *Would-be Worlds* similarly argues that:

To anyone infected with the idea that the human mind is unlimited in its capacity to answer questions about natural and human affairs, a tour of twentieth-century science must be quite a depressing experience. Many of the deepest and most well-chronicled results of science in this century have been statements about what cannot be done and what cannot be known.

(Casti 1997: 196)

Casti cites, as examples, Gödel's theorem, which says that a mathematical system is either incomplete or inconsistent and Turing's theory of computer systems which says you cannot systematically test a system and its data to say whether it will stop when processing it.

Recognizing the difficulty of dealing with highly complex questions is not new. It is a point expressed by Tolstoy (1978) in his essay on the nature of historical explanation at the end of his great nineteenth-century novel *War and Peace*. Tolstoy contended that the actions of nations are guided by individuals. Ancient historians attributed the causes of historical events first to the will of God and then to the actions of key individuals: monarchs, generals or ministers of state. However, it is not these individuals acting as forces which move nations, Tolstoy argued. That cause lies in the interactions of numerous people connected with the event all acting as autonomous individuals. 'The movement of nations is caused not by power, nor by intellectual activity, nor even by a combination of the two, as historians have supposed, but by the activity of all the people who participate in the event' (Tolstoy 1978: 1425).

The further we are removed from the event the more we can see that what appeared to be free choice was in fact influenced by the context of the event. Chains of causation of human actions thus become essentially unknowable because they depend on the perspective of the historian. As Casti (1997) more recently explains, complex systems consist of a number of intelligent, adaptive agents interacting on the basis of local information. We still await, Casti suggests, the development of a theory which will explain how complex systems work.

Another of Horgan's interviewees was the linguist Noam Chomsky. He argued that physicists can only create a 'theory of what they know how to formulate' (Horgan 1998: 152). Chomsky divided scientific questions into problems, which are at least potentially answerable, and mysteries, which are not, and he suggested we are linguistically limited in our ability to ask questions. Horgan also draws attention to the nineteenth-century German philosopher Immanuel Kant who suggested that the structure of our minds constrains the questions we ask and the answers we glean from them (Horgan 1998: 29). So the research we do is limited by the nature of human brains. Another of Horgan's interviewees, Roger Shepherd, a psychologist from Stanford University, expressed the view that science is getting perhaps too complicated. In the future, he suggested, there may be theories which even the most brilliant scientists cannot understand. Horgan asks: does the increasing difficulty of science mean it is approaching its limits? 'Maybe I'm old-fashioned,' Roger Shepherd said, 'but if a theory is so complicated that no single person can understand it, what satisfaction can we take in it?' (Horgan 1998: 234).

According to Horgan, other eminent researchers believe that there is no limit to the things we can investigate. The geneticist Richard Dawkins, for example, does not like the idea that there are some questions that should not be answered; that no one wants to understand. He believes, with others, that researchers want to understand everything and that there are only scientists to understand it (Horgan 1998: 119). Another of Horgan's interviewees, Per Bak, rebuts what he calls the 'wishy-washy' idea that problems are just too hard for human brains (Horgan 1998: 203). Per Bak says that science will look very different in the future (ibid.: 221).

Any idea that research, let alone science, has explained everything is, of course ridiculous. It demonstrates an arrogance demanding to be questioned. As we have seen, there are many things which academic research does not want to explain. We have seen that there are important areas of human knowledge to be investigated right outside those which academic research has hitherto focused on. There are important questions which academic research has not yet even begun to address. We have also seen that research has used limited ways of looking at a limited range of phenomena. There are many topics and methods of investigation needing to be explored. A transformation of the academic enterprise is urgently needed. Humility might be a more appropriate attitude.

PRODUCT TO PROCESS

The concern of academic inquiry has to be to improve our understanding of the problems we face in a world characterized by perplexity, uncertainty and super-complexity, and to develop our ability to solve them. Research should lead to a growing and deepening understanding and realization of what is of value. As such it must become a process of learning about how to live. We cannot do this by leaving ourselves out of the picture and it is not something which a small handful of academics can do alone. It is no use expert academics simply developing understanding or arrogantly asserting that all is under their control. It has to be a cooperative endeavour. Academics have to help other people understand, articulate and solve their own problems. Research thus must have both a personal and a social dimension.

How are we going to do this when, as we have seen, there are problems in doing something different, i.e. where the nature of the problems or questions challenges conventional assumptions about the very nature of research? How are we going to do it when research practice has psychopathological impulses embedded within its very nature? How are we going to do this when we are all at sea and do not have an idea of what would constitute an appropriate direction? And finally, how are we going to do this when we are conscious of the particularity of our cultural locatedness?

In Chapter Four we saw some examples of how this is beginning to happen. Let us now pursue this further. We will leave until Chapter Eight discussions of how powerful political agendas constrain research and how they put a brake on new directions. For now, let us explore what needs to happen, not why it cannot. A vision will of course have to compete, indeed is competing, in a cultural context set up to avoid it. But we need the vision in order to give expression to growing trends and avert the crisis.

In the face of critical questioning research is, as we have seen, becoming a process whereby we explore how to operate in a multifaceted, pluralistic universe. While there are particular examples that can inform other contexts these do not provide general rules about how to do this which can be applied in all situations. We now know that they never will. Research should move away from manifestations of a quantitative conception of knowledge where knowledge products are stored, to become the process of changing the way we understand the phenomena of our experience. The emphasis has to move from end products to the process of how we come to know. What this change in ideas about knowledge does is to shift the emphasis away from the implicit assumptions that we can know what truth is and can know what is true, towards the idea that understanding what truth is and creating or discovering it is part and parcel of our individual and collective inquiries. In the emerging traditions of what I have called experiential research, truth and validity are not necessarily achieved at all stages nor are they an outcome. They are instead processes to aim for. We do not know what truth or validity are in a pluralistic context. Truth is thus a process of becoming. It takes on the meaning of 'being true to'. Unlike traditional research which presents truths as fixed outcomes of research, new forms view 'truth-full-ness' as ways of proceeding. Truth is a process. It is a quality of the reality of the researcher's experience; a way of acting and a way of knowing.

Talking of inquiry as a process shifts attention away from the number of problems or questions solved or answered, towards the quality of the process of solving or answering, or indeed the morality of pursuing particular questions. The research becomes a faithful reflection of the world *as the researcher sees it*. The process is continuous. We have to do as I indicated in Chapter Four and 'look again' when we think we know. The search becomes as important as what we find. The way we search is important. The knowledge which results from an inquiry process is only a small subset of what the inquirer has come to know in the course of it. As we shall see in Chapter Nine, we should not confuse the product of an inquiry, a coherent theory which explains a set of observed phenomena, or a completed project, created object or journal article, with the knowing which the inquirer experiences in the process of its development. Critical reflection on the assumptions lying behind ideas, theories, etc., may amount to acting as if everything is relevant (my second research guideline – see Chapter Four). This can lead to further knowledge which again can be looked at in relation to what is unsaid, leading to further knowledge and so on. Coming to know is a process.

Talking of knowing as a process shifts attention away from the number of things a researcher has found or mastered towards the quality of the mastery. By analogy, learning to paint does not stop when the apprentice has painted a picture.

Learning perspective, drawing and mixing colours, etc., go on through painting many pictures. They are lifelong processes. The trick is not to confuse the end product, the painting, with the process of knowing how to paint.

In the pluralistic context of uncertainty, we must recognize that whatever we know, we know only hypothetically. Being open in this way takes account of the fact that our research may form part of the process of others' comings to know. Openness to new insights means exploring the possibilities for creative co-production of meaning by the researcher and the audience for the research. The electronic submission of theses, electronic journals and research reports provides cases where this is now to be seen. Studies produced in hypertext and multimedia (graphics, video, audio, animation), for example, mean that a reader might begin and continually return to a home page where there might be links to major subject areas, and these in turn might lead to another range of pages. How the individual navigates this process will be quite individual to them, part of that individual's process of coming to know. Such emphasis on the process rather than the product would give rise to a new form of research, the adoption of which would transform the academic enterprise, including science as we know it, our research institutions, universities and the like. Indeed, in the shift to an emphasis on process there is the germ of a means of societal and personal transformation.

VALID CONSCIOUSNESS

If research is to guide us in finding a way through a pluralistic, uncertain world characterized by multi-complexity, the researcher's awareness needs to be explicitly recognized as a growing and developing part of the research process. It is not something that you just have, which you then apply to the research you do. Nor is it something you arrive at by the end of the research. Rather the development of awareness needs to become part and parcel of the activity we call research. We are always in the process of becoming aware. There is only the journey, no destination, and certainly no golden city at the end of all of our endeavours.

Being aware as a researcher means to some degree playing with boundaries; drawing them in different ways on all sorts of levels, illuminating differing views of reality and differing realities by defining and redefining them. It means being aware of the ways the contexts in which we are framed affect us and our actions. Remembering that research is a process, researcher awareness which is knowing is engaged in the continual search for clarity, for awareness. In traditional research, the aim is be aware of subjective inputs, in order to minimize them, as mentioned in Chapter Four; what Skolimowski (1984) calls the 'yoga of objectivity'. To conduct research in the conventional way, as we have seen, we have to leave ourselves out of it. What happens though is that having accustomed ourselves to doing this, we tend to leave ourselves out of our own lives too. Working in a detached 'objective' way we become detached from our own needs, emotions and our inner knowing. We have mirrored the detachment of traditional research by becoming alienated from ourselves and others.

Research in the future needs to become a highly moral procedure. By moral I do not refer to a narrow adherence to a set of maxims. Rather, I have in mind the pursuit of whatever enhances life and gives expression to our connectedness to all actions, events, things and creatures in the cosmos. This means taking account of the mystery of our participation, not blindly assuming we have control over it. It means developing the 'yoga of participation' (Skolimowski 1984).

The importance of the quality of the knower and the shift from a detached consciousness to a self-reflective, aware consciousness is nowhere more firmly needed than in the area of the ethics of research. In the current ethical minefield this has an urgency about it, for ethical questions must be resolved in the context of the research design itself. Adherence to traditional rules means that scientists' ethical judgements do not have a place within their research. This is not to say that scientists are immoral people. Yet it is well recognized that, logically, traditional methodology can lead to a neglect of moral responsibility because it allows researchers to detach themselves from the moral consequences of their actions. In order to make a moral judgement, the traditional researcher has to go outside the methodology of their research. Many scientists I have met are well-intentioned people who care about aspects of the natural world, yet scientific and technological developments have taken place in disregard of their moral implications, and some devastating social, psychological and ecological consequences are apparent. Harding (1991) argues that a number of efforts have been made to 'absolve' scientists from the social consequences of their research: for example, by defining social desires as technological needs which then lead to legitimate scientific research; by shifting the values within science through the technologies developed to produce scientific knowledge, such as genetic engineering, nuclear accelerators, etc.; by using the information created through scientific research in applications which are by no means politically neutral. The failure of traditional research methodology to embody within it questions of value has left the academic world in a state of moral turbulence. There is now a huge number of ethical questions facing researchers. Indeed, there is evidence to suggest that the range of techniques and investigations which are possible but which raise ethical questions is increasing.

To talk about the ethics of research is to come back to the question of who is going to enforce the rules. Questions of ethics are questions about power-sharing and about who has the power to enforce what values. Ethical decision-making in relation to research has become another area of contested space. But where does the ethical responsibility lie? In order to deal with this situation, ethics committees, which in Australia, for example, have been established by the Vice-Chancellors' Committee prompted by the National Health and Medical Research Council (NH&MRC), provide a mandatory check on all research proposals involving humans and animals. The bureaucratic process in some countries may seem heavy-handed. In those disciplines and countries where ethical responsibility is thought to lie in the professional bodies, and where the professional body defines a code of conduct, responsibility for ethical decision-making rests with the individual researcher. This is the case in education and sociology in the UK and in psychology in the US (see e.g. American Psychological Association 1981, Appelbaum and Rosenbaum 1989). But what does this say about the moral judgement of researchers? While it is now clear that the investigators' research that led to the development of the atom bomb was morally indefensible, at the time it was conducted the issues were far from clear (Jungk 1960). 'Throughout the twentieth century the claim to be scientific has repeatedly been brought forward as an all-purpose justification for policies to which there were obvious moral objections' (Midgley 1997: 70).

A similar situation exists today in respect of current concerns. Critical questions about the development of antibiotics have been raised only after they have been in use for some time. In contrast, genetic engineering has been a cause for concern in society prior to its widespread use, and researchers are having to defend its development. Such defences were not deemed necessary while scientific advances were seen as *ipso facto* a good thing. The problem is that ethical questions have become extremely complex. Ethics committees are unable to deal with all of the implications. For example, social and biological projects which appear harmless in the Western world may be demeaning for aboriginal people or peoples in other, poorer cultures. Ethics committees and procedures tend to preserve the status quo because they are not set up to encourage new methodologies and may misinterpret the intentions of, for example, cooperative and participatory inquiries. There are many inquiries where getting it wrong is simply not an option. In such cases ethical questions cannot be decided *post hoc*.

Some years ago I let a room in my house to a Masters' student studying zoology. She had to get mice pregnant and then kill them to examine the foetuses. Her natural disinclination to do what she considered to be ethically indefensible had to be suppressed. What I mean by a self-reflective aware consciousness is that she would have used her feelings as a resource in her research and not suppressed them. No doubt her supervisors considered the research important. But what is important? How do we decide whether it is more important to pursue research which might ultimately have beneficial consequences for humankind, or research which enables us, as researchers, to live ethical lives? There are no grand general answers to these questions. External agencies are becoming increasingly unable to make the decisions. The issues are too complex to be dealt with on a general level. Researchers have to lead the way but do not yet know how to do it. The process of finding out how to resolve ethical questions has to become part and parcel of each research project. The dilemmas have to be addressed in research teams and laboratories by the researchers themselves. Local, context-dependent ways of dealing with these dilemmas must be found and changes made to the education of researchers to ensure they are prepared for this.

WISDOM

Traditional knowledge is inherently conservative. What is replacing it is dynamically radical and progressively transformative. Looking again introduces the idea of critical thinking into the process. This, Barnett (1997a) argues, is essential if universities are to teach us how to live in conditions of postmodernity. Research of this nature will inevitably transform itself, for it has within it the means of and suggestions for transformation. In this scenario, traditional objectivism and rationalism become subsumed in a wider context of inquiry. They are merely one of a number of tools of inquiry used to help in the process of knowing and becoming.

Many sages have suggested that true enlightenment begins when we reach the point of realizing that what we have learned through books and through experience is useless when we really come face to face with ourselves. Truly experiencing one's ignorance is the point of transformation. Paradoxically, the highest point of knowing is thus a kind of not-knowing. Traditional research teaches us to neglect this. Information comes from outside ourselves. The emphasis on products – on conclusions and on objects, for example – can now be seen as an expression of a psychological longing for each individual life to be directed towards some purpose. Midgley (1992: 222) contrasts the religious idea of timelessness which, she argues, is found in the present moment, with the 'flight from the near to the remote' of scientists when they seek to explain cosmological events in teleological terms. The meaning of life for these scientists is viewed as residing in the future and far distant. Whereas for mystics it is now and here.

Experiential research, by its very nature, questions this emphasis because it necessarily rests on a recognition of the interrelationship of personal and research issues. Many innovative theses, for example, do not present an objective, detached report of inquiry because the very nature of the questions which they set out to address precludes it. The distinction between objectivity and subjectivity breaks down in such cases.

What such research forces us to do is not only to refuse to duck difficult subjective questions which traditional research defined as outside its domain, but to critically examine the interrelationships within the research:

> the hermeneutic/interpretive emphasis on the 'subjective' instead of the objective can be seen as merely a reversal of an opposition where 'objective/ subjective' is still retained as a defining and definitive polar opposition. Instead a postmodern approach seeks to subvert this dichotomy, to show that apparently mutually exclusive polar opposites are in effect mutually implicated and to suggest alternatives which radically challenge and critique dominant epistemological paradigms and discourses in all their various forms.
>
> (Usher *et al.* 1997: 204)

This is not a question of swapping the objective perspective for a subjective one. Rather, it is as if the objective and the subjective which were thought to reside on different sleeves, have now to be merged. We have, so to speak, to turn the overcoat of knowing inside out (Brew 1988). The three guidelines developed to guide an experiential methodology and outlined in Chapter Four, provide a new framework from which we can move forward. In the serious and systematic application of these three principles, rigour in experiential research can be developed and criteria for validity derived. Yet we have to come to terms with the fact that there is no golden city at the end of the journey and that what is important are not the products but rather the processes we engage in to achieve an under-standing. The critical engagement that we witness on the way and how we as people are affected by our investigations become crucially important.

However, a dark cloud hangs over the academic community. It is not just a question of acknowledging that there are particular difficulties in publishing and gaining funding for this type of work. What we are seeing instead of new thinking is, as Lyotard realized, an emphasis on performativity (i.e. performance in the service of economic wealth). In this context what I have presented in this section may seem unrealistically idealistic. Indeed, we can see these two strands – an emphasis on products in the increasing emphasis on performativity brought about by governmental research funding formulas, and an emphasis on processes derived from breaking the boundaries of knowledge – pulling in completely opposite directions. I take up this issue when I consider economic models and discuss research as a commodity in the next chapter.

Part II

Research in context

Chapter 8

Research as a commodity

Great spirits have always encountered violent opposition from mediocre minds.

(Albert Einstein)

Darkness crept stealthily over the damp heath. A breath of wind stirred and an owl hooted. Time itself, like a ghostly apparition, mysteriously vanished. And all was still. In the valley, trees and houses languished in the all-pervading gloom. Blackness stole round corners, in alleys, down drains and into every porch of the fearful hamlet. Not a light was to be seen. Sleep conspired with Night and all was silent.

There was no succour here, no place for the needy, for the lonely or the bold. Only darkness, the darkness that imprisons and entombs. A world of nothingness. No thing. A hollow world of emptiness. And then the damp. Creeping into bones. Stifling thought and arresting movement. When dark pervades the world, it is not possible to really know what it is like in light. When darkness moves in, light does not exist. As when winter shuts out all possibility that it ever will be summer and even the brightest spark of imagination is dulled in perpetual cold.

And so he walked purposefully on. He wondered what others would think of his journey in the dark. Surely they would say: 'Why go it alone?' They would think he was not the kind of person to attempt such a daunting journey. But on he trudged, picking his way across the heathland, stepping over rivulets, barely able to see the path. With the vigilance of a nocturnal creature, he watched carefully where he put his feet, as if walking through a minefield. Each weary step squelching in the damp peat earth took him onward into emptiness. Bare trees, stark against the blackness, hovered here and there in the gloom. The way was by no means assured. There was no belief that it ever would be light. There was no assurance that the journey would ever be accomplished. The minefield of thought oppressed and censored. No matter. The journey had to be undertaken. There was no going back.

When at last it was time to take a breath, to stop for a while and rest, he sat wearily down on a large boulder. Panting for breath, he felt the cold air as it entered his gaping mouth. He uttered a sigh. As if in reply, the dark clouds parted to reveal the naked moon riding high and proud like a queen of all she surveyed. The land was infused with an eerie glow. Then as the silver monarch traversed the sky the night owl swooped on its prey. Fluid shadows emerged furtively from stones, rocks, shrubs and bushes. But their time was short-lived. Night and the Dark were in control. The curtain of clouds was drawn again and the moon, destined to ride once more in solitude, disappeared from sight.

Throughout the 1990s, reflecting the orientation known as economic rationalism, research was treated as a commodity just like any other in a global economy. This orientation is influencing what research governments and other bodies including industry choose to provide money for and this in turn is influencing what research academics choose to do and how they choose to do it. In this chapter I am going to explore this view of research and examine some of its effects.

While I am anxious to avoid the fatalism which has permeated higher education in recent years, it has to be recognized that views of research emanating from economic rationalism currently have enormous power. Pursuing our picture images, this is the billboard view of research. Like those huge advertising hoardings in our cities which clutter up the landscape and cannot be ignored, economic rationalism is, for the academic community, as the hoardings are for the motorist, a constant irritant. They are 'in your face'.

The clash between academic values and the economic model of research is the point at which the clash of contest is fiercest. Yet it is a point on which commentators are almost silent. The economic model is a given. For the new researcher trying to get a handle on what is going on and, in particular, trying to decide what research to pursue, the effects of the economic model of research are inescapable. The ways colleagues talk about research, the aspects of research they focus on, their day-to-day preoccupations, the university's requirements for promotion and advancement, the seminars that are organized by the research office to assist in various funding applications, as well as government reports and the ways research is presented in the media, are all spurred on by this economic model. In my study of senior academic researchers, it was even found that economic factors had had a far greater impact on changes to research methodology in recent years than anything else. Yet while particular government pronouncements may be the subject of discussion, there is a stark absence of critical dialogue about this model of research in general within the academic community.

Performativity

The push for what Lyotard (1984) calls performativity, i.e. performance directed at economic ends, has been the dominant feature of this view of research. Performativity is a vehicle, that has been used by many governments around the world in their various research performance exercises for changing the nature of academic work. Everything done as research is defined in terms of clearly defined and bounded projects (Gibbons *et al.* 1994). This chunking of research activity into bite-size pieces means that they can be counted for a variety of purposes. There is a push towards closure (Usher and Soloman 1999). A myth is then created that every project needs funding. Then, so the story goes, it is possible to measure the 'amount' of research done by an individual, a department or a university in terms of the dollars of funding obtained and indeed the contribution of respective governments to world research in terms of dollars spent.

Since such performance measures have been put in place, there has clearly been an increased amount of research activity focused on producing outcomes. How much of that activity has been worthwhile is hard to say. As I mentioned before, when I talk to academics across the university campus about their research, what always strikes me is the way in which they speak of their inherent fascination with the subjects they are investigating and their curiosity to know more about their chosen field of study. So why is it that they have been apparently so compliant in going along with the economic model of research?

Ball (2000) argues that in the context of performativity, action becomes fabricated and professional judgements are subordinated. We select from versions of the truth. Each researcher is faced with a dilemma. Do they do something which they believe to be worthwhile, or do they do whatever they can as quickly as possible? Fabrication, Ball suggests, has to be sustained in order to 'escape from the gaze' (Ball 2000: 2). This means, in relation to research, that we become focused on outcomes: getting research grants or publications in order to demonstrate that we are active as researchers. What we are doing in our research is less important than what we are seen to be doing. Authenticity, Ball argues, has to be forgone. Taken out of context this behaviour seems bizarre. Why should academic researchers engage in such inauthentic behaviour? There is a sense here that academics know exactly what they are doing when they take on these agendas. Academics know these agendas require them to be inauthentic but they choose to follow them. Ball suggests that what they have lost is a kind of liberty. But why do they do this?

In order to answer this we need to understand a little more of what is involved in economic rationalism and how and why it has gained favour. One argument is that postmodern critiques, including the crises in knowledge discussed earlier, have led to a vacuum which has been filled by commercial interests and government demands. Alternatively and more persuasively, economic rationalism is viewed as a product of postmodernity. The conditions of postmodernity, Usher (1997) argues, foreground seduction:

A consumer culture does not discriminate: where everything, including meaning and knowledge can be consumed, the rules of good taste and worthwhile knowledge are challenged and subverted. In the postmodern, knowledge is conceived as multiple, reflecting multiple realities and the multiplicity of experience, and generated in a multiplicity of sites. When the worthwhile can only be defined in terms of multiple and changing taste and style, knowledge cannot be either canonical or hierarchically structured. The consumer (the learner) rather than the producer (educator) is articulated as having greater significance and power. Educational practitioners become part of the culture industry, vendors alongside many others in the hypermarket of learning.

(Usher 1997: 108)

So we have moved from the Grand Hotel of Enlightenment thinking into a kind of intellectual shopping mall where notions of knowledge and truth give way to choice and the vagaries of the 'market' (Scott 1991). It is therefore little wonder there are attempts to hold on to whatever promises security. Clearly defined objectives within clearly bounded 'projects', for example, are not only 'marketable', they are controllable within an uncontrollable system. Those who allocate resources for research have the power and are in a position to manipulate academic research for their own ends (Gibbons *et al.* 1994). Unfortunately, in a situation where academics are selling their services, profits benefit discrete sections of academia, namely, those that are closely allied to powerful outside groups (Slaughter 1993).

Such a view of the postmodern condition and the capacity of powerful groups to exploit it paints a picture of powerless academics whose only option is to grin and bear it, give up traditional notions of critique and academic autonomy, behave like good boys and girls and do what governments and those with power and money demand. There is a sense in some departments that academics are thus powerlessly following the dictates of government. Yet this clearly does a disservice to the university community. We have to recognize that universities and the academics within them are, as Ball (2000: 7) points out, consciously choosing to 'play the game'. Universities know it is in their interests to do this. Individual academics are also weighing up the consequences of following or not following the agendas of those who hold the power and have been enormously successful in rising to the challenge of competition and change and of successfully meeting the economic imperatives.

One of the places where this weighing up of advantages and disadvantages is particularly acute that I have come across while talking to people about research is in establishing research traditions in higher education institutions that hitherto were mainly teaching-only institutions. This is the case, for example, in New Zealand with the government's expectation that teaching and research should be aligned if degree courses are being taught. It is also the case with the UK's new universities, i.e. former polytechnics, and in Australia with parts of institutions that were formerly colleges of advanced education. Another area where this is a major issue and concern is establishing a research culture in departments, comprising professional areas where there has not been a tradition of research, such as physiotherapy or law. In these kinds of situation, understanding not only what research is but also what it can be, is particularly important. New traditions of research establishing themselves up at a time when the economic model of research is paramount face a particularly difficult task in deciding what is appropriate. For while traditional 'research' universities are achieving high research ratings in research assessment exercises, it is easy, in non-research institutions, to believe that high scores on research ranking are achieved by carrying out traditional research. This is particularly so when the ranking appears to be based on aspects of research aligned with conservative approaches. I have spoken to many people who tell me that in order to be competitive, traditional notions of research are being promoted in a misguided belief that this is what research is about. The field of nursing has perhaps been most successful in forging new approaches to research in the face of such pressure, but it has not been easy (see for example the work of Crotty 1996).

One of the reasons academics have been able not simply to survive but also to thrive within this research marketplace dominated by economics becomes evident when we look at the variation in the ways research is conceptualized. One particular variation, which I have called the *trading variation* (see Chapter Two), gives expression to elements which are entirely consistent with economic rationalism. In other words, the economic perspective feeds the way some academics inherently think about their research. There is no inauthenticity for such researchers, no loss of liberty. For these academics, there is no conflict in pursuing government research agendas. They perceive their research to be clearly bounded in research projects, with publication being its main force and *raison d'être*. For others, who have different views of the nature of research, there can be conflict between their preferred orientation to research and the activities they are being encouraged by government, their university and their colleagues to engage in.

An assumption of this book has been that we have choices in how we view the nature of research and in the research agendas we promote. There is no doubt that the economic view of research presents a restricted view of the nature of research. Yet there is a choice in the extent to which it is both adopted and adhered to. It must be superseded if research is, as Barnett (2000) suggests, to rise to the challenges of a super-complex world and to do the work that is required of it in teaching us how to live. Later in this chapter I will highlight some of the aspects of research which the economic view inevitably neglects and with which it fiercely competes: namely, views of research as a transformative, creative process of discovery. Research which requires time to gestate before coming to fruition or research which is personally transformative will be explored more fully in later chapters. For now, let us look more closely at the economic model and explore its implications further.

INVESTMENT

Their pronouncements leave one in no doubt that governments perceive a strong relationship between investment in research and research outcomes in terms of knowledge generated. The notion of investment in research is an interesting one. It is frequently taken to mean that for every dollar that a government spends on research, there is some incremental return and that this return can be measured. That research is a commodity requiring investment is clearly expressed in, for example, the Australian Government's White Paper on research and research training published at the end of 1999:

> Competition is strengthening on a global basis and Australia's competitiveness and attractiveness to investors is increasingly determined by our relative knowledge capabilities. Research as a key source of knowledge and new ideas is central to success in the global knowledge economy.
>
> (Commonwealth of Australia 1999: 1)

A recent New Zealand Government report similarly suggests that research and development affects the country's rate of innovation and 'provides a multiplier effect for an economy' (New Zealand Government 1999):

> Recent research reports show that the economic benefits from basic research are both real and substantial. . . . Domestic R&D affects the rate of innovation and the quantity of knowledge that can be absorbed from others. . . . R&D funding explains why the United States leads Britain and Germany in manufacturing productivity. . . . Publicly-funded R&D can be viewed as an investment in a society's learning capabilities. From Finland to America and from Australia to Canada, every dollar invested in research has a multiplier effect on the macro-economy.
>
> No nation can 'free-ride' on the world scientific system. In order to participate in the system, a nation . . . needs the capability to understand the knowledge produced by others and that understanding can only be developed through performing research . . . .
>
> (New Zealand Government 1999)

Notwithstanding the tenuous links between research and 'amount' of knowledge generated what is evident here is that measures of quantity are being used to refer to unmeasurable phenomena. As Lyotard (1984) observes, using performance as a criterion is invoked by governments to justify funding decisions. Research councils are quasi government bodies steering research programmes in terms of society's problems and emphasis on, for example, 'impact' in the UK or 'economic advancement' in Australia, or 'economic growth' in New Zealand. We shall leave aside for the moment the question of whether these ideas are at all meaningful and pursue this view of research a little further.

A number of steps have been taken by governments to enhance the chances of a fruitful return on their 'investment'. These include requiring research grant applications to indicate their relevance to economic advancement; moving towards funding targeted larger research centres; proscribing priority areas for research development; and requiring research applications for funding to detail specific objectives and demanding reporting on these objectives. Indeed, the Australian paper on research quoted earlier goes as far as to suggest that its investment in research has resulted in Australia producing 2.5 per cent of the world's knowledge. Even if we assume that this statement is based on citation counts, i.e. the extent to which Australian research is cited by researchers worldwide, this is a quite outrageous statement, as all that I have discussed in this book concerning the nature of knowledge attests. Even on a basic level there are some subject areas for which citation counts are notoriously unreliable and there is, of course, no actual relationship between the number of times a piece of work is cited and the knowledge content of that work, even less of items of 'fact' within that. The 'amount' of knowledge produced by any one country is, of course, quite simply unknowable.

In an investment view of research the value of research is equated with the amount of funding awarded to support it. This practice inevitably privileges science and technology because large amounts of funding are needed simply to build the equipment for the research experiments, let alone to pay the salaries of the people who are to carry them out. Indeed, the language of science, with its emphasis on quantity and its focus on defined objectives, has been particularly successful in adapting the language of research investment to its purposes. For example, to convince society that it needs to spend billions of dollars to discover gravity waves, which some people doubt exist and which no one has yet been able to detect, when no one knows whether to do so will have any benefit to society, is an achievement indeed! Collins and Pinch (1998), discussing the case of the search for solar neutrinos (sub-nuclear particles produced by nuclear fusion in our sun), argue that there is some evidence that the predictions of the flux of solar neutrinos varied with the physicists' need for funding. Because the neutrinos do not interact with matter they are notoriously difficult to detect. However, in 1964 when the need for funding was high, a high solar flux was predicted (i.e. 40 solar neutrino units or SNUs). When the first results began to emerge three years later the prediction was much lower (19 SNUs). Collins and Pinch (1998) say that several scientists have pointed out that the project would never have been funded had the lower prediction been used. Humanities and social science research does not have the capacity to generate predictions in this way. Based on the notion that the aim of research is to develop qualitative understandings of the phenomena being investigated, it inevitably becomes the poor relation. Yet this is not to say that the problems and questions it addresses are any less relevant to society. On the contrary, they may be rather more so than some of the massively funded physical science research which is remote both from the everyday experience and the needs of human society.

Becher (1989) makes a distinction between what he calls 'urban' academic communities where there is a large concentration of researchers in one place and 'rural' communities where researchers are spread sparsely throughout a number of institutions. He makes another distinction between 'convergent' and 'divergent' disciplines. Convergent disciplinary communities have a sense of shared identity while divergent ones are schismatic and ideologically fragmented. Becher (1989: 136) argues that economic constraints and therefore government agendas 'bear more harshly' on what he calls the 'urban capital-intensive areas of big science' than on the 'rural, labour-intensive pastures of the humanities and social sciences'. On the other hand, communities which are both urban and convergent, he argues, have a better chance of competing for research funding because they are structurally constituted both to know and to advance their own interests in a way which divergent and rural communities are not. Their divergence means that they may not even have or be aware of any collective interests. They are therefore comparatively weak politically. Indeed, Becher suggests, 'good standing accrues on each scale at the end which emphasises the theoretical, the quantitative and the sharply defined' (Becher 1989: 160).

So we can see that when we talk about investment in research we are not talking about a level playing field. Some areas are inevitably privileged. The question for us here is what is the link between the investment and the 'return on the investment'. Ironically, the rate of return may be higher the less is invested. This is not an argument for not funding research, merely to say the needs of different areas of inquiry are different. The return may take many years or decades in the case of some areas and be relatively fast in others. The crucial question for us is the extent to which treating research as a matter of investment is helping us in the big jobs we have to do. Does it help us to live with the complexity of a multifaceted world and does it show us how to live? Can it find a way through multiple realities of our complex worlds and cultures? I believe that it simplifies rather than engages with the multicomplexity. Based on outdated notions of truth and knowledge, it constrains rather than liberates.

Indeed, even when lip-service is paid to nobler and broader cultural advancement, research is still viewed as being primarily for economic ends. For example, pointing to the disjunction between the New Zealand Government's pronouncements that research is both to enhance cultural insights and to promote economic growth, Harvey suggests:

> Throwing all our intellectual resource into the same contestable market fest for knowledge devalues, debases and controls ideas and research to the point where original (truly innovative?) and critical thinking becomes unwelcome and makes a mockery of any romantic notion of a knowledge society the government would like to construct.
>
> (Harvey 1999: 13)

Yet research has now become essential to human survival. So of course we need to invest in it. It is, after all, research that has discovered the hole in the ozone layer. It is research that is investigating the effects of this on the world's climate. It is through research that basic diseases have been eliminated. It is through research that we might come to know the causes of crime, the ways people in particular communities will vote, why some people develop drug dependencies, why vandalism takes place. It is research which is making life more comfortable for those with cancer. It is only through systematic research that ways of providing cover and shelter as the world's climate changes and providing food for increased populations are likely to be found. Yet, as we saw in Chapter Six, much research is not directed at solving the world's problems and this illustrates a fundamental but fascinating dilemma. There is a tension between investing in particular research projects which have defined desired outcomes on the one hand and knowing that research is unpredictable on the other. It is like aiming an arrow in one direction but finding that it can land in quite another. The results we get are not the ones we expect to get. The arrow can even redefine the universe in which it is situated. It is the nature of academic research to have unpredictable findings and to discover problems and issues which we previously did not even know existed. It is in the nature of research not to be tamed by investment strategies and strictly defined project objectives.

With the notion of investment goes the concept of risk. In the everyday decisions which researchers are having to make the risks are weighed up. However, there is evidence that researchers are choosing not to engage in interdisciplinary projects because of the greater risk that they will not be funded (McNay 1997). In addition, many research supervisors do not encourage postgraduates to engage in risky theses. This is particularly a problem in countries where there is a genuine risk of failing a Ph.D., for example in Sweden. The risk of failing to get research funding means that academics are likely to 'play safe' and choose to do mundane, strictly disciplinary, straightforward research projects.

TRADING COMMODITIES

Lyotard (1984) says that technological transformations of the nature of knowledge mean that the relationship of knowledge to knowers is increasingly tending to take the form of producers and consumers in relation to the commodities they produce and consume. You can see what this means if you think of the way information is exchanged over the Internet. In the virtual university, knowledge is information which can be bought and sold. No longer is knowledge a quality of knowing, rather it is information that is detached from people and can be traded. Through research, knowledge is and will be produced in order to be sold. The goal is exchange (Lyotard 1984).

> Capitalism solves the scientific problem of research funding in its own way: directly by financing research departments in private companies, in which demands for performativity and recommercialization orient research first and foremost toward technological 'applications'; and indirectly by creating

private, state, or mixed-sector research foundations that grant program subsidies to university departments, research laboratories and independent research groups with no expectation of an immediate return on the results of the work – this is done on the theory that research must be financed at a loss for certain length of time in order to increase the probability of its yielding a decisive, and therefore highly profitable, innovation.

(Lyotard 1984: 45)

There was a shift in the 1990s towards universities gaining income through the provision of a range of intellectual goods and services (Sutherland 1994). Taking up the idea of the production of knowledge for which there is both a demand and a supply, Gibbons *et al.* (1994) argue that a completely new kind of knowledge 'production' has come into being. To recap the argument considered in Chapter Five, they call this 'Mode 2', by which they refer to knowledge that is trans-disciplinary and institutionalized in a more heterogeneous and flexible socially distributed system than Mode 1 knowledge production which, they argue, is characteristic of disciplinary research institutionalized largely in universities. Note here that knowledge is viewed as a commodity which is 'produced'. As we have seen throughout this book the nature of academic research is by no means as restricted and contained as this picture of Mode 1 knowledge production would suggest, nor has it ever been. In Chapter Six, in particular, I showed that research has always had an ambivalent relationship with society's perceived needs. Nonetheless, Gibbons *et al.*'s analysis is useful in the current discussion of research as a commodity. They argue that universities are coming to recognize that they are now only one type of player in a 'vastly expanded knowledge production process' (ibid.: 11). In such a scenario higher education institutions require permeability. They need to be able to respond quickly, to be reactive and open to opportunities as they arise (ibid.). However, we have seen that where governments are pushing the research agenda, impermeability and inflexibility are fostered. To be open to the challenges of Gibbons *et al.*'s Mode 2 knowledge production the opposite is needed.

Gibbons and colleagues suggest that on the 'supply' side, the number of knowledge producers is vast and growing. Expansion in higher education has resulted in society being infused with experts in research, all of whom are products of universities (ibid.). Indeed, research qualifications have themselves become a commodity. There is, they argue, a parallel expansion in the 'demand' side. These demands come from society not only in the form of industrial requirements, but also in the form of public enquiries as well as government requirements, for example, to know the implications of high-risk technologies. There is a huge demand for specialist knowledge. In this scenario, academics' knowledge, like the specialist knowledge of others, can be bought and sold and it frequently is. Academics are increasingly being called upon to give opinions, state evidence in public forums, be expert witnesses in court trials, and provide consultancy advice in a wide range of contexts:

The major change to befall the universities over the last two decades has been the identification of the campus as a significant site of capital accumulation, a change in social perception which has resulted in the systematic conversion of intellectual activity into intellectual capital and, hence, intellectual property. There have been two general phases of this transformation. The first, which began twenty years ago and is still underway, entailed the commoditization of the research function of the university, transforming scientific and engineering knowledge into commercially viable proprietary products that could be owned and bought and sold in the market. The second, which we are now witnessing, entails the commoditization of the educational function of the university, transforming courses into courseware, the activity of instruction itself into commercially viable proprietary products that can be owned and bought and sold in the market. In the first phase the universities became the site of production and sale of patents and exclusive licenses. In the second, they are becoming the site of production of – as well as the chief market for – copyrighted videos, courseware, CD-ROMs, and Web sites.

(Noble 1999)

Responding to the marketplace

So where are individual researchers in all of this? While Becher (1989), writing in the 1980s, notes that many researchers perceived themselves not to be influenced by external concerns such as government agendas, in my investigations of the views of senior academic researchers, changes to research were viewed as being largely a result of pressures coming from outside the discipline in which the research was being conducted. As we saw in Chapter Two, researchers believed that the government was dictating the research agenda, not them. A number of researchers mentioned increased pressure to find funding. No longer, they believed, was it possible to opt out of research, or to do research not leading to publications or funding. The increased costs of research, or rather the devolution of these costs to the researchers, meant that the researchers considered they were having to take on more of the responsibility for getting funds which were becoming more difficult to find. This was influencing the ways in which research was defined and carried out. In my study, after the first set of interviews had been carried out, a document was prepared outlining the findings. Researchers were invited to discuss the ideas with other researchers who had been interviewed. Here is an exchange between two researchers at a meeting in which they discussed this issue:

[the document with the findings] made it all a bit clearer to me why I have – I suppose – got a bit disenchanted with the way my own research has gone over the last ten years. I've almost invariably ended up in joint projects where in fact what one does is called research management . . . one of the few things you can get is research assistants, and so research assistants end up having fun and going to the library and doing the research and you end up being this research manager. So that's where . . . I thought my own context of research would be very much the Layer one, but I find I was much more quoted in the [Trading] one, and I'm sure that is simply because the way to succeed in ARC grants has increasingly been to get involved in joint projects. (12)

I think part of what I was getting at before, about the language people speak, especially the language of people who get grants, it's a successful grant holder . . . which is that you've learnt that whole notion that . . . research equals grant equals that sort of management. It's not necessarily your own concept of research, it's more the way you are forced to live in the current climate. (20) (Discussion 1)

Let's explore what the first of these researchers calls the *trading variation* a little further because, as I indicated, it does provide a possible explanation of why the economic rationalist model of research has so successfully penetrated the walls of academe. In the trading variation, research was viewed as a commodity which is exchanged for goods and services. The trading here is like the economic market we have been exploring where various academic goods and services are bought and exchanged in a social situation for money, power or prestige. The focus in the trading variation is on the outcomes of research; on the finished product and how the researcher is going to be seen at the end of it. Whether the outcomes are conceived in terms of completed projects, publications, research grants or the achievement of objectives, these outcomes provide a constant reference point:

I'm involved in a number of projects . . . one a collaborative large ARC grant with a number of other people to produce an Oxford companion to Australian feminism . . . this is the third year of the project because we did have some DEET money and we've had a three year large ARC grant . . . so I've had to put quite a lot of time into that but because it's a large project the time has mainly been meeting to design the volume . . . (12)

. . . my objective is basically developing a humanoid . . . The potential applications, industrial applications [are] always in my mind in terms of how these things can find their way into innovative products. (23)

Well it started as a small ARC grant way back in the early '90s and I did quite a lot of work then and I've got a selection of poems coming out as a book very shortly and then all the poems together will come out as a major anthology. (04)

We have seen that one of the key features in economic views of research is the idea of the production of commodities such as publications. For those researchers who define research in terms of publications as in the trading variation, performativity is not problematic. Publications are exchanged for prestige, money or promotion:

> I think an important aspect of it is the publication in a broad sense, in the sense that meeting with other people that are interested in the same things that you're doing, because I think that, [in the] world of knowledge and the world of the particular area that you're working in, you only really progress by seeing what other people are doing and in reference to what other people are doing . . . I think that's why publication by giving papers or writing articles is a very important aspect to research because it does bring you into contact with those other people, It makes you known, and then you go on from there to other projects. (02)

> I think I started out being an academic like most people, publishing billions of papers. And . . . certainly if I was starting again I'd do the same thing, because you get promoted by publishing papers and . . . building machinery and making things work is not actually an awfully efficient way of publishing papers. (06)

I am writing this book at a time when academic publications are proliferating. So much so that it is unlikely that anyone is able to keep up with the literature in any but the smallest domain of inquiry. Government performance measures which record and reward with additional funding numbers of research publications, in particular kinds of journal and conference proceedings, may lead to an emphasis on publication for its own sake. There are concerns in the academic community that there is too much being published before it is ready. In a study of the effects of the UK's Research Assessment Exercise, McNay (1997) reported that 25 per cent of respondents overall and 40 per cent of younger academics indicated that they published prematurely. However, while the governments are rewarding this kind of superficial performance, the pressure on academics to publish will remain. Fortunately government agencies are seeing the problems associated with measures which count all publications, so that in the 1996 UK Research Assessment Exercise, for example, just the four best publications of individual researchers were taken into account. Australia appears to be likely to adopt a similar system (Commonwealth of Australia 1999).

Yet publishing itself is becoming increasingly complex with the growth, among other things, of electronic publishing. There is talk of articles being published while in progress along with pre- and post-publication peer reviews and the 'finished' article. When an article is 'finished' is also a matter of debate, raising the question of what exactly constitutes an academic article. For electronic publishing there is no limit on word length of articles; ideas are transferred rapidly; and search engines are able to deal with information overload and multiple access points which permit individual articles to be more widely read. One of the facets of this publishing scenario are services which précis information from a variety of sources. This goes beyond the use of abstracting services, which have existed for some time, providing readers, editors and technologists whose job it is to do the summaries. The character of academic research, based on in-depth study of the literature, is radically changed by this. There are implications for ideas of scholarship pursued in Chapter Three, for it raises the question of standards of scholarship carried out as the basic background reading and preparation for the research. One conception of scholarship considered there was that it was perceived as a matter of being very thorough and professional. This professionalism is compromised in this changing nature of academic publication.

Research and property

So we are moving to a situation where academic papers and summaries of academic papers are, like books and shoes and electrical goods, commodities for sale. Once you get into a situation where what academics produce is for sale, the ideas and artefacts of research become property. They belong to someone, just like any other kinds of property. The question then is: who do they belong to? Who owns the property? If a manufacturing company, for example, funds a research studentship, does it own the intellectual property which results from the doctorate? Or does the student have a right to treat the work as their own? There are implications here both for how and what is disseminated. If you talk to postgraduate research supervisors about this issue you find that there are many cases where the student is not able to publish findings because someone else claims ownership. There are also important implications for how much and what kind of collaboration is possible. These are inevitable consequences of this economically driven view of research.

A number of serious issues about copyright and intellectual property are thrown up with electronic publishing. The World Wide Web is fluid in this sense and untamable. Electronic publishers are choosing to publish their journals on the Internet. Indeed a journal without a web version is increasingly rare. There is no evidence that electronic journals result in loss of sales even though there is evidence that throughout the world university libraries are cutting journal subscriptions particularly to the specialized, low-circulation, high-cost journals. Electronic publishing overcomes many of the problems of conventional publication, such as slow information transfer given the time it takes from submitting an article to it being read by journal subscribers, high cost of printing and distribution, low impact through citation counts and information overload. If a large company like Microsoft, for example, introduces gateways to journals and periodicals as is rumoured, who then is in charge of academic publishing? These are all issues which will determine whether an academic is going to choose to put articles on the Web or not and whether indeed they wish to engage in this 'market'.

SOCIAL INTERACTION

However there is another aspect of the trading view of research which makes it consistent with the commodity view and the economic rationalist model to which it is tied. Research in the trading variation is an arena for social interaction. Social interactions create opportunities for personal advancement. This includes going to conferences and getting feedback on research from colleagues the world over. Very important to the process of research in this variation is the idea of research being for an audience. How the research is perceived, whether it is accepted or ignored by the research community, is a focus of attention. Researchers demonstrating this conception present themselves as being part of an international community and stress the importance of being valued by that community:

> the research . . . sees its fruition through publication but also by writing the paper, going through the process of writing, you find out where the shortfalls in your approach have been, you go through the peer-review process, and then you get your . . . rigorous assessment of what you've done and you learn by the rigorousness and that complements the research as well . . . I criticise people when they make value judgements on others' research, because my value judgement is based completely on 'where did they publish it?' and 'did it go through their peer-review?' and 'was it accepted by their immediate scientific community as something important and worthwhile doing?' And I think the value judgement of the research should be left to that, the peer-review, not to subjective assessment within a department or within a university, because I see this all the time, where people are criticising other people's research, but without the knowledge basis of how to criticise it in the first place. (18)

Contributing to a community of scholars with similar interests is a source of satisfaction for researchers. This might mean being known as the expert or 'being one of a group of people who are controlling the subject in the world' (14), or it might simply be the pleasure of collaboration. Research opens doors into other communities.

Frequently in the trading view, research is described in terms of what other people are or are not doing; what other people do or do not think. More often than not research is viewed in terms of relationships with other people. It is often described in terms of the activities of such people and the relationships which the researcher has with these people: research assistants, collaborators, other researchers in the field, for example:

> Since I got the large grant I've had a half-time research assistant working for the last three years and that's been enormously helpful. She's been able to do a lot of the library work and bibliographical work and . . . a lot of bits and pieces that I can easily delegate to her . . . (04)

When I worked on the Bicentennial history of Australia . . . a really big group of about twenty people, although far fewer than that ended up actually writing for the book. But we did have very wonderful exchange meetings and so on where you'd get some feedback from other people . . . everybody is at different universities . . . (12)

We can now see that the economic, commodity view of research not only has the power to dictate what research is pursued through funding and performance measures but it is also consistent with some of the key ways in which researchers think about their research, what they believe research to be and how they derive their satisfaction from it. These factors combined make it very powerful.

DISCOVERY

When research is viewed as a commodity within a national and/or international marketplace, business practices take over. This means that research which does not readily fit into this model is squeezed out. So, in the final part of this chapter, we are left to ask: what are the consequences? What does the economic view of research inevitably suppress or ignore?

The primary emphasis on performance related to economic ends within an economic paradigm of research is fundamentally inconsistent with and contrary to notions of research as discovery. If discovery was truly the primary objective, there would be an open research system. This would mean that research which did not have defined outcomes and objectives would be encouraged and funded. Yet various governments have had difficulty in funding so-called 'blue skies' or 'curiosity-driven' research which may or may not lead to new discoveries and which may or may not be of relevance to narrow governmental agendas:

So what we're doing is trying to ask fundamental questions, to just prod away . . . And because it requires a considerable technological development to be able to do anything, you've got to spend quite a lot of time building that technological base so . . . I feel about it as though I'm playing games . . . I've always had difficulty defining a research project. . . . some other people can say 'oh, yes, we're going along here to do this particular project' and I find that very difficult to do . . . In one sense I suppose I know I want to go around and fiddle around and play games with that and in a sense know what comes out of it, so . . . we're able to grow the zinc salinide layers, but we have to be able to dope them so they are conductive. We have to obtain the knowledge that says 'yes, when you set the temperatures of the cells this way you end up with certain results' . . . do enough experimenting and fiddling around . . . enough growth and enough tests to know what we're doing, establish our ability to control the process. Now, I can't say in a research project or proposal that that is what we're going to do, because we won't get funded to do that.

But on the other hand, to say that 'we are going to do this . . .' depends on our ability to do the other stuff. And then when you get in there you don't know quite what you are going to get out of it. Usually what happens is you go in there . . . I mean, when I was in Cardiff, we always said we were going to learn how to grow stuff, and then we started to fiddle around, and we grew and initially we said 'oh, look! We've got a layer.' So we fiddled around and we changed the temperatures and we found that we got a layer there and another layer here and it all sort of looked alright . . . and whatever you did you sort of got a layer and you thought 'oh, this is not too bad, this is relatively easy' but then we said 'oh, hang on, we'd better be systematic about this' and then you look at the literature and discover that half the things that are written in the literature haven't been controlled very well, and they don't really know what's going on, and they . . . and you . . . discover that there are a few people who are groping around thinking they know what's going on but are not doing a really good job on it . . . and what really surprised me was the difficulty of sitting down and deciding that we would commit ourselves to growing this particular sequence, this other thing was going to take us X weeks and what it's going to involve. I had a student working with me, so we said 'o.k., we'll go off and do this' and we grew 15 growths, it was about 4–5 weeks' work. And each one had to have a series of tests done on it. And in the end, you put it together and get a result. And we published a paper on it. So . . . in the beginning we couldn't have said we were going to go and come out with a result, it's the process of being there and in it that ultimately allows you to say 'o.k., now we can think if we go down there we are going to get it', so it's the involvement in the process. . . . so in other words, it seems to me that research is being involved and having the capability and finding the questions and trying to look for the relationships that come out of it. How do these things work? Why is it like this? How can I change the process? So it's a series of asking questions. In science it means that you have an event and try to control all the variables and say 'this is affecting this'. (52)

There is a tension between an investment view of research and a view of research as a process of stepping into the unknown which this extract exemplifies. Herein lie the dilemma and the place where the space of research is perhaps most contested. Defined outcomes limit possibilities. Indeed, in one particular government funding scheme in Australia, it is well known within the academic community that you have to have done the research *before* you apply for it to be funded because the requirements of the application are so stringent as to require specific known outcomes to be specified. These cannot be known in advance of the research being done! Experienced researchers write the application on the basis of the work they have already done and use the money to fund the next 'discovery' stage of the research.

Research which is an open process of discovery is more like a gardener sowing seeds, some of which will germinate and others of which will stagnate in the ground.

The gardener does not mind, but just sows more seeds to get the required yield. It is not like buying stocks and shares with a guaranteed dividend and a predicted rate of return. Many of the world's most significant scientific discoveries have been found by chance. You cannot plan for chance or random discoveries. You can only sow the seeds and hope that some will flower profusely in ways which will benefit society and/or solve its problems, perhaps in unexpected ways.

Recognizing that governments have a hard task deciding how to fund research, keeping to the horticultural metaphors, we could say that they have made some attempts, like farmers, to grow out imperfections in the seeds so that a larger number germinate and a higher yield can be expected. One of the ways they have endeavoured to do this in Australia, for example, is by employing the competing academic researcher's 'track record' in research as a significant factor influencing decisions concerning research funding. It is making explicit the saying of Jesus Christ often quoted in academic circles that 'to every one hath that shall be given' (Matt. 25: 29). Following the horticultural analogy Becher says that:

> A market garden is successful in so far as it cultivates a variety of produce to meet its clients' disparate needs. To drive a bulldozer through it in the interests of greater efficiency and higher productivity makes sense only if one wishes to transform it into a cornfield. Corn grows easily, but too assiduous a concentration of producing it will – as we now know to our cost – create a massive and useless surplus of one particular commodity, and a corresponding scarcity of those whose cultivation, though beneficial in its own right, happens to be more demanding, more labour-intensive and generally less easy to govern.
>
> (Becher 1989: 166)

Becher comments: 'Given the economic and military potential of contemporary scientific knowledge, such manipulation cannot be regarded with equanimity.'

We have seen in this chapter that the pressure to publish as a consequence of government research-funding policies is treated by academics whose primary view of research is in alignment with the economic view as a normal process of doing research. The trading variation, however, is only one way of viewing research. When we consider other views of the nature of research we begin to see what is forgone in this economic view. The need for research to demonstrate relevance to society and to demonstrate action through publications and income acquisition masks its potential to open up opportunities for individual and social transformation through sustained engagement with hard ideas. This tension will be differently negotiated depending on the researcher's conceptions of research.

In recent years, as a result of the government funding measures discussed in this chapter, large numbers of academics have been encouraged to engage in research publication for the first time. Yet demonstrating progress through publication may be at variance with ideas of research as a process of transformation. Indeed in this social and economic context, research as personal development may appear a self-indulgent luxury. The paradox is that a focus on action may be potentially crippling and in the end stultifying. Taking tiny steps by increasing the quantity of publications within what Kuhn (1970) called 'normal science', may prevent research from moving forward in giant revolutionary leaps.

Depending on an individual academic's conception of research, the economic rationalist view of research will be more or less problematic and, again depending on their conception, the outcomes will be different both in terms of numbers and quality of publications, research grants, etc., in terms of the nature of the ideas generated, in terms of personal and of social learning. In the short term, control of this process is in the hands of those who hold the purse strings, such as government and university funding bodies and promotions committees. In the longer term, the ultimate outcome of research is never quite what we think it is going to be.

But now it is time to look at the other side of the coin and to examine a picture of the nature of research which is almost entirely neglected in the economic perspective we have been considering in this chapter. The activity of engaging in research may include ideas, insights, learning about ourselves and about the phenomena of investigation, the development of skills, and so on, none of which show up in published work. There are many researchers who do not publish all their work, yet learn a great deal from their research. There is a balance to be struck between research as personal learning or development and disseminating requirements. In the next chapter we examine the transformative effects of research and consider whether this view is better able to teach us how to live.

Chapter 9

Research and learning

> Bring forth that which is within you. If you bring forth what is within you, what you bring forth will save you. If you do not bring forth what is within you, what you do not bring forth will destroy you.
>
> (The Gnostic Gospel of Thomas)

It was a thin autumn morning. A veil of mist hung over the world; or at least as much of it as Rosalie could see. She took the coast path. Nothing to seaward could be seen. She could hear only the lapping of the water on the beach below and the cry of the lonely seagulls. The path descended the steep chasm of the chine down to the beach. Rosalie's mind was numb. The crumbling cliffs loomed large through the mist. Clods of clay beneath her feet; a reminder that all must crumble. A lump came to her throat. Here dinosaurs had roamed in their swamp. 'Change. All is change,' she reflected.

For the past twenty-four hours Rosalie had been living in her worst nightmare. Everything she had worked so hard to avoid had happened. One thing she had learnt in her life was that things were unpredictable. She knew this indubitably. And yet yesterday she had experienced that unpredictability in all its devastation.

Rosalie prided herself on being healthy. All through her teenage years she never had a day off school and then, when she had started working, a couple of aspirin tablets had always seen off any threat of a cold. What was it the advert said: 'Don't let a headache get in the way. Get on with your day . . .'? It had been a kind of personal motto. And now, she couldn't voice the word which stuck in her throat. 'Why? Why?' She asked herself. Then disbelief. Surely there was some mistake. Yet the doctor had been adamant.

When she first went for the tests she did so with a light heart. She had been feeling tired and nauseous from time to time but didn't think anything could possibly be seriously wrong. After the first lot of tests she felt fine and was sure there would be no problem. It was as if she was going through the motions of the tests just to humour her doctor. When it was suggested she go for some more she knew there must be some mistake. She was a healthy person. She defined herself by her fitness and diet. In fact she was considered quite an expert on diet by her friends at the gym. She thought people only got ill if they smoked or lived squalid lives. She went for the next lot of tests in a very detached frame of mind as if the doctors were checking out someone else. She wasn't going to let it bother her.

And now the verdict. As she wandered along the shore, she shook her head in disbelief and despair. She knew she would have to endure some radical changes in her lifestyle but she had made changes before and was pretty adaptable. No. What she was finding so hard to face was that her idea of herself as a healthy person had been completely turned around. Over the course of her short life she thought she had learnt a lot about how to stay fit. Now her views of herself as a healthy person had been totally disproved. It was as if she had the one thing which all her life she had sought to avoid. The news didn't just tell her she was ill. It told her that she didn't know herself any more. She was not the person she had thought herself to be.

When you start to do research, it is obvious there are lots of things to learn. That is one of the prime motivations for doing it: to learn everything we can about the topic of our chosen study. Anyone who has ever embarked on a masters' programme or doctorate will also know that, in learning about how to do research and in learning about the subject they are researching, they also learn about themselves. When among their colleagues or supervisors only the outward signs are seen, new researchers may feel that only they have personal dilemmas; only they have difficulty getting down to work; only they are torn between reading and writing; only they are finding that research pervades all aspects of their lives. Researchers openly acknowledge that postgraduate students engage in learning, but they do not always carry that over to their own research activities (Brew and Boud 1995a). Like much of the learning they did as undergraduates, most of the individual learning which experienced researchers do in the course of their research remains private and not spoken about. This includes what they learn about themselves and the skills they develop, as well as findings that do not fit the overall pattern of explanation but which may inform future research. Experienced researchers may focus on getting grants and sending off work for publication, but for the novice this is all rather mysterious, and it leaves out the personal processes which researchers go through in achieving such outcomes.

The extent to which researchers see their learning as connected to their research depends on their views of the nature of research, so first we will look at their different views about what they learn while doing research. However, research also contributes to the way people in our society perceive the world around them in general. So we will examine collective, social learning. This is tied up with ideas about progress. We have already seen that the idea of accumulating knowledge is no longer viable so we need to explore different ideas about what constitutes progress before concluding that we have to give up this notion. The chapter therefore looks at the question of how research can find a new definition for itself and what needs to happen in critical questioning of this idea. I suggest that, if academic research is to teach society how to live, it must become more like learning.

The view of research as a process of personal and social learning is left out of the economic model. Indeed, looking at the ways people learn while doing research is diametrically opposed to, and in tension with, the way we viewed it in the last chapter, where the focus was on observable outcomes. In focusing attention on the relationship of research to learning on a personal and a social level, in this chapter we shall see that what we learn is unpredictable. This implies that those who control research agendas do not necessarily control what is collectively learnt. We do not always learn what we expect to learn. We do not always discover what we expect to discover. Research is full of surprises.

PERSONAL LEARNING

Research provides a range of opportunities for the personal learning of those who carry it out. It clearly accommodates and encourages a wide variety of learning styles, approaches and attitudes. Academics are autonomous, independent learners. Here is what one of the researchers in my study said when asked whether any of their research activities constituted learning:

> [I am learning] all the time. Absolutely! non-stop . . . I'm never not writing something and I'm never not learning. I mean, every single day. . . . It's not as though I don't think I'm competent to be in the job I'm in, it's just that the universe of . . . material in anybody's field . . . is just so vast . . . one . . . is always learning. . . . It's literally non-stop . . . it's every minute of the day . . . (01)

Nevertheless, researchers differ in what they report they learn when engaging in research activities. We should also note that they differ in the extent to which what they learn during research is perceived as having effects on their lives and in the extent to which they believe research transforms them as people. These ideas appear to be tied to their views of what research is.

For some academics their research and their learning are integral and they do not distinguish between them. Research is not only seen as a process of learning; research *is* learning. But the connection between research and learning is not inevitable. Other researchers have difficulty in thinking of research as a learning process. For them, research is concerned with the generation of skills or knowledge which they conceptualize as external to themselves. It has little, if anything, to do with their own learning. Some researchers keep their learning contained within an academic sphere, but for others, research is personally transformative. To follow our picture analogy, it is not just a question of whether learning is in the background or the foreground. Some researchers see themselves as looking at the research picture. Others are inside it.

The differences in perception and the reasons behind them, about which we can only speculate, as well as the ways in which these perceptions link to the social and cultural context, illustrate some important tensions in what we understand research to be. So based on what we know from my study of experienced researchers (see Chapter One), we will look more closely at how researchers conceptualize what they learn through research.

Experiencing learning through research

We saw in Chapter Two how the *domino variation* described research as a range of phenomena conceived as distinct and described as a series of separate tasks, events, activities, problems, etc. Predictably, then, sometimes research activities are conceived as resulting in the learning of facts, techniques, knowledge, skills, ideas and information, which are similarly listed as separate from each other.

> You may have to develop new skills . . . I had to learn to use generation after generation of different computer systems . . . so there is an amount of learning of skills that you need . . . (28)

> There are all sorts of things you have to learn . . . knowledge of how books and manuscripts are produced . . . physically, like how the animal skins are treated when manuscripts were prepared . . . how the leaves are folded and arranged together, how they are sown and bound to form a book and how the leaves of the manuscript are ruled or arranged to receive the written text . . . and then the study of printing . . . all these things . . . people have to learn. (14)

The *domino variation* includes the idea that although it is clearly the person who acquires them, knowledge, skills, etc. are essentially viewed as separate from the researcher as a person. While in this conception learning is taking place – in doing research new techniques and knowledge from previously unknown areas are learnt – research is not thought to impact on the researcher's life in any way and is not viewed as changing the person in any significant way. The researcher's life is viewed as essentially unconnected to the research.

In the *trading variation*, as we saw in Chapter Eight, research is an arena for social interaction. This conception views social interactions as opportunities for personal change. These opportunities include going to conferences and getting feedback on research from colleagues. They might include obtaining a job, causing a particular career to develop, providing an opportunity to organize a conference, take on a management role or meet a partner. In some cases doing research opens up opportunities for living in different cultures and this transforms lives:

> I've actually gone to England . . . to stay for several months . . . inhabit a house and get to know the local shops and . . . try to come to terms with the slightly weird . . . culture of Cambridge. . . . (It has) added to life experience . . . being aware that there's a cultural difference in Australian culture. So it's mind-blowing in itself. (20)

Also personal changes in this conception are attributed to being in a university or to the demands that research places on life, i.e. as coming about for extrinsic reasons. That is to say, it is not the research, but the whole work context, which brings about personal change.

In the *layer variation*, learning is viewed as integral to the research process. In this conception learning encapsulates the idea of research as changing perspectives to better integrate understanding. There is the sense of broadening one's intellectual horizons:

> You learn how much you don't know. (11)

> . . . you become more skeptical. (08)

> . . . although you start off fairly respectful of ideas after a while you just say 'this is a load of rubbish'. (17)

> Learning is a consequence of doing research. You do research and you learn. You learn how to view things, you learn what works and what doesn't work . . . a lot of times I've sat down and said I need to learn this bit of theory so I can do that. . . . As you read you think 'oh yes that's a useful idea' and . . . 'I want to know a bit more about that'. You read it out of interest. Perhaps it may not be of use immediately, but it may be of use in five years' time when you're doing something different. (16)

Finally, in the *journey variation*, in contrast, research questions go beyond the intellectual issues and are carried over into all aspects of life. Content, issues and processes are viewed as all contributing to the process of critical reflection. In this variation, as the name implies, there is frequently the idea of a personal journey and an emphasis on the assimilation of research into the researcher's life and understanding.

> [Research is] a good way of marrying your development as a person, your . . . personal practice with your intellectual practice. For me that's the whole point about living and doing . . . there's no point in separating them. (09)

In the journey conception, activities in which the researcher engages, whether or not they appear to have a direct bearing, are viewed as relevant to the research because they inform the life issues which underpin the research questions. Encounters with the data are viewed as transforming theoretical and experiential understandings of the issues which are the focus of interest. The researcher is transformed by this encounter.

> the whole field work experience is a much deeper basis than simply collecting a bunch of data, it actually has major transformative effects on the personality. (09)

> You go and do your field work, and however you come back you're going to be different than you were before you underwent the ritual. (38)

Unlike the layer variation where it is the ideas that are being researched which illuminate personal issues, in the journey variation the personal issues and the research issues are viewed as one and the same thing. Personal transformation comes about not because ideas are applied to the person, but because research, learning and personal transformation are viewed as different facets of the person.

> For me, research is a kind of transcendental therapy. . . . It transforms one through the process of engaging in it. . . . I'm a different person from doing field work . . . and . . . it's definitely had a transformative effect on me . . . for the better . . . even the more esoteric parts of it, the discipline requirements, the concentration requirements . . . the discipline and diligence I think, are transformative . . . It's the most intensive form of psychotherapy you can do. And for some people, they can't do it, it doesn't work, it's too confronting. (09)

Discerning critical features

Academic work can be a bit like juggling plates, moving each task on sometimes imperceptibly to maintain ongoing steady progress. Some of the learning academics do while engaged in this is, as we have seen, relatively trivial. Other learning is more meaningful, as when some ideas collide and a situation is viewed in a new way. 'Being able to see something in a certain way amounts to being able to discern critical aspects of the phenomenon and keep them in focal awareness simultaneously' (Bowden and Marton 1998: 81).

This is like Husserl (1973), as I observed in Chapter Four, when he says that when you think you know you should 'look again'. In grasping a point (an object, an idea, a theory) Husserl says, we first see vaguely, indistinctly, then we look again and again, varying perspective and distance, focusing on a particular segment, returning to patches of indistinctness, seeking clarity. What is at stake is the pattern which fuses everything into a meaningful whole. It is that pattern on which we focus, until it stands out before us. Looking again and again is a way of minimizing self-deception. In looking again, we do not take our impressions as 'true' or 'the way things are'. We continually go round the experiential research cycle, progressively deepening our understanding. Bowden and Marton (1998) suggest that when we learn something new, we come to see it in a new way. So when we are researching we keep a whole range of ideas in view and then a pattern comes into view. This idea was expressed by a researcher in my study when asked what it was about research which gave personal satisfaction:

> the satisfaction of finding an underlying pattern or simplicity in things which appear initially to be confusing or complicated. (47)

Seeing a different pattern happens because the critical features of the phenomenon appear to us in a new way (Bowden and Marton 1998). This researcher explains the process:

> So you're trying to . . . make sure that you're accurate and precise and you're also trying to assemble it into meaningful patterns and orders. . . . So you are trying to impose order on what was chaos and to impose clarity on what was hidden or murky. (31)

Sometimes this is involuntary and sometimes there is a struggle to see something differently. By entering into interaction with ideas, whether from a text or from another person, new perspectives, which are neither the one held already nor the one the other person or text held, new understandings are created. In the literature on teaching and learning in higher education this is referred to as a 'deep' approach to learning (see Marton, Hounsell and Entwistle 1997). Deep approaches to learning are about making meaning.

SOCIAL LEARNING

What individuals believe they learn when they engage in activities they call research, then, is tied to their views of what research is and we see here views ranging from the pragmatic acquisition of skills on the one hand to personal psychological transformation on the other. But the individual works within a historical and cultural tradition, and in an organizational and social context. Research is not just an individual phenomenon. It is, as we have repeatedly seen, a social phenomenon. Discussions about the learning of individual researchers leave out these social aspects.

The ways in which people in a particular society conceptualize the world around them is clearly based on their history, culture and traditions, and research contributes to this in those cultures where it is practised. The relationship between the questions that are asked, the problems that are considered worthy of solution and how communities learn is complex and problematic. New knowledge does not, of course, only emanate from academic research. Nevertheless, such research does have as a primary purpose the generation of socially useful knowledge. So academic research and academic learning both involve engaging in a dialogue through which the social construction of knowledge takes place. Researchers discern the critical features of a phenomenon in an entirely new way and share this in conversations with their colleagues, through publication, through conferences, and personal communications of various kinds. Students learn to discern the critical features of phenomena that are new to them, often through the participation of their teachers in such conversations, in discussions among themselves and also through their assigned tasks.

As far as the learning which societies experience is concerned, it is clear that a change of perception of people within a culture consists of discerning critical features of a phenomenon in a different way. But that is not all there is to the question of how societies learn. For it does not explain why some new ways of perceiving a phenomenon become common currency and others do not. If we look at how ideas become established in research communities we can see that there are a number of things which influence whether a set of researchers will accept or believe in new findings. As we saw earlier there are a number of reasons for not believing in the results of various experiments. These include faith in a researcher's experimental competence, ideas about their personality and intelligence, their reputation, their previous history of failed experiments, the size and prestige of the university they are working in, and even their nationality (Collins and Pinch 1998; Milton 1994; Latour and Woolgar 1986). So whether the new ideas even get beyond the first stage of acceptance by the academic community depends on a number of factors.

Progress

Through research, we paint a picture of the universe. The picture that has been composed is complex and intricate and by painting it, researchers have shown up aspects which hitherto were unseen. So, for example, they have shown us that the Milky Way, far from constituting the most distant stars, is now seen to be part and parcel of our own galaxy and our galaxy is seen as just one in millions of galaxies. Our conception of the universe has changed because of the pictures which scientific research has painted for us.

Much of the discourse of research output would describe this in terms of improvements or advances. In relation to the development of social or cultural understanding we are accustomed to viewing society as progressing and research as contributing to this progress. Society clearly learns as a result of research, but does it also progress and if so in what direction? Many questions have been asked about the extent to which the picture which research has painted is the correct one; whether it gives the true description. As we have seen earlier in the book, this raises many questions about what we mean by 'true' and how we tell what is true. Lots of the questions about progress are about whether the picture we now have is better than the one people had before and how we decide which is indeed better. If there are no ways to decide which is better, does that mean that all pictures are equally good? If they are not, then there is a genuine question about why we are doing research at all; a key question we have been considering in this book. So looking at the ways in which research relates to the learning of researchers is only the first step. The implications of research for the learning of societies must also be examined.

This is to acknowledge that there is no view of the universe which is independent of the social context in which that view is advanced. It goes hand in hand with the recognition that there is no society or culture which has a monopoly on the truth. We are all too well aware in the global community that in other cultures of the world people think quite differently. The need to accept the validity of views other than our own means that a Western view of progress cannot be sustained on its own, but neither can a view of the world derived from any other culture. Deciding between different ideas becomes a moral question, not an empirical one.

Nevertheless, the academic culture (as well as society at large) is still imbued with a strong sense that research leads to progress; that research findings are progressively uncovering reality; that we are learning more and more about the world we live in. Research is still dependent on ideas of progress despite the fact that what we mean by progress has shifted. The physicist Hermann Bondi expressed the dilemma like this:

> [Einstein's disproof of Newton's theory of gravitation] had a tremendous effect on the intellectual climate. It had been thought that whatever in the world might be difficult, might be complex, might be hard to understand, at least Newton's theory of gravitation was good and solid, tested well over a hundred thousand times. And when such a theory falls victim to the increasing precision of observation and calculation, one certainly feels that one can never again rest assured.
>
> (Bondi 1975: 3).

Bondi adds, following Popper, for whom this kind of refutation was characteristic: 'this is the stuff of progress'. Popper's view was that research produces better and better theories; that we get better at solving a wider range of increasingly complex problems. He argued that a new theory, however revolutionary, must always be able to explain the success, and must give results at least as good as, those of its predecessor. For him it was rationally decidable whether a new theory is better. Progress for Popper was defined as increasing the truth content of our theories (Popper 1973).

But this is a view that can no longer be sustained. For a start, we cannot compare false theories in respect to how wrong they are (Maxwell 1984). Progress in one direction can mean loss of progress in another (Feyerabend 1978). Think about it: the longer-term consequences of research are often quite contrary to the intended outcomes. The effects on germs of the development of antibiotics and the consequences of modern medicine on the immune system are just two familiar examples to illustrate this. Time and money spent exploring the farther reaches of the universe is time and money lost in solving world poverty. There is always an opportunity cost in selecting the areas we choose to investigate.

Making a distinction between phases of what he calls 'normal science', where communities of scientists work on puzzles thrown up by a particular paradigm, and 'extraordinary' or 'revolutionary' science where, following the recognition of a number of anomalies, there is a shift of paradigm, Kuhn (1970) argued that the idea of truth as a goal had to be abandoned. Truth for him was confined to particular paradigms, i.e. a matter of consensus. Kuhn's (1970) view left open the possibility that a revolutionary shift of paradigm may not necessarily produce a better or more extensive explanation. In science, for example, he suggested that the members of the community will tend to agree which consequences of a shared theory sustain the test of experiment and are therefore true, which are false, and which are not yet tested. He recognized there are no criteria of truth which are outside of any paradigm. He suggested that what was important was to see present ideas not as in some sense more advanced than those of the past, but rather to see all ideas in the context, and according to the perceptions, of those advocating them. Making value judgements about past systems of rationality from the perspective of our own were, he said, inappropriate. Our own theories are as subject to radical change as those of the past. They are not specially privileged.

Arguments have subsequently been advanced from many quarters such that nowadays it is difficult on a logical level to sustain traditional ideas of truth and progress. Nevertheless, such ideas do still play an important role in setting research agendas and in our research and cultural practices. Research proceeds *as if* truth and progress were unproblematic at the same time as the very questioning of these concepts continues. Imagine that we have two pictures of the universe both of which are consistent with what we see during the day and at night. The question is: how do we tell which is the best or the most accurate or the truest? The answer is that in absolute terms we cannot. There is no general answer. Our conceptions of what is true are tied to the context in which they are advanced. What is true in one context may not be so in another. Scientists will argue that we do know some things for certain; that there are indisputable facts (see e.g. Horgan 1998). This does not discount the fact (*sic*) that there may well be other explanations which fit the facts equally well.

There is a tension between on the one hand the desire for research to give us 'answers' – true descriptions of reality – and on the other the realization that there are none such and the recognition that what is true for one context is untrue for another. As Sonia Greger, in discussing her ethnographic research with villagers in Crete, says: 'Truth has to be negotiated among those you know and have to live with' (Greger 1997: 118). The example she gives of how truth is negotiated in the community illustrates the way the villagers negotiate three axes of meaning-negotiation: the practical (including skills, organizations, notions of what technically is the right way); the symbolic (including ritual/sacred objects, ethically the right way); and the given (aspects of the environment which are accepted because they are uncontrollable). Adjustments are constantly made in this negotiation. Greger draws attention to the role of myth-making as a vital human function and its role in defining what counts as knowledge and truth in a context of uncertainty, contradiction and confusion. We have already discussed the narratives which Lyotard, for one, argues underpin Western science. Myths define our perceptions of reality. These are enshrined in the images we use. For example, describing our universe in mechanistic images gives a different picture from describing it in terms of systems and relationships. We will explore further the question of the images and narratives sustained by and sustaining research in Chapter Eleven.

We have been looking at research as a process of social learning. Perhaps the most significant thing we can conclude from this discussion is that, like personal learning, it is unpredictable. It is what it is, not what we would like it to be. What we learn is, of course, guided by our research agendas: the problems we recognize and the questions we ask. But the answers we end up with are not tied to the answers we wish to have. It is like when we engage in the kind of critical questioning involved in research which demands personal engagement. We examine our personal relatedness to the phenomena of our study. For a while we may have the illusion of progress, then some experiences may cause a re-evaluation of everything we thought we knew and we have a sense of starting all over again (Brew 1993). We discover that even our experiences are not always cumulative. A new perspective may mean a complete reordering of the world as we knew it. We may conceptualize the world or particular phenomena in an entirely new way.

If academic research is to find a way to navigate through a postmodern world characterized by uncertainty, unpredictability and incoherence, we are going to need to engage with this unpredictability. Plurality is of the essence. There are vested interests involved in holding on to the idea that we can progress. If we give up the notion of progress, we have to face not only the question of what research is for, we also have to face fairly and squarely the realization that what is important is not some kind of golden future. What is important is how we deal with the world and live within it here and now. Research tenaciously seeks to occupy this contested space.

If research is to lead the way under these conditions of postmodernity, then research consciousness must move away from viewing everything as if it can be treated objectively and from thinking it can move towards some golden city of complete knowledge. Research consciousness must be open to entertaining multiple views of the world; juggling them and being open to yet others which come into focus. There is a need for research to balance on the one hand the need to produce socially useful knowledge and on the other its potential to transform those who engage in it. Barnett (1997a) suggests that while reflection characterizes late modernity, there are mechanisms preventing this from developing into a transformatory critique. We have examined a number of these throughout this book. So we are poised at a crossroads. Traditional ideas of progress rest on ideas of knowledge as external and separate from knowers. Pushing this view results ultimately in the opposite: refutation and redefinition of the problem or question. Yet new ideas and experiences can take us back to square one; to a redefinition of our selves in relation to the world we perceive around us. We come face to face with our ignorance and move forward again in a spiral of new understandings, which in turn result in refutation. Perhaps in late modernity, recognition of our ignorance and our inability to predict and control are what we have learned. Postmodernity arrives when we admit that learning through research is similarly a cyclical process, albeit on a social level. We do not control what we end up discovering.

ACADEMIC LEARNING

How researchers personally make sense of the phenomena of investigation is an indication of how far research must go to be in a position to do this. In Chapter Four we saw the interrelationship between the quality of the knower and the research tradition: traditional methods depending upon a detached consciousness and emergent research increasingly depending on an involved, aware consciousness. We have also noted that, while there are clearly differences in relation to the domain of inquiry (industrial sponsored research for example, perhaps presenting more limited opportunities), there is evidence that postgraduate students are increasingly addressing issues of personal relevance to them in doctoral research and growing numbers are choosing to examine their own subjectivity in relation to their research topic (Brew 1998b). Many of the newer disciplines, as we saw in Part I, are defining research questions which demand personal engagement on the part of those carrying out the research.

Maslow (1968) suggested that the mature, self-actualized knower is more likely to treat scientific discovery with awe and love, rather than being tied to neat rules and pathological defences. Realizing oneself as a person means encountering our own pathologies along the way. Examination of the inner world may be more painful than examination of the world outside ourselves. Yet this awareness is not something we either do or do not have. It needs to be developed as part of the research process. It is not something you ever arrive at. We are always in the process of becoming aware. There is only the journey (Brew 1988). All this points to a movement away from detached investigation towards research in which the researcher is personally involved.

Conservatism about forms of knowing inherent in traditional research and within the economic model obscures the richness in human knowing which can be obtained through explicit recognition of our personal connectedness to the phenomena of our investigation. Even subjective experiences under scrutiny in research become objectified by the traditional requirement of separating the research process from its product. Fortunately things are now changing. New forms of inquiry are being developed which have both a personal and a social dimension. Academic inquiry in such work is justified by its capacity to promote and support personal inquiry. We considered some examples in Chapter Four. The separation between the researcher, the research topic and the community where the work is carried out and where they apply their findings, is broken down. Such work lies, as this researcher, interviewed as part of a project on supervisory practices in relation to non-traditional thesis work recognizes, on the academic fringe:

> I live on the edge. I live on the edge as a researcher. I live on the edge as a practitioner. I live on the edge as a person. But I know the edge. . . . We're back at discovering the self. I know that I'm doing research that is really, and some day we will think it's really very basic . . . It's not intricacies and it's not subtleties. It's very stark beginnings of understanding the human condition that we know makes a difference in human survival and the quality of life for people in communities. I know it's making a few more doctors a little more respectful of a few more patients. I know that we've got a curriculum in the school which is teaching 10 year old kids how to hang on to their hope when their parents are fighting. I know that we've found ways of representing this condition, visually that we never thought we would be able to do. So that when somebody says what is this thing called hope we can say. I want you to look at these 20 pictures and then if you still have that question let me know. So that we make it visible and that's the thing that we're focusing on. How do you make hope visible in your own life, to the community and then the second thing I'm really interested in is: how do you put it in practice, if you're an educator or if you're a teacher?
>
> (Jevons 1998)

In the new forms of research we see that the emphasis has shifted towards examining the world-as-experienced; towards the idea that reality is a construct; and towards a blurring of the distinction between subjective and objective worlds. For while traditional research has resulted in a great deal of knowledge about the latter, it has, by denying subjectivity, meant that we are still very ignorant regarding the processes of human subjective experience. We have not learnt how to live. Research has told us very little about how to be happy and almost nothing about how to be wise.

We have examined the way in which research agendas are set because society wants to know the answers to certain questions or to solve particular problems. However, although social learning is tied up with what the society believes it needs to learn, we now know that the answers which are found can open up new vistas and opportunities. We may look at phenomena from a range of different directions but we do not always get the answers we wish for. That a society believes it needs to learn something or puts an emphasis on finding out about a particular phenomenon is no guarantee it will not learn something else. For example, it is well known that in response to Russia's Sputnik programme, and because of the perceived need to learn about space travel, America put a man on the Moon. Upon seeing pictures of the Earth, in its beauty, from the Moon, what we learnt most about was not the Moon, nor was it about space. We learnt most about our own world. Leaps in societal learning take place when we unpredictably shift perspective. This can happen even when there is a desire to incrementally increase our factual knowledge in one domain. The knowledge is not necessarily what we set out to make it. Research is full of surprises.

If research is to teach us how to live, it will need to become more like learning. It will need to be integrated more firmly with the researchers' own experiences of transformation. For fully taking on the implications of postmodernity is itself essentially transformative. When the Berlin Wall came down, Europeans experienced a paradigmatic shift in perspective. Their views of Europe, of particular countries in Europe and of themselves, underwent a radical rethink. The West realized that underlying a hatred of the Wall was a sense of security. We had to rethink our conceptual maps of Europe. Postmodernity presents an even more radical redrawing of our frameworks for understanding. Coping with super-complexity means being a lifelong learner. It means that through research we learn how to live not so we can make pronouncements for others; but because post-modernity requires the constant engagement at both a personal and a social level with the question: how *do* we live?

In this chapter we have considered research as learning on an individual and on a societal level. We have noted that there are different perspectives among academic researchers concerning what they learn when engaged in research activities. These range from the acquisition of skills on the one hand to personal transformation on the other. What individuals learn is likely to be unpredictable but in setting research agendas there are choices to be made about the extent to which personal transformation is a goal. We must recognize that the emphasis on increasing publications output may be detrimental to the development of researchers as individuals. On a societal level, learning is similarly unpredictable; not subject to control. It is always maverick. It can never be tamed. By setting the research agenda we can influence the fields of study but we cannot determine what is found out. There is no way that research can make society learn the things researchers or any one else wants it to learn. Progress is not a cumulative acquisition of bodies of knowledge. Rather it consists in our changing perspective and in redefining ourselves and our reality. We have noted a trend towards the development of research which is personally challenging to the researcher. I have suggested that the development of mature awareness and an engaged and involved research consciousness is imperative if research is to teach us how to live.

Chapter 10

Research and teaching

> We do but learn today, what our better advanced judgements will unteach tomorrow.
>
> (Sir Thomas Browne)

'Huh. Here she goes again. More fiction. What's she doing? Why does she keep lapsing into little bits of fiction?'

'Well, I quite like the fictional bits. It breaks it up.'

'Makes you think about things in different ways.'

'That's right. I quite like it too.'

'I know. But what does she think she's doing? Why's she doing it?'

'I don't know. I suppose, well, sometimes she creates a kind of atmosphere. Like, you know, when I read that bit at the beginning of the chapter on economics. I felt really gloomy and that's just how I feel when I think about the government and what it's doing to higher education.'

'But that's daft. This is supposed to be a serious academic book. I think fiction trivializes.'

'But perhaps it does provide a different kind of truth . . .' Jamie looked wistful and everyone sensed he was going to say more. Instead there was silence.

Ann interrupted it. 'But we're the readers. We're not supposed to be in the book. We're only supposed to be outside it. Reading it!'

'That's right. What are we doing in the book? I don't want to be in the book. I want to keep my distance. How dare she put us in the book?'

'Well it's not us, is it? Just people like us.'

'Well it reads like us.'

'Anyway it doesn't matter.' It was Jamie's good sense showing again. 'What's important is what it says about the nature of research. That's what the book's supposed to be about. What does the fiction say about the nature of research?'

Douglas, sceptical as ever said: 'Nothing! It doesn't tell you anything. It's just self-indulgent nonsense.'

'I don't agree,' Ann said. 'The further it goes on the more I think the fiction is very significant. Like, . . . well, here, for example, she's put us in the book and I think that's important because . . . isn't she saying something about the way we are both inside research and on the outside of it looking in? I mean, here we are on the outside of the book looking at the inside of the whole research culture and stuff. But we're researchers ourselves so we are inside as well.'

'Mm. That's quite profound. Is it really supposed to mean that?'

'Does it matter what it's really supposed to mean? Isn't it what you interpret it to mean which counts?'

'I still don't like being in the book. It makes me feel uneasy.'

'But it's only like looking in a mirror.'

'I don't like that either,' Douglas said and everyone laughed.

Later, when the others had left to go to the library, Ann still sat thoughtfully turning over the pages to see if she could discern any kind of pattern. Jamie moved to a chair round her side of the coffee table. He said: ' I wonder what Professor Knox would say if he read the book. I should think he would think it was a load of rubbish.'

'I don't think he'd like it either. Most of those senior academics don't really understand what it is like not to know what they're up to. I don't think he would get it at all.'

'No. It's a pity. I rather suspect there's a lot here which is quite contentious.'

'Which it shouldn't be. Really. I mean . . . one of the things my supervisor was telling me last week was about the importance of taking a critical stance. He was referring to my topic of course. I'm doing a lit. review at the moment on feminist approaches in the sociology of poverty. Anyway, he was saying you have to be critical whatever you read. And I think that what she's doing is being critical about research in general. I don't think there's any harm in that. After all, it's what we're all about, isn't it?'

'Yes, but I have a suspicion that she's tapping into a great deal of prejudice. Otherwise people would be talking about these things. We wouldn't be reading a potentially subversive book to find out what it is everyone is not telling us.'

The purpose of all research is to teach, not in the narrow sense of being available for students, but in the broader sense of teaching people in the wider community about the world they live in. Teaching provides the *raison d'être* for research. When we look around the world in which we live, there is no aspect of our daily experience which is not informed by perceptions of reality defined for us by research. Chemists, for example, have changed the way we view the air we breathe, sociologists have affected the way we perceive our relationships with the people with whom we come into contact, historians have shaped the way we relate to the street where we live. Indeed there is not one aspect of our daily lives for which our perception has not been influenced by some aspect of research. Research findings are one of the most fundamental impetuses directing the ways in which people's perceptions of the world around them change and develop. There are answers to important problems which only research can teach us about. Yet, as we saw in Chapter Nine, what society learns is not rationally decidable. Political, ideological and social factors influence the adoption of particular ideas by students, colleagues and society at large. The negotiation and communication involved in the processes of inter-pretation and construction of knowledge all contribute to the ways in which research changes ideas.

How disciplinary knowledge is formed and exchanged through the negotiation of meanings with students; the ways in which ideas are generated and communi-cated in an academic context; the ways in which research communities come into being, flourish and then die; and how, when flourishing, they define what counts as knowledge: all attest to the ways in which knowledge is generated and shared in a social context. A community of scholars still serves as an ideal. The scholar surrounded by a small group of students is viewed as the quintessential teaching and learning situation. We attempt to preserve this in the tutorial system in which we hope free discussion and debate take place. In this idealized scenario, teachers share ideas from research with their students. Teaching sits in harmony with research.

Yet this is not only an ideal. When we look at the way academics go about their work, there is still quite a bit of truth in the idea of a harmony between research and teaching. For me, as a case in point, my day begins with the walk to work. I've usually got some ideas on my mind so I try to get them straight as I stride along. I arrive at my desk and jot down an idea I had. While I am at it I also jot down one or two jobs I remember I have to do. I deal with the mail: a couple of new journals, reminders to send off conference registrations, a problem with a colleague – the usual stuff. I look at the email and send off a few messages. I do not distinguish between the ones that are setting up a research collaboration from those which are to do with university committees and the like. I finalize arrangements for the afternoon's teaching session. While waiting for the photocopying to finish, I make a telephone call to sort out the staff problem. Kept waiting on the line, I start to search the Internet: must look up that reference I came across yesterday. And so my day goes on. I make no distinction between my research, my teaching, my learning and my administration.

In the course of the daily life of the academic, research, teaching and administration are all interwoven. For many academics, teaching and research are simply different facets of academic life and it is difficult to tell where one begins and the other leaves off. As we saw in Chapter Three, some academics view teaching and dissemination simply as aspects of scholarship. Smeby (1998) suggests that the criteria for determining whether something is research or teaching depend on the intellectual level of the student, while Rowland (1996) reports that what the senior academics in his study considered 'research' and what they considered 'teaching' was determined by who the audience were.

So the relationship between teaching and research resides in the everyday minutiae of decisions which go with daily life. Sometimes the focus is more on activities which make up the teaching side of things. Sometimes, there is what seems like the 'luxury' of time for research. For some people, and at some times, these are quite separate. For others, and at other times, they seem inseparable, for example, when there is a group of postgraduate students working on topics related to the academic's research interests. Engaging in research provides nourishment to teaching. It provides a creative outlet. Take away research, and teaching can become routine. Take away teaching, and research can become remote and stodgy. In other words, when we look at academic practice we see that research and teaching are not particularly distinct in academics' minds.

> [A]lthough people normally used the terms teaching and research in a relatively unproblematic fashion, once some of them began to think of their academic activity in more specific detail, the two terms became much more closely intertwined.
>
> (Rowland 1996: 13)

CONTESTED SPACE

One theme which we have seen repeatedly throughout this book is the idea that research comes up with surprises; it does not always end up in the place we want it. Instead, it challenges us with the unexpected. Nowhere is this tension between desired research findings and what research has actually found more poignant than in debates concerning the relationship between teaching and research. Empirical studies over a number of years have consistently failed to demonstrate statistically convincing connections between research and teaching, and investigators have repeatedly questioned why there are low or no correlations. An enormous amount of literature on the subject is succinctly summed up by Hattie and Marsh when, having carried out a meta-analysis of fifty-eight studies of the relationship, they say: 'the evidence suggests a zero relationship, and there was no support for the existence of moderators' (Hattie and Marsh 1996: 530).

Perceptions of the relationship between teaching and research held within the academic community are clearly complex and subtle (Neumann 1992). The assumption in the face of everyday experience has been that there really is a link, or there ought to be one, but that we have simply failed to demonstrate it statistically. Suggesting there is a disjunction between the widely held view amongst academics that there is a connection between teaching and research, and results of empirical studies which appear to refute this, Webster (1985) says the myth that there is a link persists because we would like there to be one. Research has continued to be done because the findings appear to contradict academics' experience and be contrary to common sense. Since he suggested this, a number of further studies have substantiated his findings. Centra (1983) quoted a study in which 95 per cent of science faculty staff agreed that 'research increases teaching effectiveness by increasing awareness and currency', but they also said that a good teacher did not have to do research. However, it is clear, as Centra (1983) suggested and Neumann (1992) re-emphasized, that the belief that there is a connection is stronger than statistical evidence for it.

Clearly the acceptance of any particular interpretation of the findings is dependent on one's underlying beliefs about the link and one's conception of what constitutes scholarly work. In an attempt to explain apparently contradictory findings, Ramsden and Moses (1992) outlined three possible views of the links between teaching and research: the strong integrationist view which suggests that in order to be a good university teacher one must be an active researcher; the integrationist view which is the belief that there are links between teaching and research at the departmental or institutional level but not at the level of the individual academic; and the independence view which says there is no causal relation.

In the day-to-day work of each academic, each department and each faculty, and in the management decisions of universities, research and teaching occupy contested space. How often within the minutiae of tasks undertaken daily by academics do they pause to question the time taken up with teaching and the lack of time for research? Or the other way round? How often does spending time on research feel like time taken out of academic duties? If in no other arena, research and teaching compete for time in the life of the busy academic. Teaching takes time from research. Research is time taken out of teaching. Every individual academic who has both responsibilities has to negotiate this contested space on a daily basis.

It might seem curious to those unfamiliar with the ways of universities that academics, for whom in many countries doing research is part of their contract of employment, should ever question whether they should be spending time on research. For the experienced researcher this is less of an issue. But for academics trying to establish themselves in a new career, there are many mixed messages around. They may be encouraged to do research, but at the same time be given a heavy teaching burden. New academics may be encouraged to spend time obtaining research grants or publishing in international journals. Yet their teaching commitments may preclude spending long periods of concentrated study away from the department. They may lack the qualifications in teaching which would enable them to feel confident in that area of activity, so feel they need to spend time on building up teaching skills. Taking time for research when there is a line of demanding and needy students queuing up at the door can be difficult or seem churlish and self-indulgent. As we have seen, the prestige of the university depends on its research in the same way that the prestige of a country is linked to its research (see Chapter Eight). It is therefore probably unrealistic to argue that the prestige of individual academics should not be tied to their research reputations in spite of many moves in recent years to acknowledge and reward teaching expertise in promotions criteria. Neglecting either one at the expense of the other is rarely an option in the successful academic career nowadays.

Individual academics have to do a balancing act. Should they bring their own research and their teaching closer together or should they keep them separate? Should they focus on the one or the other now or later? The ways in which they resolve these dilemmas will depend on their views of the nature of research, the proximity of the subjects of research to the subjects taught, the level of the students, their perceptions of the reward systems within their institution and their perceptions of their career potential. While an individual's views of the relationship may not be the same as the institutional view, the balancing act also has to be performed at the level of universities. Neither the academics nor their managers may have any desire to see the connection between teaching and research severed or weakened. Indeed, recent arguments have suggested it should be strengthened as we will see a little later.

There is another balance to be struck in this connection, arising from the idea that a university should be a community of learners. For the relationship between research and teaching is tied up with a hierarchical organizational structure. Examining the nature of research in the context of its relationship to teaching is to bring into focus the asymmetrical relationship between teacher and student, and again the space is contested, needing to be carefully negotiated. If knowledge is context-bound, defined by particular communities and giving expression to the interests of powerful groups, as we saw earlier, these ideas have to apply in academic situations. For such relationships impinge on the ways and context in which students learn. I have argued elsewhere that an academic apartheid exists between academics and allied staff (Brew 1995). Yet there is another apartheid which is relevant here and that is the one between academics and students. In this context academics have a special, privileged, status. Traditionally it is the academics who define what counts as appropriate knowledge for students to learn. It is the academics who assess the extent to which students have learnt it. In a global, mass higher education system, where there is open access to information through the Internet and open choice for students to put together a range of course modules to suit their needs and interests, it is possible for students to take on more of the authority to decide what is appropriate to learn, particularly in generalist courses. The academic elite status is called into question and there is a potential crisis of authority. To suggest that the learning researchers do is similar to the learning students do, as the idea of the university as a community of learners suggests, is to narrow the distinction between novice learners and expert learners. But this comes at a price. The more research and teaching are brought together, the more students are 'let in' to the privileged domain of the researcher. Preserving the distinction between academic researcher and student researcher is a way of preserving an elite. While the rhetoric of equality is used, I do not think that the academic community is ready to take on the full implications of this at present. Yet this is essential if our new vision for research is to be realized.

While it is potentially feasible for there to be no links between teaching and research, and for the teaching and research activities of universities to be kept entirely separate, this would have significant consequences for universities, particularly in countries such as the UK and Australia, where there is a strong tradition of academic work involving book teaching and research. There are good reasons for universities in these contexts not to be staffed by two groups of academics: researchers and teachers. They include the high status and value placed on research, and the potential for academics who have teaching-only contracts to be exploited. In Sweden, where there is a tradition of teachers and research contracts being separate, these factors also apply, leading to recent demands on teachers to do research and researchers to do teaching. On the other hand, with the increased use of postgraduate student teachers, particularly in junior year courses, and increasing numbers of casual teaching staff, assumptions about the role of academics are being challenged. Ramsden and Moses (1992) suggest that separating teaching and research may, in fact, increase teaching quality. They argue that students should not be misled into thinking that highly productive research departments offer high quality courses. In contrast, Barnett (1997a) calls for teaching to become more research-like, while Shore, Pinker and Bates (1990) suggest that research may serve as a model for teaching. Hattie and Marsh (1996) suggest that marrying teaching and research by enhancing the relationship between them is a desirable aim of universities. How we negotiate these different perspectives depends, among other things, on what we understand research to be.

Arguing that what is needed is a new model for undergraduate education within research-based universities, the Boyer Commission has recently suggested that: 'inquiry, investigation, and discovery are the heart of the enterprise, whether in funded research projects or in undergraduate classrooms or graduate apprenticeships. Everyone at a university should be a discoverer, a learner' (Strum Kenny 1999: 9). The Commission's report details ten different ways in which undergraduate education can be enhanced. These include involving students more in research, encouraging the use of inquiry into the undergraduate curriculum, breaking down the barriers to interdisciplinary study, using information technology in creative ways, linking the development of skills for lifelong learning with coursework and culminating the undergraduate experience with a major research project. Following an investigation of students' conceptions of their teachers' research, Jenkins *et al.* (1998) similarly argue that not only should students have opportunities to benefit from their teachers' research, they should be more often involved in helping to carry it out, a point which the Boyer Commission echoes. Attention,

Jenkins *et al.* (1998) suggest, should be given in curriculum design to how staff research can benefit student learning. For bringing research and teaching together requires policy and management decisions. These might include policies requiring departments to monitor and identify how their research impacts upon and supports the undergraduate curriculum, and policies requiring measures of teaching quality to include how individuals integrate their research into their teaching. Hattie and Marsh (1996) suggest emphasizing the construction rather than the imparting of knowledge; encouraging a deep approach to learning; emphasizing uncertainty; ensuring the best researchers teach across all levels of students; involving students in 'artistic and scientific productivity'; rewarding teachers for the currency of their material; and ensuring public awards for teaching. They argue that creativity, commitment, inquisitiveness and critical analysis should be rewarded in both teaching and research.

For Barnett, the call to make teaching more research-like is part of the need to redefine the roles of students and teachers in the development of a culture of critical action in higher education. It is part of the process of redefining the academic role to take on the context of uncertainty; a context in which, he argues, both research and teaching need to change (Barnett 1997a).

> Rather than hypothesizing a conceptual distinction between research and teaching (which then have to be brought together in some way), teaching may be seen as an insertion into the processes of research and not into its outcomes. What is required is not that students become masters of bodies of thought, but that they are enabled to begin to experience the space and challenge of open, critical inquiry (in all its personal and interpersonal aspects).
>
> (Barnett 1997a: 110)

All of these suggestions for how research and teaching should be brought together are founded on a number of different ideas about the nature of research and about what constitutes a university education. Different views of the nature of research have different consequences for how the relationship between teaching and research is viewed and how the dilemmas we have seen unfold in this chapter are resolved at individual, group and institutional levels. So it is important to be clear what understandings of research and scholarship are being talked about. In the remainder of this chapter I consider some of the implications of the relationship between teaching and research for different views of research. This will highlight dilemmas already discussed and provide further support for the new directions that have been suggested throughout this book.

BRINGING RESEARCH AND TEACHING TOGETHER

We have seen in this book that the nature of research, reflecting changing ideas about the nature of knowledge and about how we come to know, is itself changing and is being challenged by the context of uncertainty in which we find ourselves living. We have also noted the ways in which the social and political context influences what we understand research to be. Teaching and learning in higher education are also changing to reflect these same influences.

Changes in higher education which have been affecting the relationship between teaching and research include the move to a mass higher education system (Elton 1992; Westergaard 1991) and demands on the amount of time available both for teaching and for research (Hattie and Marsh 1996), as well as changes in the nature of research and in the nature of teaching (Rowland 1996). All of these changes appear to have driven such a wedge between teaching and research that some have questioned whether that relationship still exists (e.g. Hattie and Marsh 1996). Jenkins *et al.* (1998) suggest that in these changed conditions for higher education, opportunities for motivating students through involving them in discussions of their teachers' research are frequently lost. They claim that students are often ignorant of the research their teachers are doing yet would like to know more. Elton (1992) notes that a changed policy context has given urgency to questions about the relationship between teaching and research.

In a recent article, I suggested that we have to see the debate between teaching and research as located in a time dimension (Brew 1999b). There are many variations on the way the relationship between teaching and research is negotiated and maintained. The kaleidoscopic, ever changing nature of this relationship has to be seen in the context of challenges to ideas about knowledge and knowing. For example, relationships between teaching and research in a tradition which views itself as heavily dependent on an empiricist or Enlightenment philosophy are different from those which arise and become evident within a more pluralistic tradition. When research and teaching are both viewed as being founded on a traditional empiricist framework, the relationship is always problematic. If the knowledge research generates is seen as objective and separate from knowers, it is quite reasonable to assume that it requires transmission and absorption through a separately conceptualized teaching process. If on the other hand knowledge is seen as a product of communication and negotiation, the links between research and teaching are quite different. The relationship between research and learning is more intimate. Thus a move towards a more pluralistic view of knowledge which fully takes on board the interpretive nature of academic work, then, means that research and teaching can be viewed as being in a symbiotic relationship (Brew 1999b). So what do the directions teaching and learning in higher education are taking tell us about the nature of research?

Increasing recognition that when students graduate they need to be ready to practise in their chosen profession has developed awareness among higher education teachers of the need to encourage and assess a broad range of abilities and attributes, including personal as well as academic and generic skills and attributes. The importance of lifelong learning, assessment of experiential learning and of learning skills, as well as the use of assessment which is 'authentic' (Wiggins 1989), i.e. that realistically matches the tasks the students are to undertake in their professional lives, is becoming widely recognized in higher education teaching and learning. The need for a professional approach to whatever activities are engaged in has to be taught as an explicit part of undergraduate education.

In this context the higher education curriculum is now making room for the study of unforeseeable but interconnected problems and issues. No longer is it adequate to present problems as if they are self-contained and clearly bounded, or to separate student learning experiences emphasizing discrete items of content (for example, separate lectures), or for students to merely be engaged in solving routine problems to which their teachers already know the answers. Preparing students to solve unforeseen problems is important so that, whatever they do when they graduate, they can act decisively and effectively in a complex environment.

Our understanding of the nature of research teaches us quite a bit about what is involved in taking a professional approach and what is involved in solving complex problems. Our explorations of the nature of scholarship in Chapter Three, in particular, emphasized the way professionalism is embodied in academic work. On one level this included an emphasis on giving attention to detail including logic, use of evidence, making sure work is properly referenced, etc. On another level it provided an alternative definition of rigour in a postmodern context, where rigour is viewed as an aspect of professionalism, not as a rule-bound pursuit of objectivity. For example, focusing on the pragmatic, the domino conception of research emphasized the role of the higher education curriculum as a process of developing the strategies, tools, techniques, knowledge and experience that are needed for this. It also drew attention to the ways in which complex problems are connected, to the fact that one answer leads to other questions, and to how solving one problem may illuminate or raise a range of other problems. Similarly, variation in ideas about the nature of scholarship drew attention to the importance of a thorough grasp of background knowledge as a necessary prerequisite to the development of solutions. The layer view stressed the importance of looking beneath the surface for meaning which may initially appear hidden, the trading view highlighted the importance of communities of practice in solving problems and the journey view reminded us that anything may be relevant to the solution. This close connection between the activities of research and the actions required in order for students to operate in a complex environment, signifies that research practice offers an important grounding in teaching us how to live.

Changing conceptions

Biggs (1996) argues that the most significant impact on teaching practice in higher education over the past thirty years or so has been the shift to viewing learning as a process of construction, as being about creating knowledge rather than simply absorbing it. One of the greatest challenges that higher education teaching and learning has had to face is the challenge of changing students' conceptions of the phenomena of their study (Dahlgren 1997). Teaching students to learn always to examine the context, the significance and range of possible interpretations of phenomena, and to be prepared to revise interpretations when the process of looking again reveals an alternative explanation, is vital. As teaching becomes more student-centred, negotiated, discursive and reflexive, there is a move from an emphasis on teaching towards an emphasis on the facilitation of learning. Encouraging students to take more responsibility, to become autonomous, independent learners, an emphasis on learning to learn and on reflective practice, are all consistent with new understandings of the nature of knowledge as constructed within a socio-political context.

The growing use of reflective portfolios and the development of personal and professional skills reflects this increased emphasis on teaching to advance active learning and encourage students to be critical, creative thinkers. So too does the move to resource-based, more varied and more flexible teaching and learning, including greater choice for students, flexibility of course offering, flexibility of place and time to suit their needs and interests, and so on, with limited choice being afforded through modular programmes and greater choice through individually designed learning contracts. All of these encourage greater participation by students in their own learning.

Moves towards problem-based, inquiry-focused methods of teaching and learning, particularly in professional courses, where the learner develops a personal understanding of a phenomenon by interacting with conceptions in the literature, ideas presented by teachers and others, and by personal experience within a framework of inquiry are, however, still treated with suspicion, particularly in traditional discipline areas. Attempts to move towards research-based, independent study at junior undergraduate levels have met with some resistance. Eschewing teaching in favour of research/inquiry-based approaches to learning is considered new and radical, yet such approaches move the learning of students more in line with the research activities of their teachers.

In the context of globalization, the role of academic communities of practice is increasingly being recognized as important. The growing emphasis on using information technology to build up networks of students engaged in a variety of forms of collaboration is evidence of the concern higher education teachers have in this regard and the emphasis they increasingly place on communities of practice. This is occurring both within faculties and departments and also outside the particular university in which a student is enrolled. If new knowledge is to be disseminated, students may become teachers for parts of their university life, perhaps teaching more junior colleagues and disseminating their work in a variety of ways. At the very least, engaging in communities of practice and disseminating ideas have to be seen as part of the curriculum process for students. This may indicate a role for student conferences and networks (perhaps taking a global and/or electronic form) as well as student publications such as special journals, and opportunities to engage in debates with people in a variety of locations.

The search for interpretation and meaning is vital in the super-complex world which we face. It is a skill developed in a process of research which underlines the importance of not taking things at face value, of searching for the underlying meanings in phenomena and changing conceptions dependent on what is found. In order to operate within a super-complex environment, people need to be able to make complex judgements based on evidence. They need to be skilled at bringing new interpretations to familiar as well as unfamiliar contexts. As we saw in Chapter Nine, if research is to lead the way in these conditions of postmodernity, research consciousness must be open to entertaining multiple views of the world, juggling them and being open to yet others which come into focus, changing conceptions in the light of new evidence.

Changing consciousness

In some university systems, in the UK and US for example, where students are likely to reside away from home, university education has traditionally been viewed as a process of personal as well as academic development. More recently, moves to include within undergraduate curricula the development of personal and academic skills and attributes have recognized the need to do more than leave this process to the *ad hoc* living arrangements of students. We have seen how some academics view their research as a process of personal discovery and change. In Chapter Nine I highlighted the need for research to balance on the one hand the need to produce socially useful knowledge and on the other its potential to transform those who engage in it. Making this explicit within a university education would mean that through the process of inquiry students' individual growth and personal development would become an integral part of their university study. Integration of the personal and professional means placing greater emphasis on the personal relevance of the subject of study to students, the primary goal being the development of their self-knowledge or exploration of their existential life issues. We have seen some examples in this book where postgraduates have done this in the context of doctoral research.

This points to a need in higher education teaching to focus on the processes of learning, rather than on the products of that learning. The wider implications of this, however, are far more radical and indicate a way of reconceptualizing academic work. Focusing on the personal as an integral part of the academic requires that the context of teaching and learning be characterized by relationships of trust. Indeed, such changes call into question just who are the teachers and who the learners. Authentic changes in relationships, learning perhaps becoming a collaborative process of engagement in a joint enterprise and distinctions between teacher and student becoming less clear, challenge the power relationships between teacher and student. It may also mean breaking down the distinction between teaching and learning as both teachers and students come to explore explicitly the issues which confront them and discuss these in a non-threatening, trusting environment. This means assessment might be focused on formative pieces of work, examinations being rare. It may mean a re-evaluation of the role of grades and marks, which legitimate the exercise of power by academics vis-à-vis their students.

In this book, our explorations of the tensions between different approaches and ideas about the nature of research have pointed to some essential directions for the future development of research if it is to teach us how to live within a context of uncertainty, plurality and super-complexity. Exploring the relationship between teaching and research in this context, therefore, is closely bound up with questions about what higher education is for and how it needs to grow to take on such challenges. We have seen in this chapter that bringing teaching and research together and viewing personal development as inevitably an intrinsic part of both research and teaching is therefore not just an academic exercise. It is crucial if students are to learn how to live. In other words, changes in the world in which academics operate necessitate changes in research which in turn necessitate changes in what is taught and in the relationship between teachers and learners.

However, given that the space research occupies is contested, and by powerful competing agendas, these changes are not likely to come about easily and soon. In the next chapter we will see that the very language used to talk about research pulls in directions that are diametrically opposed to those I have been advocating and that I have argued are essential if we are to avert a crisis in the academy and move research towards a position of providing leadership in teaching people how to live.

Chapter 11

Research as discourse

Let us know how Truth is developed among you.

(George Fox)

Eldred had taken the first step. He had enlisted. Not that there were any outward signs of him having done so. But that was the nature of these troubles. It was war, but no one was naming it as such. Man against his neighbour, one community against another, life had become impossible, and things were getting worse. Eldred did not know what was going to befall him. He had no idea what he would be called upon to do. Yet he knew that he had to take up arms and fight just as his brother had done. There would be no peace while the enemy was active.

The trouble was that in this war it was difficult to tell who the enemies were. Eldred had heard stories of great battles fought on foreign fields. His grandfather, who had been a soldier as a young man, had told stories of the gallantry and glory of war: the colours of the standard bearers, the sound of the drums, the red of officers' uniforms and the glint of the sun on raised swords. There the infantry were lined up waiting for the signal for the battle to begin. Grandfather had told how he had waited, with a hundred others ready to fight for the King; waiting fearfully for the signal to be given when the enemy would appear over the hill and they would charge full pelt and give them hell.

But this was different. The fields of battle were the villages and hamlets of Eldred's home country. The enemy was within, waiting to strike when you least expected it. There were spies everywhere. You had to be careful who you spoke to and what you said. There were stories going round that put the fear of God into everyone. People had talked to their neighbour and then found that very person sitting in judgement round the other side of a large desk in a sham of a trial. The labourer they had known hoeing the weeds alongside them in the fields had been the very person to carry out lurid and mind-blowing acts of human torture and degradation. Everyone was in fear and everyone was being very careful.

He had been given an address where, it was said, he would get his orders. It was his custom to go and collect firewood in the copse and the address wasn't far out of the way. So the next day he set off down the lane just as usual. He found the tumbledown house tucked away about a mile further on. Making sure he had not been followed, in trepidation he knocked on the door. 'Password!?' came a loud voice from within. He gave the password and there was an unlocking of bolts and turning of keys. The door opened. He entered. The room smelt musty. There were five or six shadowy figures ranged around the room. He recognized Sedrick, the blacksmith and little Johnny Makepeace, the wheelwright's son. Wondering if he was in the right place, Eldred furtively glanced at them all. Was this the side he was supposed to be on? The mood was sombre as they recollected recent events. There had been that family in the next village where the children had been murdered in front of the eyes of their parents; the terrible rapes that had happened to the girls over at Stanthorpe after they had rounded them up and forced them into the woods. But most of all the massacre that had been carried out in broad daylight over in the next village had shocked them all. It was too awful to even think about. That was what had led Eldred to realize he had to be doing something. There was no way out. They had to fight back. They were going to have to beat these brigands at their own game. They were going to have to be subtle and use stealth because there was no way of knowing for sure who they were. A few names were mentioned. Eldred was astonished at some of them, for they were people he considered to be upstanding citizens; people who commanded respect. Yet here was the evidence. They were putting fear and dread into the hearts of every good man, woman and child in the country.

One day, a few weeks later, when Eldred was getting used to passing messages and watching the movements of particular key individuals as he had been instructed, he was called upon to do something much more dangerous. They had to ambush the brigands as they returned from one of their dreadful forays into yet another village enclosure. Waiting, Eldred crouched behind a tree thinking that this was like a real battle. When the enemy rounded the bend the signal was given. From nowhere and everywhere his friends emerged and ran down the steep gully. It was not a pretty sight as they fought man to man on that fearful day. Eldred felt sick as he saw little Johnny lying with his throat cut in the ditch. Yet buoyed with anger and indignation at the loss of his brother, at the sight of little Johnny, he fought heartily with all his strength until at last all was quiet. It was not until his company regrouped that Eldred saw that his arm had been injured. He would live to fight another day; others would not.

I started this book by drawing attention to the fact that the nature of research is something people in academic environments tend to take for granted. Throughout the book I have drawn attention to some of the factors which drive what people do in the name of research, determine what aspects of research are valued and followed and dictate who the key researchers are. In talking about research as contested space I have exhibited some of the tensions which new researchers have to negotiate and drawn attention to some of the dilemmas which have to be faced. In exploring how research can help us to live in a confusing world characterized by uncertainty, I have suggested elements of a vision of where it needs to be heading.

Those new to higher education sometimes hear more experienced researchers, senior colleagues and politicians talking and writing about research as if they are listening to a conversation in a language they do not know very well. It is like when we learnt a language at school but had not mastered it enough to understand the slang or the double-entendres or the significance of particular phrases and constructions. The language of habit perpetuates as well as masks key aspects of the nature of research. Some of these aspects are revealed in the imagery we use to talk about it and in the assumptions we make about what does not need to be said.

It should by now be apparent that conversations about aspects of research take place in many arenas and within many different social, political and historical contexts. Different conversations, like different pictures of the same landscape, proceed alongside each other and each conversation is within other, larger conversations. A fashionable way to describe this is in terms of discourses. There is the informal discourse between academic colleagues, both in the same area of research and in different areas, and the formal discourse of academic conference papers, journal articles and books, etc. There is the discourse of research managers and the wider academic community regarding institutional and national policies for research. There is also the discourse of funding providers: charitable institutions, foundations, research councils, as well as government agencies. There is the discourse of politicians and there is the discourse of journalists. There is the discourse of people outside the academy including industrialists, public servants and professionals as well as people in other corners of society. Research, as we have seen, touches everyone's life one way or another, so we must expect conversations about it to take place any time and any where by any body. Among these discourses there are discourses which support and sustain each other, and there are contested ones where discourses compete or undermine each other. The language of habit means that we hardly notice some of these contests.

Any discussion about what kind of discourse research is should not be constructed as an attempt to describe what all these people are talking and writing about. Sometimes, when I run workshops for people who are trying to make sense of the research scene so they can begin to develop a research career, one of the first things we do is to brainstorm the words associated with the word 'research'. This enables us to identify all the voices: all the people who are implicitly or explicitly telling the new researcher what they should and should not be doing. Some of these are to do with the methodology of research (being objective, finding knowledge, new ideas, etc.). Some are to do with the research culture of universities (grants, money, promotion, etc.) We have seen throughout this book that we have to reject the myth of neutrality in research and examine ways in which its discourse serves to skew the areas of investigation into particular domains at the expense of others (Spanier 1995; Wertheim 1995). Identifying the voices in this way, we encourage workshop participants to make choices about the voices they want and do not want to listen to. They need to be able to rationally evaluate which agendas they will follow and which ignore. Sometimes it is a question of choosing to follow a particular agenda, knowing they are doing so for a particular purpose – to get a grant, for example. For academics, their work is more often than not bound up in their sense of personal identity. Getting going on a successful academic research career sometimes means recognizing that part of their personal identity has to be suppressed in the effort to take the next step. Knowing about underlying assumptions provides, as I have argued throughout this book, the possibility of challenging and changing them, and increases the possibility of choice about different directions. So, what I am concerned to do in this chapter is to examine the kind of language that is being used to talk about research and to highlight some of the implicit assumptions not normally talked about which drive and direct it.

Foucault argued that thinking, doing, theory, practice, action, knowledge, power and meaning were all combined in discourses (Usher 1997). So it is not just that research leads to a number of discourses. Research is discourse. Notice I say 'research is discourse' and not 'is a discourse' or 'is discourses'. For as Lyotard says: 'Il n'y a pas de "hors texte"' (Lyotard 1984). In other words, there is not anything which is not discourse. All discourses are framed within another discourse. This is not simply a question of the language used and the way it is used, although discourse analysts have tended to focus on these aspects. For Foucault, the discourse creates a world and prescribes what is possible and desirable and what is not. The nature of the discourse describes the phenomenon.

> The constraints function to filter discursive potentials, interrupting possible connections in the communication networks; there are things that should not be said. They also privilege certain classes of statements (sometimes only one), whose predominance characterizes the discourse of the particular institution: there are things that should be said and there are ways of saying them.
>
> (Lyotard 1984: 17)

What is not said is an important clue to what is suppressed. For power, says Foucault (1979), is only tolerable when it masks part of itself. Discourse sustains power by making it invisible. The discourse considered acceptable is the discourse that supports the interests of the powerful. One of the ways in which the power is sustained is by holding to the silence. As we have seen throughout this book, there are many subjects on which research is silent. We will return to this a little later.

NARRATIVES

In Chapter Six we considered Lyotard's idea that what gives knowledge its legitimacy is the fictional story or epic on which it is based. Recognizing the narrative element in research is not to say that everything we do or say about research is fiction and that one fiction can substitute for another, or that the fictions are equally good (Slaughter 1993).

> Scientific narratives shape the possibilities of science even as science puts some limits on available narrative structures and conventions. . . . [They] contain an inseparable and powerful mixture of fact and fantasy, ideas and emotions, action and plot that merge private and public worlds, individual enterprise and historical agency whereas . . .
>
> (Slaughter 1993: 283)

Lyotard argued that two narratives underpin traditional academic inquiry. One is political. The idea is that the spread of knowledge through society leads to people having increased freedom within a political system governed through democracy. The other Lyotard describes as a more philosophical narrative, where knowledge is legitimated through reason. In this narrative, scientific knowledge is given credibility because it represents the logical unfolding of the pursuit of truth. We have explored many elements of this narrative throughout this book. Lyotard argues that there is now 'incredulity towards grand narratives' (Blake 1997:157). Recognizing and questioning these narratives provides a basis for overturning them. This is the postmodern condition.

While we may have incredulity about those narratives we recognize there are others which are perhaps less easy to detect. The closer we are to them, the more difficult they are to see. In a study of addresses by presidents of universities to the US Congress in the 1980s, for example, Slaughter (1993) identifies two narratives with echoes of those Lyotard drew attention to. The addresses were, she suggests, occasions when academic science representatives gave an account of the public purposes of science. She argues that, in the 1980s, narratives of science policy changed from concern with fundamental science to a language of entrepreneurialism, thus reducing the centrality of basic research. The two major narratives which emerged from her analysis of the presidential testimony were: the 'fruits of research' narrative and the 'orders of magnitude' narrative.

In the 'fruits of research' narrative the language was of wonders. As in a fairy tale there was a single prohibition that if violated would cast a blight over the land and cause the fruits of research to wither. Basic science produced plenty of fruit but only so long as university researchers were left alone. Science could solve problems in unpredictable ways, so undirected basic research is important. Hard work was done by imaginative and skilled scientists. Slaughter argues that the term 'basic science' was used as a metaphor for autonomous science, so this narrative kept university science in the hands of the scientists. This meant operating without constraint: independent decision-making on the part of scientists and a clear distinction between the university and industry. Private industry simply did not figure in this narrative. Basic science, unquestioningly supported by society, was the cornucopia, spilling over with the fruits of research and making progress possible (Slaughter 1993).

The second way of describing science found by Slaughter was the 'orders of magnitude' narrative. In this narrative the idea is that fewer workers would result in greater productivity. 'Academic participation in the product innovation process became the key to economic prosperity' (Slaughter 1993: 289). There was a recognition in this narrative that science could not be left to the academics. The language used was about a partnership between business and higher education; the idea was that science would rescue America from economic decline. It is a narrative which blurred the boundaries between the private and public sectors, between science and commerce, between the university and the corporate world. The idea of basic science was redefined so as to have an applied dimension. This legitimated collaborating with industrial partners (Slaughter 1993).

In considering economic views of research in Chapter Eight, I discussed the idea that knowledge was 'produced' (Gibbons *et al.* 1994), and examined the ways in which countries saw research as 'investment'. I asked why the academic community was apparently so compliant in adopting the language of the marketplace characteristic of economic models. I suggested that it gave expression to one of the variations in the ways in which academics think about research, namely, the trading variation. We can now see that this is framed within an 'orders of magnitude' narrative of research policy.

The dangers of this narrative are noted by Slaughter. Commercial science, she suggests, becomes separated from the mainstream of higher education. The profits from commercial liaisons benefit particular sections of higher education, notably, those that are closely allied to the powerful outside groups. This results in a 'privileged enclave of market-related science policy makers and scientists', leading to increased separation of various kinds: between physical sciences and other fields; between elite universities and others; between men (who are disproportionately located in physical sciences) and women; and between various racial groups. These arrangements challenge the power arrangements embedded in the fruits of research narrative, where scientists rather than institutional leaders were key players (Slaughter 1993: 298).

However, not only are there general narratives which apply to the whole process of creating knowledge through inquiry. There are also particular narratives which are sustained in each field of study. Each research investigation is located in a fictional story of how it fits into what has gone before and why it is significant. So for example in the field of teaching and learning in higher education, the story tells how the way out of the darkness and confusion surrounding ideas about cognitive styles, learning styles and approaches to study was found in a single defining moment in the 1970s, when researchers at the University of Gothenburg in Sweden presented the idea of deep and surface approaches to learning (Marton and Säljö 1976) and all became light. The story then goes on to suggest how, helped by key individuals, these ideas led the way in influencing and changing the whole of teaching and learning in higher education. Of course the narrative is selective and linear, but it is a story that would be recognized by anyone with a background in this field of study.

These narratives are sustained by various textual strategies in academic writing and in discussions at conferences and meetings. Later in the chapter we will see how new textual strategies are providing a basis for changing the nature of the discourse of research.

LANGUAGE

We do not consciously notice the language of habit. But the language we use influences what it is possible to do, or what it is desirable to think. Images and metaphors are not just literary terms for which we could substitute value-neutral language and retain the same meaning. They extend the boundaries of theories into wider arenas. They dictate what is possible and what is considered desirable in our relationships to the world and to other humans (Harding 1991). Images and metaphors sustain conventional notions of what knowledge is important. They, like underlying narratives, are powerful influences in policy formation and maintenance. Importantly, they define who are, and sustain the interests of, the powerful. In the language which is used, people's intentions are displayed.

The language of science

Much of the discourse of research and research policy is steeped in the language of the natural sciences. Indeed, the word 'science' is frequently equated with 'research'. The more the scientific discourse dominates research the more difficult it is to make the case for funding humanities and social science research. It leads, as we have seen, to increased separation between physical sciences and other fields (Slaughter 1993). Also noticeable is the predominance of scientists and engineers amongst policy-makers and higher education managers. This suggests that the language we use strengthens the standing of particular people. In an attempt to reclaim this discourse, Harding (1991) foregrounds 'science', arguing that the social and political nature of science and the fact that everything scientists do or think is part of the social world means that we have to come to see science as one of the social sciences, and not the other way round as has traditionally been the case. In contrast, in this book I have foregrounded 'research', locating the discussion in the context of higher education. By focusing on 'research' there is no way the relationship of research to ideas of politics, power and the interests of dominant groups can be escaped. It is evident that we are looking at a social phenomenon. Indeed, the very labelling of research as 'science' feeds dominant agendas at the expense of others.

This is not just a question of confusing the terms 'science' and 'research'. The discourse of research is frequently the discourse of science *laboratories*. This is evident in the UK's funding method (HEFCE 1999) for example, which is dependent upon measures of 'volume'. Volume of research is measured by numbers of 'research active' staff, research students, research assistants and fellows. The volume of research is then 'weighted' to determine 'quanta'. Weights and volumes, products and processes, quantities and measures all resonate ideas of laboratories. Drawing on images from chemistry and biology, we talk of developing a research 'culture' that is based upon research 'strengths' where there are 'concentrations' of researchers.

In addition, the use of the language of engineering to refer to aspects of research privileges technology and technological solutions. The idea of the body as a set of interconnected mechanisms (such as the idea that the heart is a pump, the lungs are bellows, etc.) enables modern medical knowledge to develop in such a way that humans can be treated in similar ways to cars: with 'procedures' and 'techniques' and replacement parts, etc. Engineering metaphors are carried into genetics, conveying a sense of inevitability about manipulation. The language of mechanism allows for depersonalization in areas such as psychiatry, with the resulting implication that physical operations may be carried out without consent (Midgley 1997) – electro-convulsive therapy is one example of this.

Is research a gendered discourse?

In Chapter Two I suggested that there were perhaps some more obvious authors than myself of a book on research. Admittedly when I think about this, what comes to mind are senior, Western males. Is this a coincidence? Feminists have argued that it is not; that the discourse of research or 'science' is a gendered discourse. Indeed, some have argued that the very structure of our language is gendered; that language reflects masculinist ideologies, values and culture and that the simple act of naming is itself a masculinist project (see e.g. Code 1991; Spender 1999). Belenky *et al.* (1986) argue that the visual metaphors which characterize Western epistemology such as light, illumination and seeing are in contrast to the metaphors of speaking and listening that women use to ground their knowledge. Visual metaphors, she argues, suggest a camera statically recording reality from a distance. Speaking and listening suggest closeness and interaction.

Harding (1991: 69) argues that metaphors of control and domination of nature are more fruitful for men in dominant groups than for women as ways to think about nature. She suggests that mechanistic metaphors carry sexual meanings and that these meanings are central to the ways (male) scientists conceptualize inquiry and nature. Ideas of causation and control are associated with desirable male personality traits (ibid.: 45) while the female body is thought of as a factory that derives its value from the quality of its products, i.e. babies. These writers draw attention to the need to be vigilant in relation to the ways in which images and metaphors reflect and sustain dominant agendas.

Tracing the development of what she calls the mathematical sciences, Wertheim (1995) shows how women were excluded from this discourse across the centuries. Arguing that science and religion are not, as has commonly been supposed, alien to each other, but rather that physics developed as 'a religiously inspired enterprise' (1995: 7), she suggests that physicists were treated to all intents and purposes like an alternate priesthood. Wertheim's tale is of repeated exclusion of women from the social and the intellectual life of scientists. For example, during the eighteenth century, she says, much of the discussion of scientific ideas took place in the salons and in this arena there were many intelligent and knowledgeable women. However, scientific ideas, she suggests, were increasingly expressed using symbolic and mathematical language:

> there is nothing innately feminine about a poetic style of writing; in other ages poetry has been seen as distinctly masculine. The issue here was that science was being increasingly defined in opposition to whatever was seen to be associated with women, and, reciprocally, women were being associated with the things cast out of science.
>
> (Wertheim 1995: 147)

The result is that today, Wertheim argues, only 3 per cent of physics professors are women and only 9 per cent of the physics workforce are women. Harding (1991), however, contends that the issue is not the fact that there are so few women in science, it is that there are so few women directing the agendas of science.

But is it just physics where there is a problem? After all, Wertheim admits that 41 per cent of biological and life scientists are women and 36 per cent of mathematicians. Perhaps the gendered discourse is only in physics. Yet Spanier (1995), as we saw in Chapter Six, analysed the concepts and theories of molecular biology suggesting that it is involved with a gendered discourse which emphasizes polarized differences, hierarchical relationships and the domination of one group (males) by another.

> In some cases, scientific metaphors or paradigms are 'wrong' in a technical sense – for example, when bacteria are labeled 'male' and 'female,' or when 'sex' is superimposed onto macromolecules, such as hormones or carbohydrate metabolites. In other cases, such as a centralized hierarchy of control of life at the molecular and cellular level, it is the power of the metaphor that systematically skews conceptualisation of the cell and the meaning of living processes.
>
> (Spanier 1995: 96)

Harding (1991) notes in this context the use of the language of immaturity or pathology in describing women's reproductive systems, while Martin (quoted in Code 1991: 69) observes that most disciplines exclude women from their subject matter, distort the female according to the male image of her and deny value to characteristics the society considers feminine. Code (1991) argues that textual practices still exist to silence women's voices. These include defining research as 'feminist', so keeping it in a separate domain, and predominantly quoting male sources. Another way in which women have been silenced is in the use of predominantly male subjects for research even when conclusions are made in relation to the general population (see e.g. Belenky *et al.* 1986; Harding 1991).

There is another aspect of the gendered nature of the academic discourse which merits a mention here. Notwithstanding the private exchanges which are part of the process of social intercourse which comprises academic life, much of the communication about research takes place in public discussions. Feminist writers have pointed to the difficulty many women have in operating in that arena. Studies on gender differences in language suggest that women more frequently do the listening while men do the talking (Belenky *et al.* 1986; Tannen 1994).

> The most interesting examples are not just the now popularly recognized uses of the generic 'man' and 'he', which undoubtedly reflect and maintain women's invisibility. That example is part of a larger picture of language as an enforcer of women's powerlessness. . . . Sociological evidence about male control and dominance in 'private' conversations and about the contestedness of women's right to speak in 'public' together with the difficulties they face in claiming this right – reveal a stark power differential constituted along gender lines.
>
> (Code 1991: 59)

Such arguments suggest that for the new researcher, vigilance is desirable. For recognition of the ways in which our language shapes our experience provides a basis for choice. Whether or not these arguments are valid is not the point. As we have seen, images and metaphors sustain dominant agendas and it is clearly the case that many of these are advanced by men.

Colonial discourse

However the discourse of research is not only a masculinist one, it is also a colonialist one. Here we need to draw on what has been termed the myth of rescue and redemption. 'History shows Western "man" making steady advances in knowledge, morality and social organisation – as he emerges from the dark of earlier ignorance and superstition into the light of a social life organized according to reason and science' (McWilliam *et al.* 1997: 4). Thus science will save humankind from ignorance and redeem us through finding unifying ideas which will explain all things in the universe. Allied to these ideas, Midgley (1992) refers to the idea of science as salvation because, she argues, there is now a romantic notion that science has obtained a kind of spiritual power. The idea of linear progress towards some all-encompassing knowledge has imbued key scientists with a kind of priesthood and they have become and are behaving like gurus dispensing wisdom. That which is near and now is to be despised in this narrative, in favour of the far and timeless. The narrative of rescue and redemption is a narrative of conquest. Exploration is built into the nature of research: exploring ideas; conquering domains of discourse; journeying into the unknown.

The idea of research as value free, rational knowledge (see Chapter Five) has been used as a reason to assume that it is applicable everywhere. Such knowledge, Harding argues, devalues local practical knowledge which has developed within communities over time (Harding 1998). Within every research encounter, there is a power relationship. This is subsumed in the language of neutrality. However, every time we use the language of 'subjects', for example, we are using a colonialist metaphor. Doing research on people in this way has been critically questioned by many writers and there are now many examples of cooperative and participatory methodologies where there is an attempt to equalize power in the research relation-ship (see e.g. Reason 1994). For within every encounter between researcher and researched, power has to be negotiated.

Research seeks out phenomena, including the infinitely small and the infinitely large, and names them. In naming, whether or not it is meaningful to do so, the act carries a sense of ownership. Jones (1983) draws attention, for example, to the way in which in naming and giving attributes such as 'colour' and 'charm' to infinitely small phenomena such as 'quarks' we are giving expression to, and then forgetting, our own creativity. Naming makes the unknown and unknowable appear real. It gives us a sense of ownership. Yet the naming is not arbitrary. It echoes the known and the knowable. We cannot talk of 'dark matter' in the universe, for example, without echoes of the idea of 'darkest Africa'.

I am constantly struck by the way in which researchers looking at the planets and stars, for example, uncritically use the language of colonization to describe the phenomena of their experience. When I have challenged scientists on this, they have pointed to human traits of exploration and conquest. Yet these are funda-mental colonialist traits. The idea that the universe in some sense belongs to us and that we can explore it just as explorers 'found' parts of the Earth as they journeyed into places they had not visited before is enshrined in discussions of the solar system and the universe. Frequently discussions centre on which planets we could colonize and survive on. For example, it is readily assumed that we can smash a probe into Europa or Io, moons of Jupiter, or that if we could find a way to live there, we could colonize Mars. Just as the eighteenth-century Europeans who, for example, thought Australia was theirs to exploit, the assumption is that the universe is there for us to do what we like with.

Colonization is an escape from the here and now to somewhere which is perceived as ultimately better. We saw in Chapter Seven that research can be a defence against those things we do not want to know: a way of protecting ourselves from the things we fear to know. This discussion of the metaphors we use to talk about the phenomena of our experience in academic discourse underlines the habit of avoiding the sense of our locatedness in a particular place at a particular time with the concomitant acceptance of our mortality. The language of escape permeates research. Indeed, in an intriguing book entitled *Physics as Metaphor*, Jones (1983) argues that the motive behind scientific metaphors is the avoidance of death:

> We are driven by the terrible inner contradiction we feel: each of us is an infinitely expansive symbolic self imprisoned in a decaying and death-bound body. We must struggle and fight heroically to claim our own meaning and value with every symbolic weapon in our arsenal.
>
> (Jones 1983: 173)

Jones argues that 'space' is a metaphor for being; for existence and in the sense of astrological space it makes us feel related to the rest of the universe. Our very sense of existing as independent beings is tied up with the idea of space. 'Construing ourselves as existing in space is a kind of insurance against nonexistence, against death' (Jones 1983: 187). 'Time', he suggests, symbolizes persistence or endurance hinting at our immortality; while 'matter' is our metaphor for stability and security and number represents unity and diversity. We can thus 'see our deepest subjective yearnings abstracted, objectified and canonised in the physical sciences'. Through the conservation laws of energy and mass, of electric charge, momentum and spin, for example, 'the theme of immortality and endurance is singled out as the most important characteristic of the structure of physics' (Jones 1983: 190).

Research as sport

In this book I have used the metaphor of contested space to describe the nature of research. I have drawn attention to many tensions, many areas where there is competition. In this sense I have played on the common usage, within the discourse of research, of sporting metaphors. Any discussion of research in the corridors of our universities, in the popular press or in academic literature is permeated with them. For example, research is frequently carried out in 'teams'. We talk of the 'field of study', 'setting the boundaries' of the investigation, fishing for ideas, being 'on target' in relation to a research project, 'getting up' or 'winning' in relation to being successful with grant applications. If someone is the first to publish a particular idea, we talk of them 'getting over the line' first. We talk of the 'spin-offs' in terms of patents and inventions and of the ways in which governments publish research 'league tables'. All of these are sporting terms.

A recent Australian Government White Paper on research and postgraduate education places emphasis on what it calls 'research training'. When I see this I always imagine the pink gravel of a running track. It is another example of the language of sport being used to describe an aspect of research. It is not that learning how to do research is the same as learning to run a race. But using the language of sport uncritically binds into the process assumptions about what is involved in it and places limitations on practice. For example, the idea of learning how to do research as a process of open exploratory inquiry is, if not precluded, at least restricted in the research training metaphor. Another common sporting metaphor is the idea of a research 'track record'. This could be further evidence for the dominance of masculinist perspectives in research, since the idea of the single career track implied here is rarely a common experience of female academics, even of those who are not balancing career and family. Be that as it may, the images used to describe research are predominantly from sports in which men dominate.

Research can readily be seen as a sport. Clearly there are rules and there are winners and losers. Like sports, those who are winning, perhaps in terms of the number of awards (research grants or publications) they have received, tend to accumulate more of the same. The rules are generally known or assumed by everyone who participates. This makes it very difficult for newcomers to establish themselves without a sponsor, supporter or mentor. It is not that research is a sport, but there are some aspects of research which are sports-like. Indeed, new researchers are often helped when we encourage them to treat research as if it were a game, rather than the whole of life.

Many sports are competitive yet require teamwork and cooperation. Research similarly involves both team collaboration – discussing ideas, peer review, team working, etc. – and competition. Sharing ideas and understanding with people of similar interests is, for many academics, how they conceptualize research (see Chapter Two). Where large amounts of equipment are concerned this is an imperative. Researchers are poised, like footballers, between competition and cooperation.

The discourse of war

But are these just harmless images of sport or is there something much more pernicious afoot? Sport is, albeit sometimes fiercely fought, only sport. What is far more worrying is that some of the same language is the language of war. Competition and cooperation in teams is consistent with images of battle, where combat, teamwork and camaraderie also coexist. Research projects may live or die on the research battlefield. Researchers' careers may flourish or wither. Most worryingly, the outcomes of research may well be a matter of life or death in relation to the effects on the planet.

Discussions of research 'impact', the 'targeting' of research, research 'strategies' all employ metaphors of war. Drawing on the idea of sporting awards, which originate from the idea of medals being awarded after combat, research awards are given to the brightest students. In Australia the term 'University medal' is used to refer to these awards, again drawing on images of war.

The convention of detaching the researcher from the ideas and phenomena of the research permits ideas to be treated as if they belonged to no one. Research findings have to be located within a tradition so new work has to be related to old.

This is usually done in the form of an academic jousting match. 'Argument' is an integral component of academic research. First you show the weaknesses or inadequacies of your opponents and then you put up your own flag 'mapping out your territory'. Since the argument takes place in a detached, highly impersonal manner, it is possible, indeed desirable, to critically 'attack' and 'destroy' the opponent's argument or show its inadequacies before claiming victory. Feyerabend (1978: 131) called it the 'civilized strangulation of the opponent'. Otherwise mild-mannered academics, referring to the ways in which their ideas are treated by their colleagues, frequently talk of getting 'slaughtered' in seminars. Lakatos (1981) talked of a 'battleground' between rival research programmes. Under the polite veneer of the university, cut-throat competition is afoot. The 'field of study' is no polite paddock. It is a field of battle where you mass behind your 'standards'. Feminists have drawn attention to the images of rape captured in traditional epistemologies on the one hand and descriptions of particular phenomena on the other (see for example the work of Spanier discussed in Chapter Six). In the subjugation of the human vis-à-vis the physical sciences, in the separation of subjective and objective, including denial of the subjective self in research as mentioned above, in the language and practices of destruction (breaking down matter to study it; fragmentation of knowledge into different discipline domains; etc.) we witness a war going on. It is sustained by the language of mechanization. Destruction and combat are endemic to academic life.

The drive towards competition, fuelled by government agencies and funding bodies, feeds on traditional rules of detachment and non-involvement. The shortage of research funding and the highly competitive nature of the grant applications process; restrictions in the numbers of high-level university positions (e.g. professors); research assessment exercises which determine university funding; all add to the competitive nature of research. Many new researchers I have encountered in the numerous workshops I have conducted are bruised by their early experiences of trying to establish a research career. It comes as a shock to them to realize that under the polite veneer of universities there is such ferocity. They come to realize that successful researchers are frequently those who have been able to 'pick themselves up' after an 'attack' on their ideas, or after being 'knocked back' over a grant proposal or article submitted for publication. It is not just new researchers who 'suffer'.

CHANGING THE DISCOURSE

The vision I have sketched in this book contradicts many of the images of battle. Research cannot do as Barnett (2000) suggests and help society how to live in a context of uncertainty and super-complexity while it is steeped in warlike behaviour. For, as Skolimowski (1994b) says, 'what you participate in, that you become'. We need new language, new narratives and new images if we are to encourage new ways of researching to grow. My hope is that being aware of warlike language and behaviour used in the name of academic research and its achievements may mean we can choose to research and therefore to live more peacefully in future.

Yet there are no general ways of doing this. New language and new ways of resolving conflicts must be explored and developed in each context. Fortunately this is beginning to happen, and in the remainder of this chapter I want to look at some of the ways in which discourse strategies are changing.

Traditional textual practices established the validity of an academic text outside of the text. Academic writing took place in specific places according to defined rules. Authority, as we have seen, resided in notions of logic and rigour hidden in impersonal argument. Traditional academic writing is an attempt to convince; to convey ideas; to communicate them in such a way that they will be understood as the author intends but without the author intruding. The language is sanitized by foregrounding the notion of a rational discourse based on evidence. Impersonality in language established the authority of the narrative.

Increasingly, academics are recognizing the pretentiousness of much of this kind of writing, and are not only questioning but also deliberately setting out to change it. We have noted a number of examples in this book. Authenticity, which was assumed within the traditional impersonal discourse, has become problematic. Indeed, postmodernism has not only questioned the power of grand narratives, it has, as Bicklen (1999) says, problematized the privileged position of the narrative authority itself. Authority is now having to be established within the text. Truth has become the outcome of various textual strategies (McWilliam et al. 1997).

These new strategies, Bicklen suggests, include researchers eschewing the language of impersonality and telling things about themselves, foregrounding the troubling work of the writing by writers drawing attention to the status of the text as a text, and taking account of individual personal experiences and knowledge which other people bring to the reading. A 'biographical/autobiographical turn' is occurring. Researchers are using their own perspective, making explicit their own position, gaining authority through rhetoric, describing their vulnerability, and/or their ignorance. These strategies rest on 'believability' as a criterion of narrative authority rather than the authority of faceless rationality. However, they raise the question of how believability is to be established; where the authority to speak comes from. Bicklen (1999) argues that this is a particular problem where the author cannot claim to belong to the group they are writing about, for example, in areas such as youth ethnography.

One of the effects of the shift in attitude towards a freeing of textual practices in relation to research writing has been to create a form of communication which has a greater chance of respecting the knowledge and perspectives of readers. The work then is recognized to be a resource for reflection rather than an imperialist vehicle for propagandizing a particular viewpoint. In doing so a new perspective is created which is neither the one the author had already, nor the one the other person had, but a dynamic, creative combination. Through such strategies, academic writing, which was traditionally about telling, is now becoming more a process of transforming.

Another way in which the discourse is changing is through the role of information technology. Multimedia undermines the narrative tradition that is embedded in culture (Laurillard 1995). The freedom to publish anything on the Internet means that in engaging with a subject of study the reader can begin anywhere and go in any direction. The linear nature of the narrative is broken down. This is being exploited through the non-linear reporting of research which is now emerging in hypertext theses. In these, the reader may return to a navigation page but explore the research in multiple ways. No two readers would be likely to take exactly the same route through the material. The wide availability of information on the Internet means that novices may become familiar with particular subjects of study without those in authority steering them or defining for them the significance in terms of the overarching narratives. Readers therefore exercise freedom and choice.

But in addition, the kinds of discourses which researchers are being required to engage in are changing and increasingly go beyond the impersonal discourses of academic journals and books. Academic discourse has frequently been so specialist that it can only be understood by those who are closest to the research. However, not only are researchers now required to provide academic papers for discussion by colleagues, but they are being seen in television studios, giving analysis of events or accounts of leading edge research. Increasingly, universities are exploiting the economic opportunities of their research programmes. Some university researchers, for example the physicist Stephen Hawking, have even become millionaires or pursued lucrative patents or set up companies to market products. Perhaps the public faces of key researchers is a way of convincing society that public money is well spent. These are some of the effects of Mode 2 knowledge (see Chapters Five and Eight). The enormous growth in science studies and popular magazines and books on a range of scientific topics is a consequence. Many researchers view this role of popular writing and communication as outside the purview of their research. But the need to communicate with a wider audience is now enshrined even within the process of applying for grants itself. For example, in Australia each application for funding under the two major government funding schemes requires a summary to be written in layperson's language. The summary is to be used for publicity but it also has to ensure that politicians who are not versed in the topic of the research are able to understand what they are funding.

But that is not all. Academic researchers are not only being asked to give an account of themselves. They are increasingly being asked to entertain. Postman saw emerging a culture in which all public discourse had become a mode of entertainment where all symbolic life was a variant of showbusiness (Abbs 1997). Research is part of this phenomenon, as anyone who reads a newspaper or watches television can testify. The entertainment may take the form of whole programmes devoted to a scientific topic (nature programmes, programmes about the environment, about intriguing aspects of history – the history of the popes, the history of the century, great moments in the history of music, etc.). Such programmes have been entertaining the population for some time. What is now also in evidence are programmes which use the audience for experiments. One example I saw recently was a study of whether when you see a smile you become happy. After only five minutes 50,000 people had telephoned their answers and the hypothesis was confirmed. Another aspect of academic research being used as entertainment is the reporting of research findings on topics which the general public have wondered about. Does walking the dog make you fit? Does taking tiny babies on aircraft lead to cot deaths? How is the immune system affected by feelings of guilt? Many of these examples have novelty value.

The ways in which research is presented in the media affects public perceptions of the nature of research. Future research agendas are likely to reflect the research the community at large is interested in. Yet we should be wary of the view of research which is presented on television. For example, Collins and Pinch (1998: 147) argue that, even though in a television discussion of the work of the CERN team who discovered the 'z' particle, the messiness of the process of discovery was displayed, the overall message was that 'triumphalism ruled'. It was hailed as a great scientific discovery.

I was asked recently in a workshop on design as research whether a pedestrian precinct could be considered research. I must admit I have difficulty in getting my head around this notion. I believe that there is something over and above the creation of an artefact such as a painting or a building or a performance of a piece of music, or a pedestrian precinct for that matter, which determines whether something is considered to be the outcome of an academic research process. But this may be set to change if current debates in design and performance disciplines are anything to go by. What we can say, however, is that there are no grand theories about how research should be recorded and reported. These questions have to be continuously negotiated in each context. We have no idea what strategies will be used in the future to share ideas generated in research. What we do know is that the variety of forms of expression is likely to grow.

Chapter 12

Research and the future

You have asked three questions. But you have not asked the questions which you need to ask.

(Richard Wagner)

'But why, Grandad?'

Silence.

'Why?' Then again, insistently poking the old man's shoulder, the little boy again asked: 'Why, Grandad?'

The old man, head bowed, felt the heavy weight of censure on his shoulders.

The little boy tried a different tack: 'Those people . . . all those people . . . they spent such a lot of money and time. They did such a lot of work . . . and . . . and . . . they didn't even think about how it would be for us.'

Shaking his white head, Grandad in low tones: 'No.'

He couldn't himself remember the twentieth century. He had been but a little boy, even younger than young Seth here, at the turn of the millennium. How could he now explain to one so young what it had been about?

Seth said: 'I suppose because there were so many terrible wars, they had to spend their time working out how to escape to other planets. That's probably why they spent such a lot of time discovering stars.'

'I don't think anybody thought they were going to escape. Oh well, there were some cranks who thought they were going to colonize Mars, but generally . . . no, I think it was more to do with getting caught up with just the thrill of discovering things. You know like when you find out something you get excited about it.'

'Oh come on!' Graham protested. 'Surely you're not going to end with a kind of doomsday scenario: human beings wipe out earth's ecology leading to the destruction of the environment. Little boy wonders why the dramatic climate change, people either dying of earthquakes, erupting volcanoes, storms, flooding, tornadoes, etc., or being taken over by AIDS or some other dreaded disease yet to be discovered? Research leads to devastation and destruction. Human life almost wiped out!'

'Well no,' I countered. 'But it's tempting. I mean we're poised here, aren't we? Things could go one way or the other.'

'Or they could just go on being neither one thing nor the other.'

'Mm?' I wasn't sure what he meant.

Graham continued: 'Well, you know. Things could just potter on. That's what we do isn't it? Just soldier on, politicians and the like mucking things up from time to time, failing to understand the nature of the academic profession, wanting to tame it, wanting to . . . oh I don't know, keep it under wraps.'

'Well you can't blame them. They have got limited resources. They want to make sure universities use the money wisely.'

'Well that's true but it's premised on thinking that people are not working very hard. Everyone I know wants to come up with a Nobel prizewinning idea. They're all working like slaves to finish this or that project.'

'Yes but are they solving the world's problems?'

'Oh, that's it, is it? Perhaps there will be a disaster and humans will be wiped out.'

'Well no, I'm not . . .'

Graham cut in: 'And perhaps there won't. All the government wants to do is to count what we do; measure it. Or something. They don't care if we solve problems. I don't think they believe we can solve any serious problems. I just wish they'd let us get on and do our jobs. They're always trying to predict research outcomes; to sort of second-guess what the answers might be. But they don't believe in us. They don't even see the problems we are trying to solve. It would take us all our energy to convince them that the problems were problems. So we might as well do what we've always done and just get on with things as we see them.'

'Well I think that's a bit defeatist,' I countered. 'I mean, things could go the other way. I mean, suppose people started to say "okay, the purpose of research is to solve the world's problems. Let's tackle them." Poverty, say, that's one we haven't cracked yet. Let's have a major world initiative to really work on solving that. Then war. Put bags of resources and energy into really knowing the causes and really working on that, then climate change, disease, famine and so on.'

> 'Yes but in the first place you have to have people acknowledge that these are solvable problems.'
>
> 'Aren't they?'
>
> 'Well we haven't solved them yet!'
>
> 'No but that's because we have been looking in the wrong places. We have had methods for doing research which avoid the things we don't want to know. So we haven't solved problems we don't want to know can be solved. We need some new ways of doing things.'

This book has been concerned with the fascinating and absorbing process whereby academics in universities investigate and come to know the world and with the contexts in which that process operates. I have argued, following Barnett, that in a world characterized by uncertainty, complexity and plurality, academic research must go beyond existing methods and agendas to develop new forms of research, to expand existing frameworks of knowledge and knowing, and to teach society how to live. All the way through the book we have seen the nature of research presented as a picture of a complex, puzzling, kaleidoscopic landscape. It engages the brightest minds, but puts brakes on their thought, requiring them to define problems and issues within narrow boundaries. It is at one and the same time the source of creativity and of constraint. It is heavily dependent on long-term processes yet demands short-term outcomes. It influences people's thinking in society in a profound and fundamental way, yet is almost invisible to those same people. Throughout the book, through the discussion of the different issues, it has become apparent that a number of conflicting, incompatible agendas are being pursued.

Academic research, by its very nature, is a critical pursuit. It is reflexive, generating critiques of itself. This has led to the current sense that research has lost its way. For example, we have observed increasing consciousness of the social role of research and at the very same time increasing scepticism about what it has achieved and what it has to say. Through the activities of researchers on social thought and philosophy, critical perspectives such as postmodernism have been defined. Yet these traditions pull research up by its roots, tugging at the very core of its being. Academic research is living the postmodern condition of uncertainty. In addition, the critical self-questioning of science in the popular scientific literature manifests some deep concerns within the academic community itself about the progress and viability of large scale research projects. Such work, as we saw in Chapter Seven, has even questioned whether the really important questions have been answered. Other writers, in the face of postmodernist claims that there are no grand theories explaining everything, have propounded grand theories which purport to explain everything! There used to be strong social biases towards the idea that anything scientific is a good thing (see e.g. Midgley 1992). These having been critically questioned inside and outside the academy, scientists are critically questioning what they themselves do.

I think the self-referencing critique of research is something many of the politicians of the 1980s and 1990s have failed to grasp. Demands for accountability in research are understandable given pressure on public expenditure but they do not take account of the fact that the process of discovery sooner or later questions and then reinvents itself. What we understand research to be clearly changes with different generations. Historical analyses of the way research has evolved seem to suggest that it goes in 30–50 year cycles. Perhaps this is too long for many politicians. The critiques may take place in different areas of study and they do not necessarily emanate from within particular disciplinary areas. But ultimately, they have to be taken account of by all.

To understand the nature of research we have had to engage with many ironies and contradictions. This is a paradox since, as we have seen, research is often thought to be inherently a rational procedure. We have also seen that within the indeterminate, confusing and conflicting tensions, there are new ways of researching waiting in the wings. Let us review some of the paradoxes that have emerged in earlier discussions. Then we will be in a position to consider future directions.

First, although research has been intimately tied to what we want to know (the questions Western society considers important to answer and the problems considered important to solve), frequently researchers have asked and answered questions no one else is asking or wanting answered. This is seen most clearly when, for example, researchers interest themselves in other cultures and practices to their own, where there are people in their own culture who have no interest in them and no desire to know the things the researchers seek to know about them. Intrusive colonial research on indigenous peoples is a legacy of this and is perpetuated in the so-called 'Human Genome Project'. So there is always the question of who wants to know and, as we have seen throughout this book, this is tied to who holds the power.

A frequent assumption has been that an increase in knowledge implies a retreat of ignorance and that there is a direction to the way knowledge is going. The idea that we can know everything there is to know about the universe was based on the idea of a coherent, continuous reality which obeyed laws we could discover that applied at every point of space and time near and far, and the idea that all future events are determinable and predictable. What research has shown us, however, is that this is all impossible. We always look from our own vantage point, and there are many phenomena and events we cannot predict. Indeed, 'to every increase in knowledge there corresponds an increase in ignorance; to new types of knowledge there correspond new types of ignorance' (Ceruti 1994: 25).

It used to be assumed that time is linear and irreversible and that the development of knowledge was linear and cumulative. The organization of research projects should accordingly be designed on such a linear assumption of time so that research advances sequentially. Yet time is part of the equation. Time can be polyphonic, personal, or viewed as cyclical (Brady 2000), like the Australian aboriginal conception of time: not necessarily linear nor unidirectional. As modern physics has shown us, on certain scales it can be discontinuous and reversible.

Research practice shares these paradoxes. Ironically, funded projects with defined objectives mean that research is likely to move more slowly and be out of date when the project is finished. Even slower is the application to practice. We have seen an example of this in our earlier discussion of the ways that postmodernism, while having enormous influence theoretically, is taking much longer to influence research actions. Since in research you have to transcend the starting point, you do not know where it is going. Research is a systematic planned procedure yet it is always coming up with unexpected surprises.

In Chapter Seven we saw that problems which depend on a complex set of decisions made by independent agents cannot be solved by traditional methods of analysis. Even the most sophisticated and complex computer modelling can fail to predict what will happen (Casti 1997). Yet believing we are omniscient, Ceruti (1994: 16) says, we think it is possible to translate the universe into a 'finite domain of discourse' and the more we endeavour to do this the more we 'come to know the universe as infinite'. As Bronowski elegantly puts it: 'one aim of the physical sciences has been to give an exact picture of the material world. One achievement of physics in the twentieth century has been to prove that the aim is unattainable' (Bronowski 1976). But it is not just the material world we cannot picture exactly. In this book we have touched on many traditions of thought which are telling us loud and clear there is no one vantage point from which to view the physical, social and psychological world around us. We are destined to look from a variety of limited perspectives, we are tied to our particular cultural spectacles and we are doomed to eternal debate.

In some ways that would suggest we are freed from the constraints that finding an 'exact picture' entails. We have more freedom, but that at one and the same time is also a constraint. Postmodernism, for example, in freeing us from 'foundational discourses', constrains the kinds of explanations which are possible. Overarching grand narratives, for example, are not. There is, as we have persistently noted, a tension in academic research between freedom and control, creativity and constraint.

We have seen throughout this book, however, that notwithstanding critical questioning of traditional research boundaries, there is evidence at the margins of a freeing up of notions of what research is and what it can do. Slowly, almost imperceptibly, new research is breaking the rules and defining new ones. Studies which break conventions are burgeoning. But it is not a question of 'anything goes'. Rather, as we have seen, there is serious questioning going on, particularly in the newer disciplines, about what can be called research. The results can be seen, for example, in the ways what is called 'qualitative research' is changing. Such research is now often a far cry from the days where it was conceived as an alternative to quantitative research. Much of what used to be called post-positive research might well now come under the qualitative research heading. This is a way of making what I have called 'experiential research' accepted within the mainstream. Or rather the mainstream is redefining itself.

In addition, research conventions are changing. There are slow shifts in university rules governing thesis presentation, which are being exploited by adventurous students. My university recently agreed a policy of accepting theses submitted electronically. This soon resulted in an Internet-based thesis (Greenwood 1999). This kind of work is opening up the possibility of different kinds of research discourses, ones which question the narrative tradition, as we saw in Chapter Eleven. There are increasing numbers of journals being developed which encourage or accept different kinds of writing of articles. It is slowly becoming easier for those whose research methodology is highly innovative to have their work published. Electronic publishing is also opening up all kinds of opportunities for different kinds of research publications and communications, for example, journals that publish papers in progress, as we saw in Chapter Eight.

HAVE WE ASKED THE QUESTIONS WE NEED TO ASK?

We see academic research taking on the conditions of postmodernity, but still grounded in Enlightenment thinking. When we look closely at research practice and its relationship to society, we cannot escape seeing an outdated epistemology infusing practice. Consistent with the idea of a knowable universe discussed above, modern research holds to the idea that one day all would be solved. True there are many positives and we should not neglect them: elimination of basic diseases, convenience of modern living, etc. Yet along the way we have created horrors and we are living the consequences. An epistemology based on fragmentation, which cut humans off from the world of which they are a part and which denied the value of their experience, has unfortunately created a world which reflects such methodology, values and ethos.

> Many of the taken for granted improvements in the quality of human life and many of the benefits of technological advance, can be traced back to their origins in academic enquiry and exploration. On the darker side, physicists may share a particular sense of responsibility for the creation of atomic and nuclear weapons, and engineers for the dubious blessings of nuclear power. Chemistry has given rise to its own forms of weaponry: biology to the possibility of bacteriological warfare and, along another pathway to the ethical uncertainties of genetic engineering. The pure and applied sciences are not alone in their openness to such accusations. The appeal to history lies behind some of the most bitter territorial and racial disputes; sociological theorizing has given birth to powerful and sometimes destructive ideological movements; economics shares some of the blame for disastrous financial policies as well as some of the credit for successful ones. All in all, the outcome of research must be rated as a mixed blessing to humanity.
>
> (Becher 1989: 132)

Distinguishing between the process of discovering new knowledge and the act of using it, academic researchers have been able to distance themselves from its consequences (Becher 1989). Yet the more research has advanced, the more distrustful people have become of it. Nowhere is this more evident than in the debates about the genetic engineering of foods. Fuller (1998), in an article in the *Independent on Sunday*, highlights a key paradox. At the same time as books which popularize science have been selling millions of copies, he suggests, there has been a dramatic slowing down in enrolments in science courses at universities (Fuller 1998:71). He argues that the power of science rests on first its distinctive social organization, then its 'concerted political effort to apply the results of scientific research to all aspects of society and thirdly, the control which scientists have hitherto exerted over how their history is told'. One of the ways in which they do this is to misinterpret things which non-scientists say about science, attributing their pronouncements to ignorance of its practices. However, Fuller argues:

> The failure of science to live up to its own manufactured expectations has probably done more harm to science's social standing in recent years than anything science studies has ever done. Science studies had nothing to do with the PR disasters associated with Aids and BSE research.
>
> (Fuller 1998: 71)

Fuller argues that those who call themselves scientists who engage in specialist activities and communicate with their peers in a narrow circle of colleagues and acquaintances are rather alien from people's everyday concerns. Yet without others, including politicians, physicians and policymakers who use science more or less as it was intended and 'ordinary' people in society who are the 'consumers' of science, science would not enjoy the power that it has (Fuller 1998). Yet, as Fuller demonstrates, scientists have a contempt for such people and misinterpret their intentions when they say things about science. This is leading people to distance themselves from it. The arrogance of modern research has been its downfall.

Graham was tying his shoelace. I seized the opportunity his silence presented. 'We've got to find a way through this incoherent, kaleido-scopic, ever-changing world to lead the way. I mean . . . like Barnett says, research in academic settings has to lead the way.' Graham sighed and shook his head. I decided to try again: 'The failure . . . the huge failure of the Western research tradition is that it hasn't made us wise. We need wisdom.'

'So, you're saying that in this kind of pluralistic uncertain world, academic research has to take a lead in showing how to develop wisdom? It can't do that. It's not set up to do that.' Graham was adamant and for a moment I felt the argument had been swept from under my feet.

But I wasn't going to give in that easily. 'But it's changing. You can see that,' I said tenaciously. 'If we consciously give encouragement to the way it is changing then it can. If we do and if we can find a way whereby research can lead us to become wise, then we will have not only learnt how to research in conditions of postmodernity, we'll also have learnt how to live.'

'I think that's just too idealistic', Graham, now looking distracted, said. He got up and went over to his computer which had just indicated there was a new email message. He clicked the mouse and read the screen, pulling a face as he did so. Returning to his chair he said: 'With all the pressure from governments and funding bodies to adopt atomistic, outcomes-oriented approaches to research . . . er . . . and as you yourself have argued, and all the support there is for the idea of research as a commodity, how can you possibly convince senior academic managers that research should be free to find ways to develop wisdom? It's just not on.'

Ignoring the fact that I thought I had made it clear that I was writing for new researchers, not people managing research, I protested: 'But we have a choice. We can move towards more transformative, holistic approaches to research within the academy if we want to enough.'

'But we've got to follow outside agendas. If we are going to get the funding we need then we have to apply for grants and publish and do all the things that the university and the government require of us. Research is not isolated from political agendas. You've argued this strongly in your book.'

'Yes, but I've also argued that we have a choice in the way we reconcile the different agendas for research: social, personal, academic and governmental. As I say, we've got a choice. Researchers have got a choice. Universities have got a choice. Governments have got a choice. It's not all inevitable. It doesn't just happen.'

'Mm.' Graham didn't sound convinced.

I continued: 'By pursuing the idea of research as occupying contested space I hope I have shown the different and conflicting visions being pursued.'

'And you have also shown that which things are pursued is related to who's got the power.'

'I know. Well the aim of the book is to be thought-provoking. I mean . . . I'm not going to resolve all the issues. I actually hope that my readers will continue thinking about all these things after the covers are closed. I'm not looking for a grand theory! Methodologies for research which endeavour to contradict these ways and which value process not products are, as I have shown, waiting in the wings, but they are on the margins. Whatever you say, there is a desire for harmony, beauty, wisdom, integrity and coherence.'

'Oh yeh! . . . and all is disharmony, fragmentation, fear and incoherence,' Graham parodied. 'There you go again. Getting into your gloom and doom scenario again.'

'No, I'm not. I really think the groundwork has been laid for new methods to be implemented.'

'But the next article must be sent off; the next funding application polished.' Graham's practicality was a hard nut to crack.

'I think we just have to have more time to sort out the mess; to come up with some new ideas. Individually, and in research teams I mean. The idea of research productivity skews the research towards the short term and the trivial.'

'But you've got to have outcomes.'

'Whether or not the work is ready for it? Research is a long-term investment. Or it should be. The government has a three-year plan for higher education. Our university has a five-year plan. The Tasmanian Forestry Commission has a 500-year plan!'

'Well it's obvious you can't grow trees overnight and that huon pine trees take hundreds of years to mature.'

I was now feeling Graham might be getting the message, so continued: 'It's less obvious with research that long-term strategies are needed. If we're committed to solving the world's problems we have to allow time for creativity. I believe that academic research has to continue to be in a position to deal with the big issues. Academics have to be free to engage in sustained study and thinking, and this takes time. They shouldn't be tied to trivial short-term outputs and demands that they demonstrate performance every year or so. That's like trying to speed up the growth of trees. Academic research has to resist demands for short-term quick results.'

'It sounds like you're advocating a return to some kind of golden age like in the days when academics spent much of their time sitting in the Mediterranean sun reading and chatting to the locals throughout a long summer vacation of idleness.'

'Well in my experience there never was such a time, however much the myth was asserted.'

Graham, still toeing the institutional line, argued: 'Anyway, I don't think that there's a case for academics saying they are doing research and yet not having anything tangible to show for it.'

'But when they did this, I think it was more likely to have been because they were giving more time to teaching than because they were idle. I think governments have a lot to answer for in their inability to understand what is involved in engaging in a sustained piece of study. It's like in David Lodge's book *Nice Work* where he asks her how many hours she works and she says, "I work all the time."'

Graham nodded and smiled, then suggested lunch.

On the way to the staff lounge I reiterated my firm belief that we have to find new ways of researching that are not based on tired notions of knowledge and methodology but which embody our values. 'I know it's a tough task,' I said. 'There are no overarching theories either to direct our actions or to aspire to finding, so who we are, how we act and how we communicate are all important.' We each got a ploughman's at the bar and as we sat munching our way through cheese and French bread I explained my ideas about the relationship between how we research and what we research, and the importance of paying attention to research communication, research action and research consciousness. By then Graham was in a receptive mood. Deep down, he too knew that the current situation was unworkable in the long run. He was sceptical about how it could change but his heart was in the right place. He wouldn't admit it to his departmental colleagues but instinctively he was looking for an escape from the treadmill of grant and article writing. Wistfully he said: 'We can't do research if we are not free to explore . . . if there is not time for reflection. If only there were the freedom of timelessness so that true consideration could be given to problems and issues, as they deserve.'

'I agree. There are some important problems to solve and creative minds need to be free to solve them.'

WHERE TO NOW?

Surely the outcome of academic inquiry should be what Maxwell describes as: 'our enhanced capacity to solve our fundamental problems of living' (Maxwell 1984: 73). For no intelligent person can escape the fact that there are enormous problems facing the people of the world. Research has been as much responsible for drawing attention to problems as it has been responsible for solving them. Indeed, academic research has been exceptionally successful in delineating problems. Problems of global warming, for example, are evident because researchers are able to measure air quality, calculate ozone emissions, measure the hole in the ozone layer and so on. Similarly we understand more now about the relationship of war to poverty and hunger. Scientists and social scientists in particular have explained complex interactions of physical phenomena and social events, and a literate, articulate public has through the media, learnt of complex and difficult problems for which there are, as yet, no solutions. The facts of their existence are inescapable to anyone in the world who has a radio receiver or can read a newspaper or a book. What research has not taught us is how to solve such problems. But it is not just the solving of problems or the answering of questions that is needed. Academic research, as we have seen, has been straitjacketed in narrow methodologies, circumscribed by distinct disciplinary explanations, restricted within a narrow range of acceptable phenomena available for investigation, and imprisoned in narrow notions of explanation, all of which have limited the development of our capacity to solve existing, let alone unforeseen, problems. For even if all of today's world problems were to be solved there will always be another clutch of problems waiting in the wings, 'every new breakthrough quickly becoming the source of more problems' (Fuller 1998: 71).

As we have seen throughout this book, all researchers have their own ideas about what research is and what they are doing when they carry it out. These ideas are their attempts to make sense of the conventions of research and the context in which they are working and living. The ways in which researchers think about their research reflect the changes as well as the dilemmas posed by old and new ideas about research and by the fact they are increasingly being asked to give an account of themselves. University researchers are caught between their governments' funding emphases on performance, product and output, and their desire to get on and do their research as they see fit and given their capacity for critical reflection, for they too are part of the very society which seeks to question their activities. In this book we have seen that many academic researchers are ignoring the conditions of postmodernity, getting on with their research as best they may, treating postmodernism either as simply generating new content areas or as having no relevance to their discipline or to the next laboratory experiment or paper. Performance has frequently become the chief imperative. Like many other researchers I have been applying for research grants. It is a process of learning the rules and then working very hard to apply them. In most cases it is an activity doomed to failure. But like the mythical Sisyphus who was destined forever to keep rolling a rock up a mountain, when we are knocked back, we keep on picking ourselves up and starting again. That is the world we are in. It is a crazy world. But it is a world of our own choosing.

Yet one thing we know about creativity in research is that answers frequently come unexpectedly and from unplanned sources inside and outside the university. In attempting to understand the world in which we live, we have frequently learnt about it in ways we did not expect. In exploring the role of intuition in science Marton *et al.* (1994) examined Nobel prizewinners' conceptions of scientific intuition. A number gave expression to the way in which unexpected insights occur when least expected. Careful planning towards known goals is contrary to this. Notwithstanding that there are many people jumping up and down to maintain the status quo, a quiet revolution is taking place. If in this book I have shown that the narrow way is not the only way and if I have given courage to any creative minds to exercise that creativity, then the book will have been worthwhile.

If new researchers have found in it a way of reflecting on the culture and practice of research in ways which enlarge the domain over which they can exercise freedom of choice, then I will be more than pleased. We have choices over the directions in which research is heading, both in terms of the topics we choose to explore and the ways in which we choose to explore them. To be constrained by narrow agendas because we are unaware of alternatives or afraid of retribution is unforgivable. I hope that in this book I have encouraged, indeed or opened up possibilities, for new thinking, for new kinds of knowledge, new kinds of scholarship and new learning, for defining new rules, for creating new methodologies as yet undreamed of, for developing new forms of expression of research outcomes, for solving old problems in new ways as well as opening up new questions and creating new discourses, and for involving the person in the process. Research is clearly going to remain contested space for some time to come, but the weaker voices must grow stronger if the stronger voices are to lose some of their power.

When gardeners sow seeds, they sow many more than are going to germinate. Animals and birds have more offspring than are likely to survive. Millions of human sperm result in one fertilized egg. In order for academics to contribute to the solving of important questions, it has to be recognized that some of the seeds will fall on stony ground. Much of the research which is done in universities may not have a direct outcome. But the useless stuff may prove useful in the end (Brady 2000). The person who does not succeed in bringing new knowledge to light in publications may be a superb mentor of a postgraduate student who in turn may turn up a major discovery. The teaching of new researchers is an important task and much research has to be carried out by such teachers in order to prepare them to educate the next generation of researchers. You may need to have lots of researchers doing research on lots of things for just one good idea to emerge, because you can never predict what a particular project or a particular researcher will end up discovering. The outcomes are rarely what we think they are going to be. This is the excitement of research.

In a world characterised by uncertainty and super-complexity, a vital task of a university education is to prepare students to solve a range of interconnected, frequently unforeseen problems that will persist long after the student leaves university (Barnett 1997b). Tolerance of ambiguity is a necessary requirement of a super-complex, uncertain world where there are no right answers. Personal and professional studies in which the student of the future will thus be engaged, will be conducted amid uncertainty and blurred boundaries. To learn how to operate in a context of confusion and ambivalence is an important task facing the higher education of the future and its students. For leadership is required in teaching society how to do it too.

'What you participate in, that you become' (Skolimowski 1994b). We move towards and we become what we think about. The way we research affects our potential. The way I talk to myself affects my potential. The way societies think of themselves and the world around them affects their collective potential. You can see what this means when you consider the effects of becoming able to leave Earth and travel in space in the twentieth century. Now that we have the possibility to rise above the Earth and to view it from above, we are able to conceive possibilities which hitherto were closed to us. Indeed, perhaps the most influential factor fuelling the ecological movement and the conception of the planet as in danger came into play when we viewed its fragility and beauty from outside. We are now able to conceptualise the Earth as a whole. This influences our actions towards it. It influences the ways in which we think about the past and about the future. It underscores the choices we have in moving forward in directions which are socially and ecologically harmful or in ones which lead to harmony and wisdom.

We have a choice whether we leave ourselves out of our own thinking or whether we involve ourselves fully in coming to know not only the world in which we live but also ourselves. Academic research, as a key influence on the ways in which people conceptualize the world and ourselves in relation to it, can similarly choose participation and integration or fragmentation and destruction.

We must have the courage to behave as if the utopian vision were here now. The shift from dystopia to utopia will come about only if researchers have the courage to speak up for and practise change. This is not just about being resistant; it is about creating new ways of doing things, of researching. Not just doing what is needed to survive, and fabricating practice as we noted in discussing research as a commodity in Chapter Eight, but thriving and being creative in new ways.

As I rummaged in a bookshop while researching for this volume, a book entitled *Quakers and Nazis* leapt out of a sale to grab my attention (Schmitt 1997). It documents the ways in which German Quakers worked within the Nazi regime to uphold a way of life diametrically opposed to it. They lived a humanitarian vision: hiding Jews, alleviating suffering, worshipping with Nazis present and helping people to escape. The new ways of researching I have been sketching in this book stress new ways of being, acting and communicating, developing new consciousness through what Barnett (1997a) calls critical action. It is vital that we have the courage to do this through new forms of research within an academic regime still characterized by an emphasis on performativity, competition and the accumulation of dubious rewards. For as Veronica Brady (2000) says, 'we ought to be difficult people'. Our values are important in moving research forward and these will undoubtedly be contested. Recognizing that our values are mediated by our gender, our class, our sexual orientation and our ethnicity, we now know that there are no external criteria of truth we can apply. Among other things, I think this means listening carefully (and really hearing) those who have different gender, class, sexual orientation and ethnicity. Attempting to reconcile views we cannot truly grasp with our own is a difficult process. I believe we need to find new pathways to explore different truths. But we should not suppose we will ever reach perfect understanding or complete agreement. It is the journey that matters, not what may lie at the end of it.

FACTS AND FICTIONS

At the outset I indicated that this book was to be idiosyncratic and influenced by my personal concerns, and this it has clearly been. My efforts to understand what drives research are clearly rooted in my personal experiences within the academic community and the ways in which these were shaped by the diverse influences on my life. As I bring the book to a close I am led to ask: is the argument about research as contested space just an argument about me and my research, my journey, my experience? Do I suggest that research occupies contested space because for me personally it is contested space and have I objectified this personal concern born of my history and my career, writing it large for an academic audience using logic and example to back up my personal interests and dilemmas? So is the argument that research is contested space my fiction?

Clearly it is. Yet in owning this, I believe I illustrate a facet of the nature of research which I cannot otherwise demonstrate, and which research (by its very nature!) more often than not denies. Research *is* about exploring our personal concerns. Think about it. Much research is a hard slog. Day after day the researcher is engaged in routine and, to the outsider, what may seem boring tasks. What keeps us going is the inherent fascination we feel about the subject of study, the ideas we come up with while engaged in the boring searches, the routine laboratory work, the transcribing of umpteen interview transcripts and so on. Research has to become part of the people who carry it out. It is through the systematic and sustained engagement with ideas that new realities are made. It is through the interpretations made by creative individuals that new 'discoveries', new fictions, emerge. For research is the creating of fictions which we then attempt to live. Whether our 'fictions' are also 'fact' is not the point. Some are. Some are not. Within a particular frame of reference some are. Within that same frame of reference, some are not. There are no facts or fictions which are not within any frame of reference. So we create a fiction and this then becomes our reality.

Ultimately through my research I come to know myself. If in coming to know myself I also help others to know themselves or to know the world in which we live so much the better. Another aspect which I have pointed to throughout this book is that research both needs to and has this power to change the lives of those who carry it out. Academics are people with influence over students and over universities, so this is not a trivial thing to say. In this book I have argued that how we do research is as important as what we research and as important as what we find out. For research has to go beyond the academy and teach us how to live. Research inevitably has both a personal and a social dimension. New forms of academic inquiry have the power to explicitly promote and support personal inquiry. I am not just talking about social scientific or psychological research here. As Ceruti says, 'the reintegration of the observer into his or her own descriptions gets to the root of the most important developments of the physical and biological sciences in this century' (Ceruti 1994: 24). If anyone has learnt how to operate in a context of uncertainty and super-complexity, it is those new researchers who have pioneered the way to new research methods and new domains of discourse. These are the researches which are now teaching us how to live.

If through the research I do solve any of the world's problems or if I help others to move a step closer to solving the world's problems, that is great. But I contend that I cannot help to solve the world's problems without coming to know myself. For many of the issues academic research addresses are escapes from ourselves: our humanity and our essentially special, yet nothing particularly special, place in the cosmos. For example, whether or not elements of life on Earth are found elsewhere in the universe is irrelevant to our need to learn to recognize the special nature of the Earth's biodiversity and to live peacefully and harmoniously with each other and with our particular planet. If we do not then we will continue to use research as an escape from the realities of our existence. We will not solve the world's problems if we continue research traditions which are an escape from who, what and where we are. In other words, we will not solve the world's problems if we continue to run from those things we fear to know. We will not solve the world's problems if we continue to practise research which is a defence against knowing those things we do not want to know. Neither will we be in a position to teach society how to live.

The book has suggested that the process of research must move us beyond the despair of postmodernism and the drudgery of commodified knowledge to discover anew how to inquire in ways which not only take forward our collective understanding of the world but provide exemplars of how others might live. It has also provided suggestions about how research must change to do this. Research must acknowledge its disasters as well as its achievements; its rigidities as well as its creativity; its power and its powerlessness; its openness and its dogmatic blinkers. A shift of focus is needed if research is to be of value to the academy and to society in the future. That shift of focus is coming about by a changed appreciation of the value of the processes of research; critical questioning at every stage of the relationship of the research to society; definition of rules for research within each research project; making ethical behaviour and critical understanding of the nature of knowledge part of research discourse in each local context. The shift of focus is coming about by recognizing that research has hitherto investigated in limited ways a limited range of phenomena. And it is coming about by being open to new problems and new questions. In the activities carried out as research, in the ways research is communicated and in the consciousness of the researcher, inquiry is becoming increasingly conscious of its reflexivity, and this is set to continue. In such ways the academy can provide a new justification for its existence: teaching society how to live in a climate of uncertainty.

There is now a new millennium before us. It presents as near as the human race ever gets to a new chance; a chance to start again. Surely we must direct our research efforts to making the world a better place. There might not be any grand theories to direct how we do this but we have some clear ideas about what would be a better world. I would put freedom from poverty and hunger, respect for the environment, harmony and love on my list. I would put valuing each individual unique person including ourselves and I would also put respect for the wonder of the presence of life on earth. We must ask a wider range of questions; we must direct our research energies into solving problems and not just understanding them; and we must put ourselves back into the picture. Research presents the ablest and most creative minds in the world with the possibility of helping to make our life on this planet harmonious and happy and fulfilling. Let us, in humility, use the opportunity wisely.

References

Abbs, P. (1997) 'The arts, postmodern culture and the politics of aesthetic education', in Barnett, R. and Griffin, A. (eds) *The End of Knowledge in Higher Education*. London, Cassell, 128–38.

American Psychological Association (1981) 'Ethical principles of psychologists', *American Psychologist* 36: 633–8.

Appelbaum, P. S. and Rosenbaum, A. (1989) 'Tarasoff and the researcher: does the duty to protect apply in the research setting?' *American Psychologist* 44 (June): 885–94.

Ball, S. (2000) 'Performativities and fabrications in the education economy: towards the performative society', *Australian Educational Researcher* 27 (2): 1–23.

Bannister, D. (1981) 'Personal construct theory and research method', in Reason, P. and. Rowan, J. (eds) *Human Inquiry*. London, John Wiley, 191–9.

Barnes, B. (1982) *T. S. Kuhn and Social Science*. London, Macmillan.

Barnett, R. (1997a) *Higher Education: A Critical Business*. Buckingham, Open University Press and Society for Research in Higher Education.

—— (1997b) *Realizing the University*. Inaugural professorial lecture. London, Institute of Education, University of London.

—— (1997c) 'A knowledge strategy for universities', in Barnett, R. and Griffin, A. (eds) *The End of Knowledge in Higher Education*. London, Cassell, 166–79.

—— (2000) *Realizing the University: In an Age of Super-Complexity*. Buckingham, Open University Press.

—— and Griffin, A. (1997) (eds) *The End of Knowledge in Higher Education*. London, Cassell.

Bauman, Z. (1992) *Intimations of Postmodernity*. London, Routledge.

Bazeley, P., Kemp, L., Stevens, K., Asmar, C., Grbich, C., Marsh, H. and Bhathal, R. (1996) *Waiting in the Wings: A Study of Early Career Academic Researchers in Australia*. Commissioned report No 50. Canberra, Australian Government Publishing Service.

Becher, T. (1989) *Academic Tribes and Territories: Intellectual Enquiry and the Cultures of Disciplines*. Buckingham, Society for Research into Higher Education and Open University Press.

Belenky, M. F., Clinchy, B. M., Goldberger, N. R. and Tarule, J. M. (1986) *Women's Ways of Knowing: The Development of Self, Voice and Mind*. New York, Basic Books.

Bicklen, S. (1999) 'Markers of validity: the narrator's authority in qualitative studies', Keynote address to the Association for Qualitative Research Conference: Issues of Rigour in Qualitative Research. Melbourne, Vic.

Biggs, J. (1996) 'Enhancing teaching through constructive alignment', *Higher Education* 32: 1–18.

Blake, N. (1997) 'Truth, identity and community in the university', in Barnett, R. and Griffin, A. (eds) *The End of Knowledge in Higher Education*. London, Cassell, 151–64.

Bondi, H. (1975) 'What is progress in science?' in Harré, R. (ed.) *Problems of Scientific Revolution*. Oxford, Oxford University Press, 1–10.

Bowden, J. and Marton, F. (1998) *The University of Learning: Beyond Quality and Competence in Higher Education*. London, Kogan Page.

Boyer, E. (1990) *Scholarship Reconsidered: Priorities for the Professoriate*. Carnegie Foundation for the Advancement of Teaching. Princeton, NJ, University of Princeton.

Boyer, E. (1996) 'The scholarship of engagement', *Journal of Public Service and Outreach* 1 (1): 11–20.

Brady, V. (2000) 'Transformations of the expectation: the quest for the internal combustion of higher education', in James, R., Milton, J. and Gabb, R. (eds) 'Cornerstones of higher education', *Research and Development in Higher Education Vol. 22*. The Higher Education Research and Development Society of Australasia, Canberra, ACT, 5–11.

Brew, A. (1988) 'Research as learning', unpublished doctoral dissertation, University of Bath, Bath, UK.

—— (1993) 'Unlearning through experience', in Boud, D., Cohen, R. and Walker, D. (eds) *Using Experience for Learning*. Buckingham, Society for Research into Higher Education and Open University Press, 87–98.

—— (ed.) (1995) *Directions in Staff Development*. Buckingham, Society for Research in Higher Education and Open University Press.

—— (1998a) 'Understanding research: exploring different conceptions', in Higgs, J. and Cant, R. (eds) *Writing Qualitative Research*. Sydney, Hampden Press, 9–20.

—— (1998b) 'Moving beyond paradigm boundaries', in Higgs, J. and Cant, R. (eds) *Writing Qualitative Research*. Sydney, Hampden Press, 29–45.

—— (1999a) 'The value of scholarship', paper presented at the Annual Conference of the Higher Education Research and Development Society of Australasia, Melbourne, Vic.

—— (1999b) 'Research and teaching: changing relationships in a changing context', *Studies in Higher Education* 24 (3): 291–301.

—— (submitted for publication) 'Disciplinary affiliations of experienced researchers'.

—— (in press) 'Conceptions of research: a phenomenographic study', *Studies in Higher Education* 26 (3).

—— and Boud D. (1995a) 'Research and learning in higher education', in Smith, B. and Brown, S. (eds) *Research Teaching and Learning*. London, Kogan Page, 30–9.

—— —— (1995b) 'Teaching and research: establishing the vital link with learning', *Higher Education* 29: 261–73.

Bronowski, J. (1976) *The Ascent of Man*. Boston, MA, Little Brown & Co.

Casteneda, C. (1968) *The Teachings of Don Juan: A Yacqui Way of Knowledge*. Harmondsworth, Penguin.

Casti, J. L. (1997) *Would-be Worlds: How Simulation is Changing the Frontiers of Science*. New York, John Wiley.

Centra, J. A. (1983) 'Research productivity and teaching effectiveness', *Research in Higher Education* 18 (4): 379–89.

Ceruti, M. (1994) *Constraints and Possibilities: The Evolution of Knowledge and the Knowledge of Evolution*. Lausanne, Switzerland, Gordon and Breach.

Code, L. (1991) *What Can She Know? Feminist Theory and the Construction of Knowledge*. Ithaca, NY, Cornell University Press.

Cole, K. C. (1998) *The Universe and the Teacup: The Mathematics of Truth and Beauty*. London, Abacus.

Collins, H. and Pinch, T. (1998) *The Golem: What You Should Know About Science*. Cambridge, Cambridge University Press.

Commonwealth of Australia (1999) *Knowledge and Innovation: A Policy Statement on Research and Research Training*. Canberra, ACT, Australian Government Publishing Service.

Compte, A. (1971) 'The positive philosophy', reprinted in Thompson, K. and Tunstall, J. (eds) *Sociological Perspectives*, Milton Keynes, Open University Press, 18–32.

Crosby, A. W. (1997) *The Measure of Reality: Quantification and Western Society, 1250–1600*. Cambridge, Cambridge University Press.

Crotty, M. (1996) *Phenomenology and Nursing Research*. Melbourne, Vic., Churchill Livingstone.

Dahlgren, L.-O. (1997) 'The outcomes of learning', in Marton, F., Hounsell, D. and Entwistle, N. (eds) *The Experience of Learning*. Edinburgh, Scottish Academic Press, 19–35.

Davis, W. E., Chandler, T. J. and Chandler, L. (1998) 'Beyond Boyer's *Scholarship Reconsidered*', *Journal of Higher Education* 69 (1): 23–64.

Denis, M. (1979) *Toward The Development of a Theory of Intuitive Learning in Adults Based on a Descriptive Analysis*. Ed.D. thesis. Ontario Institute for Studies in Education, University of Toronto, Canada.

Elton, L. (1986) 'Research and teaching: symbiosis or conflict?' *Higher Education* 15 (3–4): 299–304.

—— (1992) 'Research, teaching and scholarship in an expanding higher education system', *Higher Education Quarterly* 46 (3): 252–67.

Feyerabend, P. (1975) *Against Method*. London, Verso.

—— (1978) *Science in a Free Society*. London, Verso.

Foucault, M. (1972) *The Archaeology of Knowledge*, translated from the French by Sheridan Smith, A. M. London, Tavistock Publications.

—— (1979) *History of Sexuality*, trans. R. Hurley. London, Allen Lane.

—— (1995) *Discipline and Punish*. New York, Vintage Books.

Fox Keller, E. (1985) *Reflections on Gender and Science*. New Haven, CT, Yale University Press.

Fuller, S. (1998) 'The human touch', *Independent on Sunday*, 28 June, p. 71.

Gibbons, M., Limoges, C., Nowotny, H., Schwartzman, S., Scott, P. and Trow, M. (1994) *The New Production of Knowledge: The Dynamics of Science and Research in Contemporary Societies*. London, Sage.

Glassick, C. E., Huber, M. T. and Maeroff, G. I. (1997) *Scholarship Assessed: Evaluation of the Professoriate*. An Ernest L. Boyer Project of the Carnegie Foundation for the Advancement of Teaching. San Francisco, Jossey-Bass.

Greenwood, J. R. (1999) *Pyridazinediones and Amino Acid Receptors: Theoretical Studies, Design, Synthesis, and Evaluation of Novel Analogues*. Ph.D. thesis, University of Sydney, NSW. URL http://gabacus.pharmacol.usyd.edu.au/thesis/.

Greger, S. (1997) 'Negotiating truth: some insights from applied social anthropology', in Barnett, R. and Griffin, A. (eds) *The End of Knowledge in Higher Education*. London, Cassell, 113–26.

Griffin, V. (1996) Personal communication.

Habermas, J. (1987) *Knowledge and Human Interests*. London, Polity Press.

Haines, G. (1969) *Essays on German Influence upon English Education and Science, 1850–1919*. New London, CT, Connecticut College.

Haldane, J. (1997) 'Higher education after ideology: whose crisis?' in Barnett, R. and Griffin, A. (eds) *The End of Knowledge in Higher Education*. London, Cassell, 53–66.

Harding, S. (1991) *Whose Science? Whose Knowledge: Thinking from Women's Lives*. Milton Keynes, Open University Press.

—— (1998) *Is Science Multi-Cultural: Postcolonialism, Feminisms and Epistemologies*. Bloomington, IN, Indiana University Press.

Harré, R. (1981) 'The positivist–empiricist approach and its alternative', in Reason, P. and Rowan, J. (eds) *Human Inquiry: A Source Book for New Paradigm Research*. London, John Wiley, 3–17.

Harvey, S. (1999) 'A decade of change for tertiary education and science research in New Zealand: who benefits?' Paper presented at Annual Conference of the Australian Association for Research in Education, Melbourne, Vic.

Hattie, J. and Marsh, H. W. (1996) 'The relationship between research and teaching: a meta-analysis', *Review of Educational Research* 66 (4): 507–42.

Hawking, S. (1988) *A Brief History of Time: From the Big Bang to Black Holes*. London, Bantam Press.

HEFCE (1997) *Research Assessment: Consultation* (Report No. RAE 2/97) Bristol, Higher Education Funding Council of England.

HEFCE (1999) *Research Assessment Exercise 2001: Assessment Panels' Criteria and Working Methods*. (Report No. RAE 5/99) Bristol, Higher Education Funding Council of England.

Heron, J. (1992) *Feeling and Personhood: Psychology in Another Key*. London, Sage.

Hesse, H. (1973) *Siddhartha*. London, Pan Books, Picador.

Hesse, M. (1980) *Revolutions and Reconstructions in the Philosophy of Science*. Brighton, Harvester.

The Holy Bible. The Revised Version. Cambridge, Cambridge University Press.

Horgan, J. (1998) *The End of Science: Facing the Limits of Knowledge in the Twilight of the Scientific Age*. London, Abacus.

Husserl, E. (1973) *The Idea of Phenomenology*. The Hague, Martinus Nijhoff.

Jenkins, A., Blackman, T., Lindsay, R. and Paton-Saltzberg, R. (1998) 'Teaching and research: student perspectives and policy implications', *Studies in Higher Education* 23 (2): 127–41.

Jevons, R. (1990) Personal communication.

Johnson, R. (1996) 'Feeling the fear', in Boud, D. and Miller, N. (eds) *Working with Experience: Animating Learning*. London, Routledge, 184–93.

Johnson, R. (forthcoming) *Emotional Fitness*. London, Metro Books.

Jones, J. (1992) 'Undergraduate students and research', in Zuber-Skerritt, O. (ed.) *Starting Research – Supervision and Training*, Brisbane, Qld, Tertiary Education Institute, University of Queensland, 50–68.

Jones, R. S. (1983) *Physics as Metaphor*. Minneapolis, MN, New American Library, Meridian.

Jungk, R. (1960) *Brighter than a Thousand Suns: A Personal History of the Atomic Scientists*. Harmondsworth, Penguin.

Kant, I. (1953) *Prologomena to any Future Metaphysics that Will Be Able to Present Itself as a Science*, translated by Lucas, P. G. Manchester, Manchester University Press.

Kirkman, M. (1999) 'Authors of our own lives: rewriting the autobiographical narrative after infertility', paper presented at the Association for Qualitative Research Conference: Issues of Rigour in Qualitative Research, Melbourne, Vic.

Kuhn, T. S. (1970) *The Structure of Scientific Revolutions*. 2nd edn. Chicago, University of Chicago Press.

Lakatos, I. (1981) 'Falsification and the methodology of scientific research programmes', in Lakatos, I. and Musgrave, A. (eds) *Criticism and the Growth of Knowledge*. Cambridge, University of Cambridge Press, 91–196.

Latour, B. and Woolgar, S. (1986) *Laboratory Life: The Construction of Scientific Facts*. Princeton, NJ, Princeton University Press.

Laurillard, D. (1995) Public lecture. University of Technology, Sydney.

Leatherman, C. (1990) 'Definition of faculty scholarship must be expanded to include teaching, Carnegie Foundation says', *Chronicle of Higher Education* 37 (14): 16–17.

Lenoir, T. (1997) *Instituting Science: The Cultural Production of Scientific Disciplines*. Stanford, CA, Stanford University Press.

Lincoln, Y. and Guba, E. (1985) *Naturalistic Inquiry*. London, Sage.

Lodge, D. (1988) *Nice Work*, Harmondsworth, Penguin.

Lorimer, D. (ed.) (1998) *The Spirit of Science: From Experiment to Experience*. Edinburgh, Floris Books.

Lovelock, J. E. (1979) *Gaia: A New Look at Life on Earth*. Oxford, Oxford University Press.

Lumby, J. (1994) *Exploring the Experience of a Life-Threatening Illness*. Ph.D. thesis, Deakin University (Geelong), Vic.

Lyotard, J.-F. (1984) *The Postmodern Condition: a Report on Knowledge*, translated from the French by Massumi, G. and Bennington, B. Minneapolis, MN, University of Minnesota Press.

McNair, S. (1997) 'Is there a crisis? Does it matter?', in Barnett, R. and Griffin, A. (eds) *The End of Knowledge in Higher Education*. London, Cassell, 27–38.

McNay, I. (1997) *The Impact of the 1992 RAE on Institutional and Individual Behaviour in English Higher Education: The Evidence from a Research Project* (Report No. M 5/97). Bristol, Higher Education Funding Council of England.

McWilliam, E., Lather, P. and Morgan, W. (1997) *Headwork, Field Work, Text Work: A Textshop in New Feminist Research*. Kelvin Grove, Qld, Queensland University of Technology.

Marton, F. and Säljö, R. (1976) 'On qualitative differences in learning. I. Outcome and process', *British Journal of Educational Psychology* 14: 4–11.

Marton, F., Fensham, P. and Chaiklin, S. (1994) 'A Nobel's eye view of scientific intuition: discussions with the Nobel prize-winners in physics, chemistry and medicine (1970–1986)', *International Journal of Science Education* 16 (4): 457–73.

Marton, F., Hounsell, D. and Entwistle, N. (eds) (1997) *The Experience of Learning*. 2nd edn. Edinburgh, Scottish Academic Press.

Maslow, A. H. (1968) *Toward a Psychology of Being*. Princeton, NJ, Van Nostrand.

Maxwell, N. (1984) *From Knowledge to Wisdom: A Revolution in the Aims and Methods of Science*. London, Basil Blackwell.

Midgley, M. (1992) *Science as Salvation: A Modern Myth and its Meaning*. London, Routledge.

—— (1994) *The Ethical Primate: Humans, Freedom and Morality*. London, Routledge.

—— (1997) 'Visions of embattled science', in Barnett, R. and Griffin, A. (eds) *The End of Knowledge in Higher Education*. London, Cassell, 68–83.

Milton, R. (1994) *Forbidden Science: Exposing the Secrets of Suppressed Research*. London, Fourth Estate.

Mooney, C. J. (1990) 'Higher-education conferees applaud Carnegie plan to broaden the definition of faculty scholarship', *Chronicle of Higher Education* 36 (30): 11.

Mourad, R. P. Jr. (1997a) *Postmodern Philosophical Critique and the Pursuit of Knowledge in Higher Education*. Westport, CT, Bergin and Garvey.

—— (1997b) 'At the forefront: postmodern interdisciplinarity', *The Review of Higher Education* 20 (2): 115–40.

Nelson, A. (1995) *The Role of Imagination in Autobiographical and Transformative Learning*. Ph.D. Thesis. University of Technology, Sydney, NSW.

Neumann, R. (1992) 'Perceptions of the teaching–research nexus: a framework for analysis', *Higher Education* 23 (2): 159–71.

—— (1993) 'Research and scholarship: perceptions of senior academic administrators', *Higher Education* 25: 97–110.

New Zealand Government (1997) *Tertiary Education Review Green Paper: A Future Tertiary Education Policy for New Zealand*. Auckland, New Zealand, New Zealand Government, www.mined.govt.nz/web/document_page.cfm?id=4710.

—— (1999) *The Knowledge Economy: A Submission to the New Zealand Government by the Minister for Information Technology's IT Advisory Group*. Auckland, New Zealand, New Zealand Government, www.med.govt.nz/pbt/knowledge_economy.

Noble, D. (1999) *Digital Diploma Mills*. URL http://communication.ucsd.edu/dl/ddm1.html.

Norris, C. (1997) *Against Relativism: Philosophy of Science, Deconstruction and Critical Theory*. Oxford, Blackwell.

Oliver, P. (1997) *Teach Yourself Research for Business Marketing and Education*. London, Hodder and Stoughton.

Paulsen, M. B. and Feldman, K. A. (1995) 'Toward a reconceptualization of scholarship: a human action system with functional imperatives', *Journal of Higher Education* 66 (6): 615–40.

Pellino, G. R., Blackburn, R. T. and Boberg, A. L. (1984) 'The dimensions of academic scholarship: faculty and administrator views', *Research in Higher Education* 20: 103–15.

Plank, M. (1981) *Where is Science Going?* Woodbridge, CN, Ox Bow Press.

Popper, K. R. (1972) *Objective Knowledge*. Oxford, Clarendon Press.

—— (1973) 'The rationality of scientific revolutions', in Harré, R. (ed.) *Problems of Scientific Revolution*. Oxford, Oxford University Press, 138–40.

—— (1980) *The Logic of Scientific Discovery*. London, Hutchinson.

Powers, B. A. and Knapp, T. R. (1995) *A Dictionary of Nursing Theory and Research*. 2nd edn. London, Sage.

Prigogine, I. and Stengers, I. (1984) *Order out of Chaos: Man's New Dialogue with Nature*. London, Fontana Flamingo.

Ramsden, P. and Moses, I. (1992) 'Associations between research and teaching in Australian higher education', *Higher Education* 23 (3): 273–95.

Reason, P. (1988) *Human Inquiry in Action: Developments in New Paradigm Research*. London, Sage.

—— (ed.) (1994) *Participation in Human Inquiry*. London, Sage.

—— and Marshall, J. (1987) 'Research as personal process', in Boud, D. and Griffin, V. (eds) *Appreciating Adults Learning: From the Learner's Perspective*. London, Kogan Page.

—— and Rowan, J. (eds) (1981) *Human Inquiry: A Source Book for New Paradigm Research*. London, John Wiley.

Reese, W. L. (1980) *Dictionary of Philosophy and Religion*. Atlantic Highlands, NJ, Humanities Press.

Rice, R. E. (1992) 'Towards a broader conception of scholarship: the American context', in Whiston, T. G. and Geiger, R. L. (eds) *Research and Higher Education: The United Kingdom and the United States*. Buckingham, SRHE and Open University Press, 117–29.

Rowan, J. and Reason, P. (1981) 'On making sense', in Reason, P. and Rowan, J. (eds) *Human Inquiry: A Source Book for New Paradigm Research*. London, John Wiley, 113–37.

Rowland, S. (1996) 'Relationships between teaching and research', *Teaching in Higher Education* 1 (1): 7–20.

Ruscio, K. P. (1987) 'The distinctive scholarship of the selective liberal arts college', *Journal of Higher Education* 58 (2): 205–22.

Schmitt, H. A. (1997) *Quakers and Nazis: Inner Light in Outer Darkness*. Missouri, MO, University of Missouri.

Schön, D. A. (1995) 'The new scholarship requires a new epistemology', *Change* 27 (6): 26–34.

Scott, D. K. and Awbrey, S. M. (1993) 'Transforming scholarship', *Change* 25 (4): 38–43.

Scott, P. (1991) *The Postmodern Challenge*. Stoke-on-Trent, Trentham Books.

Sheldrake, R. (1987) *A New Science of Life: The Hypothesis of Formative Causation*. London, Paladin, Grafton Books.

—— (1994) *Seven Experiments that Could Change the World : A Do-It-Yourself Guide to Revolutionary Science*. London, Fourth Estate.

Shore, B., Pinker, S. and Bates, M. (1990) 'Research as a model for university teaching', *Higher Education* 19: 21–35.

Simpson, R. (1983) *How the PhD Came to Britain: A Century of Struggle for Postgraduate Education*. Research into higher education monographs: 54. Guildford, Society for Research into Higher Education.

Skolimowski, H. (1983) 'The model of reality as mind', in Van der Merwe, A. (ed.) *Old and New Questions in Physics, Cosmology, Philosophy and Theoretical Biology*. New York and London, Plenum, 769–88.

—— (1984) *The Theatre of the Mind: Evolution in the Sensitive Cosmos*. Wheaton, IL, The Theosophical Publishing House.

—— (1985) 'The co-creative mind as a partner of the creative evolution', paper presented at the First International Conference on the Mind–Matter Interaction, Universidada Estadual De Campinas, July 21–24. Campinas, SP, Brazil.

—— (1994a) *EcoYoga: Practice and Meditations for Walking in Beauty on the Earth*. London, Gaia Books.

—— (1994b) *The Participatory Mind: A New Theory of Knowledge and of the Universe*. London, Arkana, Penguin.

Slaughter, S. (1993) 'Beyond basic science: research university presidents; narratives of science policy', *Science, Technology and Human Values* 18 (3): 278–302.

Smeby, J.-C. (1998) 'Knowledge production and knowledge transmission. The interaction between research and teaching at universities', *Teaching in Higher Education* 3 (1): 5–20.

Sokal, A. and Bricmont, J. (1999) *Fashionable Nonsense: Postmodern Intellectuals' Abuse of Science*. New York, Picador.

Spanier, B. B. (1995) *Im/Partial Science: Gender Ideology in Molecular Biology*. Bloomington and Indianapolis, IN, Indiana University Press.

Spender, D. (1999) *Man Made Language*. 2nd edn. London, Rivers Oram Press.

Stove, D. (1998) *Anything Goes: Origins of the Cult of Scientific Irrationalism*. Paddington, NSW, Macleay.

Street, A. (1999) 'Rigour in discursive analysis: the practices of euthanasia', paper presented at the Association for Qualitative Research Conference: Issues of Rigour in Qualitative Research, Melbourne, Vic.

Strum Kenny, S. (1999) *Reinventing Undergraduate Education: A Blueprint for America's Research Universities*. Stony Brook, NY, Carnegie Foundation for the Advancement of Teaching.

Sundre, D. L. (1992) 'The specification of the content domain of faculty scholarship', *Research in Higher Education* 33 (3): 297–315.

Sutherland, S. (1994) 'The idea of a university?', in *Universities in the Twenty-First Century: A Lecture Series*. London, National Commission on Education and the Council for Industry and Higher Education.

Tannen, D. (1994) *Talking From 9 to 5: How Women's and Men's Conversational Styles Affect Who Gets Heard, Who Gets Credit and What Gets Done at Work*. London, Virago.

Tolstoy, L. (1978) *War and Peace*. Harmondsworth, Penguin.

Usher, R. (1997) 'Seductive texts: competence, power and knowledge in postmodernity', in Barnett, R. and Griffin, A. (eds) *The End of Knowledge in Higher Education*. London, Cassell, 99–111.

—— Bryant, I. and Johnston, R. (1997) *Adult Education and the Postmodern Challenge: Learning Beyond the Limits*. London, Routledge.

—— and Solomon, N. (1999) 'Disturbing the ivory tower? Educational research as Performance and Performativity'. *Mimeo*.

Van Ginkel, H. (1994) 'University 2050: the organisation of creativity and innovation', in National Commission on Education and the Council for Industry and Higher Education (eds) *Universities in the Twenty-first century: A Lecture Series*. London, National Commission on Education and the Council for Industry and Higher Education, 65–86.

Webster, D. S. (1985) 'Does research productivity enhance teaching?' *Educational Record* 66: 60–3.

Wertheim, M. (1995) *Pythagoras' Trousers: God, Physics and the Gender Wars*. New York, Random House, Times Books.

Westergaard, J. (1991) 'Scholarship, research and teaching: a view from the social sciences', *Studies in Higher Education* 16 (1): 23–8.

Wiggins, G. (1989) 'A true test: toward more authentic and equitable assessment', *Phi Delta Kappan* 71 (9): 703–13.

Wilson, E. O. (1998) *Consilience: The Unity of Knowledge*. New York, Vintage.

Index

M7134-TN

10